OOKS

IORY

tudies
s also
Their

EDWARD T. LINENTHAL

PRESERVING MEMORY

The Struggle to Create America's

Holocaust Museum

PENGUIN BOOKS

PENGUIN BOOKS
Published by the Penguin Group
Penguin Books USA Inc., 375 Hudson Street, New York, New York 10014, U.S.A.
Penguin Books Ltd, 27 Wrights Lane, London W8 5TZ, England
Penguin Books Australia Ltd, Ringwood, Victoria, Australia
Penguin Books Canada Ltd, 10 Alcorn Avenue, Toronto, Ontario, Canada M4V 3B2
Penguin Books (N.Z.) Ltd, 182–190 Wairau Road, Auckland 10, New Zealand

Penguin Books Ltd, Registered Offices: Harmondsworth, Middlesex, England

First published in the United States of America by Viking Penguin,
a division of Penguin Books USA Inc. 1995
Published in Penguin Books 1997

10 9 8 7 6 5 4 3 2

A portion of this work first appeared as "The Boundaries of Memory:
The United States Holocaust Memorial Museum" in *American Quarterly*.

Title-page photograph courtesy of Beth Redlich,
United States Holocaust Memorial Museum.

THE LIBRARY OF CONGRESS HAS CATALOGUED THE HARDCOVER AS FOLLOWS:
Linenthal, Edward Tabor, date.
Preserving memory: the struggle to create America's Holocaust Museum/
Edward T. Linenthal.
Includes index.
ISBN 0-670-86067-0 (hc.)
ISBN 0 14 02.4549 9 (pbk.)
1. U.S. Holocaust Memorial Museum—History. 2. U.S. Holocaust Memorial
Museum—Exhibitions. 3. Holocaust, Jewish (1939–1945)—Exhibitions. 4. Holo-
caust memorials—Political aspects—United States. 5. United States—Politics and govern-
ment—1981–1989. 6. United States—Politics and government—1989–1993. I. Title.
D804.3.L56 1995
940.53´18—dc20   94–23410

Printed in the United States of America
Set in Sabon
Designed by Francesca Belanger

for Aaron Johannes Linenthal
and Jacob Arthur Linenthal

and to the memory of
Erwin A. Glikes

ACKNOWLEDGMENTS

THIS BOOK WAS BORN in the spring of 1990, when Professor John Roth of Claremont McKenna College encouraged me to talk with Michael Berenbaum, at that time project director of the United States Holocaust Memorial Museum, about the possibility of my writing a history of the project. After we met, Berenbaum agreed that my interest in the interrelationship between place and memory would serve me well. He first introduced me to Marian Craig, whose experience spans the history of this project: as staff assistant to both the President's Commission on the Holocaust and the United States Holocaust Memorial Council, assistant director to the Council, director of the Days of Remembrance program, and director of the Office of Council Relations. I met museum Director Jeshajahu (Shaike) Weinberg—who had been out of the country during my first trip—several months later. I recall this meeting well. I introduced myself, said, "It is nice to meet you," and with his wry grin, Weinberg responded, "We'll see."

Although many people gave generously of their time and enriched this book in many ways, my first debt of gratitude is to these four. Without John Roth, I probably would not have been led to the museum. Michael Berenbaum always made time for me in the midst of his frenetic schedule, introduced me to supporters and critics of the museum, opened his own files to me, and shared with me his experience both with the President's Commission and in his recent work at the museum. He has been both friend and intellectual critic throughout. Marian Craig became a good friend as well during these years. I could not have written this book without the benefit of her remarkable memory and insightful analysis of so many episodes, people, and issues. I will always have fond memories of both of us wading through dusty boxes of files in a Maryland warehouse, and the excitement we felt when coming across some "goodies" that filled out part of the story. In the limited space of an acknowledgment section, it must be enough to say that this book is as much hers as it is mine.

The book could not have been written without Shaike Weinberg, who, without knowing me well, was trusting enough to allow me to sit in on exhibit design meetings and stagings, and at a council meeting, and always let me enter into the daily life of those responsible for creating the museum. Shaike spoke with me often about various issues, allowed me access to exhibition files, and generously granted me use of some of the museum's photographs for the book. It has been a pleasure to work with him during these years.

Crucial to my work was financial support from the National Endowment for the Humanities, in the form of a summer stipend; support from the Faculty Development Program at the University of Wisconsin, Oshkosh; support from the Oshkosh Northwestern Chair of Liberal Arts at the University of Wisconsin, Oshkosh; and a grant from the Wisconsin Society for Jewish Learning.

In January 1991, I had the opportunity to join Jeff Bieber of WETA-TV in Washington, D.C., Ralph Appelbaum, Jacek Nowakowski, and Martin Smith in an unforgettable ten-day trip to Poland to visit Warsaw, Chełmno, Majdanek, Łódź, Bełżec, and Auschwitz. I had spoken with all of these people in the United States, but being with them in Poland was an experience I shall never forget. It changed me and the book in significant ways.

I have fond memories as well of the important time that I spent with Albert Abramson, Rouben Adalian, David Altshuler, Joe Brodecki, Anna Cohn, Emily Dyer, Yaffa Eliach, Sam Eskenazi, Raye Farr, Maurice Finegold, James Freed, Monroe Freedman, Stephen Goodell, Irving "Yitz" Greenberg, Radu Ioanid, Arnold Kramer,

William Kline, David Luebke, Genya Markon, Harvey Meyerhoff, Cindy Miller, Sybil Milton, Set Momjian, Lance Morgan, Micah Naftalin, John Pawlikowski, Joan Ringelheim, Arthur Rosenblatt, Steven Weintraub, and James Young. Their insights were helpful in many ways.

In our conversation, Elie Wiesel reminded me how important the work of the President's Commission on the Holocaust was. I had been unable to locate the transcripts of these meetings, crucial documents for my project. Wiesel not only invited me to his Boston University office to read his copies of these transcripts; he also generously opened his commission and council files to me, which enriched the book immeasurably. I also greatly appreciate the kindness of Raul Hilberg, who spent a weekend with me in Burlington, Vermont, and whose support of the book has meant a great deal. In addition, I appreciate the kindness of Miles and Chris Lerman, who spent a day with me in Atlantic City, New Jersey. Benjamin Meed, who, with Miles Lerman, has been one of a group of Holocaust survivors intimately connected with this project for many years, gave generously of his time and allowed me access to his papers in his New York office.

A number of people read part or all of the manuscript, saved me from historical errors, quarreled with my interpretations—which led me to rethink and alter some but not others—and offered suggestions for other issues to think about. For this I thank Ralph Appelbaum, Michael Berenbaum, David Chidester, Anna Cohn, Marian Craig, Emily Dyer, Yaffa Eliach, Raye Farr, Maurice Finegold, James Freed, Monroe Freedman, Raul Hilberg, Radu Ioanid, Arnold Kramer, David Luebke, Cindy Miller, Sybil Milton, Klaus Müller, Martin Smith, and Elie Wiesel.

It was also my good fortune, at the University of Chicago, to meet Professor Peter Novick, who is finishing a book on the evolution of Holocaust consciousness in the United States. We met on a number of occasions—each time I left regretting that our time together was so limited—and he helped me in numerous ways: sharing some extremely important articles I had not known about, carefully reading the whole manuscript, and responding in insightful ways as I reached for various formulations of issues. I am extremely grateful for his friendship and generosity.

From the first day I walked into the museum offices—then at 2000 L Street—I knew full well that time was an extremely precious commodity. The museum's April 1993 opening date loomed large, and it was clearly an exhausting race to see if the deadline could be met. In the midst of this, I asked people to spend time reflecting on their work—to create, in essence, thoughtful space for us to think together despite their frantic schedules. In addition, many people either formerly associated with the museum or having an important connection to the project gave freely of their time. Never was a question or request of mine met with anything but a willingness to help. For all of this— and for the friendships I made—I am extremely grateful.

Only some of the contributions, often in the form of interviews, will become clear in the book. Accordingly, I here thank Barbara Abramowitz, Robert McCormick Adams, Raye Allen, Charles Atherton, Edward Balawajder, Jonathan Baron, Harry Barone, Alan Berger, Norman Bernstein, Charles Blitzer, Sara Bloomfield, Hyman Bookbinder, Vivian Boxer, Sandra Bradley, Claudine Brown, J. Carter Brown, Robert McAfee Brown, Christopher Browning, Nick Capasso, Sandra Carey, Harry Cargas, Brewster Chamberlin, Betsy Chock, Noam Chomsky, Joseph Corn, William Duna, Zalman Enav, Ann Farrington, Alexa Feldman, Anna Fine, Aleisa Fishman, Benjamin Forgey, Margaret Gaynor, Gerald George, Alan Gilbert, Dara Goldberg, Ellen Goldstein, Susie Graber, Rachel Greenman, Robert Gresham, Ralph Grunewald, Gerald Gurland, Yechiam Halevy, Ian Hancock, Kevin Hanretta, Martha Hauptman, Charlotte Hebebrand, Susannah Heschel, Elaine Heumann-Gurian, Kathryn Hill, Severin Hochberg, Mieczysław Jędruszczak, Ivan Karp, Carolyn Keane, C. M. Kicklighter, James Kitchens III, Debbie Klingender, Elizabeth Koenig, Sue Kohler, Aaron Kornblum, Tomasz Kranz, Corinne Kratz, Norbert Krieg, Björn Krondorfer, Gary Kulick, Lawrence Langer, Annette Lantos, Hillel Levine, David Linderman, Hélène Lipstadt, Franklin Littell, Deirdre

McCarthy, Margaret MacDonald, Tom Mack, Charles Maier, Yitzchak Mais, David Mandel, Michelle Rae Marinelli, Michael Marrus, Peter Martz, Donald Meyer, Jennifer Mitchell, Deborah Dash Moore, Susan Morgenstein, Klaus Müller, Michael Neufeld, Jacob Neusner, Peggy Obrecht, Sarah Oglivie, Krystyna Olesky, Marc Pachter, Naomi Paiss, Carol Palmer, John Parsons, William Parsons, Lydia Perry, Jack Porter, Adam Prill, Stanley Prill, Czesław Rajca, Beth Redlich, Jerry Rehm, Wendy Resnick, Tony Richardson, Gerhard Riegner, Kevin Roche, Fernando Rondon, Liz Rose, Joan Rosenbaum, Alvin Rosenfeld, Richard Rubenstein, James Russell, Rochelle Saidel, Bennett Samson, Jonathan Sarna, Richard Savignano, Michael Schudson, Jeffrey Shandler, William Shulman, Mark Siegel, Mark Silk, Toby Sonneman, David Strauss, Sigmund Strochlitz, Janet Adams Strong, Laura Stutz, Kalman Sultanik, Kali Tal, Mark Talisman, Deneen Taylor, Keith Torney, Lawrence Vale, Eric Ward, Debra Warner, Judith Weinraub, Steven Weintraub, Chris White, Judith Whittlesey, and Warren Zimmerman. Special thanks go to Naomi Paiss and Liz Rose for their thoughtfulness during the museum's opening week ceremonies.

One of the unexpected pleasures arising from my many trips to Washington, D.C., has been my friendship with Tom and Leslie Freudenheim and their sons, Adam and Sascha, with whom I often stayed. From them I learned a great deal about museums, Washington culture, and the pleasure of fine dinners and good conversation.

I thank other friends for their help: James Blight, Paul Boyer, David Chidester, John Dower, Marc Ellis, Tom Engelhardt, James McNamara, and Jeff Sonnleitner. At the University of Wisconsin, Oshkosh, I thank Erin Czech, Cindy Schultz, Victoria Simon, Don Weber, and Michael Zimmerman.

I shall always be thankful that Jules Chametzky put me in touch with literary agent Mildred Marmur. Her advice, support, and enthusiasm have been invaluable, and I owe her a great deal. I also wish to thank Gillian Ellis, of Mildred Marmur Associates, for handling complex copyright issues with grace and good humor.

I also have a sad memory associated with this book. Less than two weeks after we celebrated the news that Erwin A. Glikes, who had just moved to Penguin USA to start a new nonfiction trade imprint, would publish my book, I received the terrible news that he had died suddenly. I dedicate this book to his memory. Marion Maneker, who had worked previously with Erwin Glikes as an editor and had joined him in this new venture, handled a difficult and painful period with dignity and sensitivity. I am grateful for his good advice and his sure hand.

Finally, to my family in Oshkosh and in Boston, my thanks for living through this book with me.

CONTENTS

PRESERVING MEMORY

INTRODUCTION

On April 22, 1993, the Holocaust became an event officially incorporated into American memory. After fifteen long years, the president dedicated the United States Holocaust Memorial Museum as a physical container to preserve the memory of the Holocaust for all Americans. The dedication was an international event of major proportions. CNN broadcast the ceremonies throughout the world. Journalists from many countries covered the opening; presidents and prime ministers of twelve countries and representatives of twenty others attended the ceremonies. That week, in fact, the nation's capital was flooded with commemorative events and museum exhibits about the Holocaust. On Sunday, April 18, an ecumenical worship service was held at the National Cathedral, and Senator John C. Danforth, an Episcopal priest, delivered the sermon, just as he had done at the first commemorative service held in the cathedral, in 1979. The Holocaust echoed throughout the nation: many churches rang bells simultaneously at the end of this service in memory of Holocaust victims.

The annual Days of Remembrance ceremony was held as usual in the Capitol Rotunda on April 20, marking the fiftieth anniversary of the Warsaw Ghetto revolt. The next day, a tribute to liberators and rescuers was held in the Arlington National Cemetery Amphitheater. John S. D. Eisenhower read a letter in which his father, former President Dwight D. Eisenhower, described the horror of encountering Ohrdruf, a subcamp of Buchenwald, in the latter days of the war in the European theater. Actress Liv Ullmann, whose grandfather had been sent to Dachau for hiding Jews, delivered a moving reading of the acclaimed writer Chaim Potok's "America Remembering," written especially for this event. That evening, the night before the opening, a concert was held in honor of the dedication of the museum at the John F. Kennedy Center for the Performing Arts.

Various Washington museums contributed to the capital's focus on the Holocaust. A symposium on "The Bombing of Auschwitz: Should the Allies Have Attempted It" was held at the National Air and Space Museum. The exhibits "Sacred Image, Sacred Text: Art of the Holocaust" and "Everyman a Hero: The Saving of Bulgarian Jewry" opened at the B'nai B'rith Klutznick Museum. And "GIs Remember: Liberating the Concentration Camps" opened at the National Museum of American Jewish Military History.

The dedication of a museum located adjacent to the ceremonial center of the nation, the Washington Mall, emphasized the Holocaust's place in the official memory of the nation. Dedication day was unseasonably cold. A raw wind greeted the ten thousand people who gathered on the Washington Mall side of the museum, including vendors hawking items like a blue button with yellow letters declaring "Raoul Wallenberg Lives, Rescue the Rescuer," or buttons and literature passed out by a smiling Holocaust denier declaring that the Holocaust never happened. The museum would begin its life as the focal point of Holocaust memory in the U.S.

The fleet of dark limousines that brought President and Mrs. Clinton, Vice-President and Mrs. Gore, and the other heads of state was a vivid sign of the unprecedented attention devoted to the opening of a cultural institution. Their presence signified that the Holocaust not only was a crucial memory for survivors or members of the public, but also might help those entrusted with affairs of state to navigate through troubled waters. Perhaps a repository of Holocaust memory, symbolized in part by this museum, could prove to be therapeutic for nations as well as individuals.

The limousines were unsettling, however. It seemed somehow

inappropriate that this manifestation of state power was converging on an institution whose purpose was to bear witness to the danger of the unlimited power of a state. As the limousines passed, policemen kept those heading for the ceremony huddled on the street corner until the way was clear. Among them were a husband and wife, survivors, for whom the dedication ceremony was less state event than symbolic burial of those murdered and affirmation of their own suffering. These two contrasting images—the massive might of official remembrance, and the quiet, intimate remembrance of individual survivors—capture the complexity and volatility of Holocaust memory. They echo the quite different characterizations of the meaning of the museum project: according to Elie Wiesel and others, the museum would be a sacred institution, entrusted with containing and expressing the mystery of the Holocaust, a mystery available only through the witness of the survivors; for some others, the museum would be a symbol of the deft use of Holocaust memory to advance ethnic power, expressed most crassly in a comment made to me that the museum was a way to remind congressmen how to vote on issues regarding the State of Israel.

Neither one of these voices—the sacred or the secular—seems appropriate for this book. The museum needs neither additional praise—it has already received much deserved recognition from many—nor reduction to some crass political purpose. Nor does it require detailed description of the type that can be found in other accounts.

The need this book seeks to address is a portrayal of the boundaries of Holocaust memory incorporated into the museum. The book excavates the layers of struggle to define and delimit the ideas, objects, persons, and representations that best capture the meaning of the Holocaust. These struggles are portrayed in all their exquisite detail, which inevitably raises larger questions about the production and use of Holocaust memory. The story moves from the negotiations over the terms and conditions of constructing national Holocaust memory—issues such as membership on the President's Commission and Holocaust Memorial Council, and the creation of a definition of the Holocaust, immediately became contentious—to the struggle to locate and design the memory: in what city, at what site, in what kind of building. It focuses on the agonizing discussion about how to narrate the Holocaust to the wider public in a federal museum, and with what artifacts to fill the space of Holocaust memory. It examines the ways in which those who shaped the permanent exhibition faced dilemmas about how to begin, what level of horror could be appropriately portrayed through photograph and artifact, how perpetrators could be portrayed without glorification, how various victim groups could be represented appropriately, and how to end without enshrining either despair or redemption. The story offers readers the opportunity to be "present at the creation" of an institution of Holocaust memory. It offers interpretive comment throughout, concluding with my thoughts on the role of official Holocaust memory: to what end, finally, the museum.

By the time the President's Commission was created in 1978, a canonical reading of the Holocaust had already been established in American culture, thanks largely to the eloquence of survivor and writer Elie Wiesel. For him, the Holocaust could never be understood but, for the sake of humankind, had to be remembered. It was an event that transcended history, almost incapable of being represented except through survivor testimony. When one was speaking of the Holocaust, it was unwritten etiquette to begin by saying that no one could understand the Holocaust, but it needed to be spoken of so "it" would not happen again, or be forgotten. The Holocaust was not only a transcendent event, it was unique, not to be compared to any other genocidal situation, and its victims were Jews. Any comparison of event or linkage to any other victim group could be, and often was perceived as, if not the murder of memory, at least its dilution. Moreover, the story ended with a kind of redemption, the creation of the State of Israel.

This is a story of boundaries defined, attacked, defended, preserved, redrawn, and re-established. It is a story of the still-continuing negotiations over the boundaries of memory. When, in the postwar years, the memory of the Holocaust was solely the possession of

American Jews, the boundaries of Holocaust memory were firmly established and could be preserved. But when the memory became a national trust, the boundaries became at one and the same time more firmly established—in response to fear of dejudaization—and yet more permeable—because of the pluralistic ownership of the memory.

Locating Holocaust Memory in American Culture

" IN THE BEGINNING," wrote historian Raul Hilberg, "there was no Holocaust. When it took place in the middle of the twentieth century, its nature was not fully grasped." From 1933 to 1945, the years of the implementation of the Nazis' murderous vision, failure of imagination was coupled with moral cowardice and the fervent desire of so many not to react to the "public secret" of what was happening to people at risk in Europe. This was followed, in the spring of 1945, by the equally passionate public desire to ignore the unforgettable images that had greeted the troops when they encountered the camps. Even for hardened combat veterans, the reality was almost unimaginable, and they felt, wrote historian Robert Abzug, "an almost unbearable mixture of empathy, disgust, guilt, anger, and alienation," engendering the urge both to remember and bear witness to the horrors encountered, and to forget, to distance oneself from unacceptable images and inconceivable realities, to turn away from what seemed the futile task of communicating this to a war-weary American public. Consequently, what came to be known as "the Holocaust" was often indistinguishable, in the immediate postwar years, from the millions of noncombatant casualties due to terror bombing of civilian populations, epidemic illness, or starvation. It was considered by most as simply part of the horror of war.

In addition to the tortured recollections of those who encountered the camps, shards of memory existed, but had not yet been distinctively shaped into a narrative. There were official documents—

which would make up the archival memory of the Holocaust from which Hilberg and others would relentlessly describe the process of destruction—and survivor testimony, which, if mentioned at all, surfaced primarily in intimate gatherings of those who had suffered. Benjamin Meed, president of the American Gathering/Federation of Jewish Holocaust Survivors and the Warsaw Ghetto Resistance Organization, survived the war in Warsaw by passing as a Christian, was active in the Jewish underground, and witnessed the destruction of the Warsaw Ghetto. He came to America in 1946, and long afterward recalled, "Our first years were hard. Everytime we heard car tires screeching, we froze. . . . We even had to adjust to the ringing of door bells. For us the echo of the old world of fear and death reverberated many times a day. . . . For years we were alone. Our fellow Jews regarded us as 'green'—the newest immigrants. Americans treated us as refugees. 'Forget the past,' we were told, 'it can only hurt you.' So we reached out to each other and remembered alone."

Rabbi Irving "Yitz" Greenberg, president of the National Jewish Center for Learning and Leadership, recalled attending Holocaust remembrance services in the late 1950s and early 1960s. The language of the ceremonies was Yiddish, he observed, and outsiders were painfully aware of their peripheral status. "It felt," remarked Greenberg, "like we were crashing a funeral."

Survivor memories were of another place and another time, displaced memories attached to those euphemistically characterized as "displaced persons." Adapting to American culture, survivors generally wanted to turn away from the horror they had lived through, become Americans, build a new life, and take advantage, cautiously, of the American dream.

There also existed the rubble of the concentration and death camps, which provided material evidence of the murderous work of the Nazis. These places had not yet become pilgrimage destinations for American and Israeli Jews. They would not emerge as places of memory until the Holocaust emerged as a distinctive event, and even then these emplaced memories often ignored Jewish Holocaust victims. Survivors' fears of again being victimized through the murder of memory—expressed throughout the making of the museum—had roots in such expressions of intentional forgetfulness.

Consequently, the Holocaust had not been constructed as a discrete "event," because the motivation to forget was too strong for survivors, perpetrators, and bystanders, the implications of what had happened were too threatening for public analysis, and the underlying guilt for not having done more was too great among some Americans, Jews and non-Jews alike. Fear of mass extermination engendered by newsreel photographs of piles of bodies bulldozed into mass graves in the camps led not to considered reflection on the contemporary significance of the Holocaust, but, rather, to contemplation of the more immediate threat of nuclear annihilation. Indeed, if the Holocaust "lived" in postwar American life, it often did so in the subterranean anxieties surrounding meaningless mass death, with the Bomb replacing the gas chamber as the agent of extermination, and in the transformation of the survivor's status from unwanted guest to a witness whose testimony revealed terrible truths the world dare not forget.

Forgetfulness, however—the treachery of memory—became a strategic ally in the postwar holy crusade against the Soviet Union, as West Germany quickly became a symbol of miraculous transformation to democracy and a bulwark against Soviet aggression. Russians became "Nazis"; Germans became freedom-loving allies. Active memory of the Nazi past was considered a needless complication in the struggle to win the Cold War. Even legal memory was short. Despite various postwar trials by Allied nations, observed historian Henry Friedlander, "the central crime of the Holocaust—the systematic extermination of the European Jews and other selected groups—did not receive the attention it demanded." The invisibility of the Holocaust also extended to serious scholarship. In the 1950s, Leon Poliakov's *Harvest of Hate* and Gerald Reitlinger's *The Final Solution*—published in England and receiving only scant attention in the United States—were the only comprehensive histories of the Holocaust in English.

Even in the American Jewish community, the Holocaust was virtually invisible. "The American Jewish suburban community," wrote historian Deborah Lipstadt, "was concerned with manifestations of unity and not diversity, universalism and not particularism. They were more concerned about acting as Americans than as Jews." This assimilationist mood did not favor disagreement with American foreign policy toward Germany; nor did many Jews find it attractive to identify with those victimized. The assimilationist trend extended to religious Jews as well, for, as Judaism became a faith comfortably situated within the acceptable boundaries of respectable religion, "there was," Leon Jick argued, "hardly a place . . . for the traumatic memories of recent horrors." Historian Stephen Whitfield observed that, in a 1961 *Commentary* symposium, "Jewishness and the Younger Intellectuals," only two of thirty-one participants "placed any stress upon the impact of the Holocaust in their lives," and the twenty-one participants in *Judaism*'s 1961 symposium "My Jewish Affirmation" avoided the Holocaust "almost completely."

The only widely available popular memory of the Holocaust was the story of Anne Frank, softened and universalized for wide acceptance. What originated as the story of a Jewish girl betrayed by an informant and murdered by the Nazis became a triumphant story of Everyperson's triumphant spirit soaring over a faceless evil.

A few people insisted on remembering publicly. Rabbi Greenberg's attention was drawn to the Holocaust in the early 1960s and represented a religious turning point for him: "I couldn't be a Jew in the same way," he said, "after the Holocaust." A Fulbright Scholar in Israel in 1961–62, he read intensively about the Holocaust at the Yad Vashem Heroes and Martyrs Memorial Authority in Jerusalem, the central institution for Holocaust memory in Israel. Upon his return to Yeshiva University in New York City, it took Greenberg two years to gain approval to teach a course on the Holocaust; he was successful only when he agreed to title the course "Totalitarianism and Ideology in the Twentieth Century."

Occasions of remembrance emerged in the 1960s. The widely publicized trial of Adolf Eichmann in Israel in 1961 proved a public forum for the dramatic testimony of over one hundred survivors. A Gallup poll reported that 87 percent of the American public was aware of Eichmann's capture, and, wrote Dorothy Rabinowitz, for many American Jews the trial was a "galvanizing force, bringing them face to face with emotions theretofore repressed, with events whose full scope and reverberations had been kept, rumbling, beneath the surface of consciousness." Also, during the mid-to-late 1960s, American Jews became less reticent about being Jews in public, as ethnic particularism became an accepted form of cultural expression.

By far the most important event in the resurrection of Holocaust imagery in American life, however, was the Six-Day War. Egyptian President Gamal Abdel Nasser mobilized his army on May 15, 1967, and declared on May 26 that his goal was the annihilation of Israel. The indifference of Western nations awakened dormant memories of the Holocaust. Though short-lived, the anxiety was intense. Another Holocaust seemed in the making. The distinguished Jewish scholar Abraham Joshua Heschel, who had emigrated to the United States in 1940 to serve on the faculty at the Conservative Jewish Theological Seminary, one of the most influential theologians of the postwar period, captured the sense of foreboding: "Terror and dread fell upon Jews everywhere. . . . Will there be another Auschwitz, another Dachau, another Treblinka. . . . In those days many of us felt that our own lives were in the balance of life and death . . . that indeed all of the Bible, all of Jewish history was at stake, the vision of redemption, the drama that began with Abraham." It was, said Heschel, "an awesome time, the collapse of complacency."

After Israel's military victory, complacency did not return. "Never Again" was heard not only from the Jewish Defense League, but also from the mouths and pocketbooks of many American Jews. This time they could celebrate a different ending to a potential Holocaust, and the restoration, on June 9, of access to the ancient Temple wall in Jerusalem. For Israelis, at least, the Six-Day War provided the satisfying resolution to what historian of religion Jacob Neusner has called "the Judaism of Holocaust and Redemption." The Holocaust could not come into being as an event, argued Neusner, until an act of redemption had taken place. "The point at which the myth . . . becomes compelling is the moment at which the redemption appears to be credible, not 1948 . . . but 1967."

It should come as no surprise that, in this period of American Jewish assertiveness, less is heard about Anne Frank, the universalist symbol of the Holocaust, and much more about Elie Wiesel, who insisted on the centrality both of Jewish experience in the Holocaust and of the survivor as witness to the Holocaust.

In 1973, the same year the United States ended its direct military intervention in Vietnam, the Yom Kippur War reignited fears of the extermination of Jews in Israel and smashed the illusion of Israeli military invincibility. For some years, Holocaust imagery had been used by elements in the antiwar movement. Some of the more radical called the nation "Amerika," but even for moderate antiwar people, noted Dorothy Rabinowitz, peace marchers carried signs that "referred as a matter of course to Auschwitz, to Himmler, and to Eichmann . . . for prominent among the themes debated during and after the Eichmann trial was the issue of individual conscience: whether the individual had a duty to refuse obedience to a system which perpetrated crimes against humanity."

Throughout the war, mainstream America was assaulted with terms like "genocide" and "race war" to describe American activity in Vietnam. The widely publicized massacre of women and children at My Lai weakened the traditional American belief in the righteousness of the American fighting man. It is certainly no coincidence that portrayals of the plight of the American Indian gained popularity during the war. Dee Brown's *Bury My Heart at Wounded Knee*, for example, a litany of persecution of American Indians, became a best-seller. Popular films such as *Soldier Blue* and *Little Big Man* also portrayed the conquest of the West as a series of genocidal acts.

Consequently, American actions in Vietnam were framed as only the latest eruption in a long, dark narrative that directly contested the righteousness assumed to have been at the core of American culture. The Holocaust provided people an example of evil seemingly unlike any other, against which this nation's—or any nation's—actions could be measured. This, Raul Hilberg believed, largely explained the growing popularity of Holocaust courses among university students. He recalled that he had modest goals when he began team-teaching such a course at the University of Vermont in the early 1970s with a colleague from the English department: he thought the class would last for perhaps two years. Its popularity convinced him to continue the course by himself. Why, he asked himself, was the subject so popular? Why were almost half the students non-Jewish? "After the disorientation of Vietnam," he argued, "they wanted to know the difference between good and evil. The Holocaust is the benchmark, the defining moment in the drama of good and evil." Putting it succinctly at a lecture at Syracuse University, Hilberg remarked, "Against this single occurrence, one would assess all other deeds. And so, memorialization began in earnest, that is to say it became organized."

Nineteen seventy-eight was a crucial year in the organization of Holocaust consciousness. Americans witnessed the drama unfolding in Skokie, Illinois, as a threatened march by Chicago-based American Nazis brought the principle of free speech into conflict with what seemed common decency, the recognition of survivors' feelings. Survivors promised to halt the march by any means necessary, to protect their community from the contamination of the Nazi uniform and flag.

American legal memory was awakened through the creation of the Office of Special Investigations, whose purpose was to bring Nazi war criminals living in the United States to trial for the purpose of deportation. Its first director, Allan Ryan, characterized this work as different in kind from other forms of Holocaust memory. Rituals and physical memorials were, he said, "retrospective in nature. There is nothing retrospective or abstract about OSI's work; real people are investigated, placed on trial, stripped of their citizenship, deported. It is the invocation of official action that makes this initiative unique." Revocation of citizenship was perceived as an act of penitential remembrance on the part of a government guilty of allowing murderers into the country after the war, and was intended as a symbolic act of national purification—"the civil equivalent," Ryan observed, "of excommunication."

On April 16–19, 1978, NBC aired a nine-and-a-half-hour miniseries, *The Holocaust*, with an estimated audience of approximately 120 million. Fierce debate raged over the show. Critics attacked it as an example of the obscene trivialization of the Holocaust in popular culture. *Time*'s Lance Morrow, for example, criticized the intrusions of commercials. "Viewers drawn back into the most painful darkness . . . would suddenly, repeatedly, find themselves jolted into the clusters of ads that seemed almost deliberately designed to offend." Morrow noted that in one scene Adolf Eichmann complained that the stench of burning bodies made it impossible for him to enjoy his dinner. Immediately following, a character in a Lysol commercial informed a housewife that she had odors in her kitchen. Elie Wiesel characterized the show as "an insult to those who perished, and to those who survived."

Others believed that the television show was almost singularly responsible for awakening interest among people ignorant of the events. In film historian Judith Doneson's judgment, for example, "people in Idaho, North Dakota, New York—throughout the United States—were now initiated, albeit in a simplified manner, into the world of the Nazi genocide against the Jews." Irving Greenberg argued that the inevitable vulgarization of commercial television was preferable to the contrast to the previous decades of "indifference, silence, and even shunning of survivors which preceded it."

When President Carter announced plans to create the President's Commission on the Holocaust in 1978, he signaled that the Holocaust had moved not only from the periphery to the center of American Jewish consciousness, but to the center of national consciousness as well. Too important a story to be bounded by ethnic memory, it was, by virtue of its awesome impact, its poisonous legacy, and its supposed valuable "lessons," worthy of inclusion in the official canon that shaped Americans' sense of themselves.

This plan to make Holocaust memory part of the official legacy of the American experience intensified criticism in some segments of the American Jewish community. There were already concerns about the growing emphasis on the Holocaust in university courses, in popular culture, and now in a plan for a national memorial. Some believed that the fixation on the Holocaust was debilitating for the spiritual life of Jews. Jacob Neusner, for example, was convinced that American Jews' use of the "myth of Holocaust and Redemption" served up no spiritual nourishment for them. Since they had not themselves experienced the birth of the State of Israel as the redemptive fulfillment of this drama, Neusner asked, "what is the point of dwelling on suffering without consolation, on death without rebirth? . . . We speak of someone else's death in Europe and someone else's rebirth" in Israel.

Even some who would eventually become important figures in the development of the museum worried about the popular function of the Holocaust for American Jews. Yaffa Eliach, for example, survived the Holocaust as a child in Lithuania, and eventually became professor of history at Brooklyn College and founder of the first Holocaust center in the United States. She became a member of the President's Commission on the Holocaust, and her own incredible story—which I will tell in chapter four—contributed to one of the museum's most acclaimed exhibits, a tower of photographs depicting murdered Jews from her town. Writing in 1979, Eliach declared that American Jews had discovered the "vast educational and financial potential of the Holocaust." It was, she said, "an instant Judaizer, shocking people back into their Jewishness. . . . One may sadly reflect that 'there is no business like Shoah business.' "

Others argued that the rich history of Judaism as a civilization would be ignored as more and more attention was paid to the Holocaust. Jews and non-Jews alike would remember only how Jews were exterminated, not their contributions so central to the development of Western civilization. And, practically, the obsession with the Holocaust would cause funds to be diverted to memorial projects that should more appropriately be used to aid Jews still suffering from anti-Semitism in foreign lands, or used in education, to help fortify Jewish identity for those struggling to remain Jewish in a secular culture.

There was fear that interest in the Holocaust was driven by a grotesque competition for status as "first and worst" victims among American ethnic groups, vying for the "fruits" of officially recognized suffering—that is, the deference of others and the assumed moral righteousness of members of the aggrieved community. Some saw this as ironic, that an influential and affluent American Jewish community perceived itself as a potential victim of another Holocaust. Some worried that remembering the Holocaust too well would complicate Jews' relationship with non-Jews.

Sociologist John Cuddihy, for example, argued that, prior to the civil-rights movement, the Holocaust conferred the "honor" of supreme-victim status upon American Jews, which often led to official compensatory gestures—America's "special relationship" with Israel, for example. In the 1960s, however, black Americans began to argue that they either shared the position of supreme victim, or occupied this privileged position alone. They appropriated Holocaust imagery to make the point—James Baldwin's highly controversial comparison of black activist Angela Davis to a "Jewish housewife headed for Dachau," for example. In response, American Jews reacted strongly, arguing that the Holocaust was "unique." They used it, said Cuddihy, as a secular form of chosenness, in order to claim an "attitude of moral superiority." The argument that the Holocaust was a unique event—an enduring item of debate throughout the museum story—registered for Cuddihy as simply a claim for superiority. "This exemption from comparison," he said, "is a heady privilege. . . . Among the many items selected by culture to symbolize status, incomparability alone is inimitable."

Others worried that the Holocaust would be inappropriately used as a filter for contemporary political issues. Not every opponent was Hitler, not every conflict potentially genocidal. Jewish theologian Marc Ellis, for example, cautioned that reading present realities— particularly the Israeli-Arab conflict—through the lens of the Holocaust was dangerous. He criticized vigorously the use of the

Holocaust as a weapon by which Jews claimed innocence and righteousness through their suffering. This, he argued, blinded them to the injustice they inflicted on Palestinians. Reflecting on this question as he stood in Auschwitz, Ellis wondered if the Holocaust had become a "safe haven" for Jews. "For if we dwell in Auschwitz, if we freeze our history at Auschwitz, we silence the questions others have of us and in fact we have of ourselves. In this way Auschwitz becomes for us a place where we can hide our accountability in the present, even as we demand it insistently of others for their past actions."

Not surprisingly, there were strong disagreements among American Jews about institutionalizing Holocaust memory. Neusner thought the idea of Holocaust centers and museums "nihilistic and obsessive," but Irving Greenberg argued that Jewish memory had always been expressed through institutions: first the Temple, then the synagogue, and now, he believed, through Holocaust centers, "places where memory is preserved, where the story is told, where the acts of mourning and continuity are publicly expressed."

All of these arguments had to do with the appropriate location of Holocaust memory in American culture. Where was it "in place"—only in written or ritual expressions of survivors, or, more widely, on national television and in monuments, memorials, and Holocaust centers throughout the nation? Did it fit comfortably into Jewish conceptions of salvation history—tragic, but no more so than a medieval pogrom—or was it out of place, something registering as unique, new, an orienting event no less profound than God's revelation at Sinai? Many of those concerned with examining the implications or legacy of the Holocaust, Jews and Christians alike—Elie Wiesel, Irving Greenberg, Michael Berenbaum, Emile Fackenheim, Richard Rubenstein, Franklin Littell, Robert McAfee Brown, Roy and Alice Eckardt, and Harry Cargas, for example—maintained that the Holocaust was not merely another in a long litany of historical tragedies, but altered fundamentally the relationship of Jews and Christians to their tradition, and called into question the beneficence of technology and the reality of social progress.

CHAPTER ONE

The Decision to Remember

THE CARTER ADMINISTRATION'S DECISION to create a commission whose task it was to recommend an appropriate national Holocaust memorial is often characterized as "political," implying that the underlying motivation had little to do with interest in Holocaust memory and everything to do with the domestic political priority of appeasing Jewish interests. For the White House, the idea certainly looked like politics at its best *and* at its most convenient. Carter would use the power of government to do something many would perceive as "good" and, at the same time, reach out to an increasingly alienated ethnic constituency. An act of commemoration could, fortuitously, also serve more pragmatic political ends.

These mixed motives were apparent when, in the spring of 1977, Mark Siegel, deputy assistant to the president, was asked by Chief of Staff Hamilton Jordan if he would become the president's liaison to the Jewish community. Carter's evangelical Christianity and his comments—both as a candidate and as president—about the Palestinian right to a homeland had disturbed many American Jews. Passions were inflamed further when Carter linked the sale of aircraft previously promised to Israel to the sale of aircraft to Egypt and Saudi Arabia. Hoping to heal the wounds, Siegel told Jordan, "Yes, if I can also be the Jewish community's liaison to the administration." That same spring, Siegel had asked Ellen Goldstein, who worked for Chief of Domestic Policy Stuart Eizenstat, to find out what nations had built Holocaust memorials. On June 21, 1977, Goldstein wrote Siegel, "There is no U.S. memorial to the victims of the Holocaust although many synagogues and temples in this country burn lights in memory of the victims." Goldstein had turned to the Center for Holocaust Studies in Brooklyn, New York, for this information. Begun in 1976, it was the oldest Holocaust center in the country, and was headed by Yaffa Eliach. "Perhaps," Goldstein mentioned to Siegel, "President Carter can begin to heal the rift between himself and the Jewish population by visiting the Center on his visit to New York." Siegel then suggested to Jordan that a panel be formed to recommend a Holocaust memorial which would be announced at the same time as the hoped-for ratification of the Genocide Treaty.

Carter's troubles with the Jewish community increased in the latter part of 1977. Menachem Begin became prime minister in May 1977. In August, Carter announced that the United States had made contact with the Palestine Liberation Organization, and that they would be acceptable partners in the Geneva peace talks. On October 1, 1977, the United States and the Soviet Union issued a joint statement which spoke of the "legitimate rights of the Palestinian people." Siegel was asked to support the administration's position, and, specifically, to "sell" the weapons package to various Jewish groups. This was a painful process, and he recalled being booed at a Young Leadership Conference of the United Jewish Appeal. The State Department had told him that the F-15 could be sold to the public as a defensive weapon. Eventually, he called the Pentagon and asked them about this. "When they stopped laughing," he said, "I realized I had been lied to." Despite his respect for the president, Siegel resigned on March 1, 1978.

Later that month, Goldstein was moved to think again about Holocaust memorials when she read columnist William Safire's acerbic commentary on the controversy regarding Nazis marching in Skokie, Illinois. "America has no vivid reminder of the Final Solution," said Safire, "but we have a reminder that not even Israelis can boast: our own homegrown handful of Nazis." Goldstein informed Eizenstat that the nation had no memorial, and, she argued, were the administration to announce a plan to build one, "it might be an appropriate gesture in honor of Israel's thirtieth anniversary and a symbol of the United States' support of Israel's birth and continued life. The idea deserves consideration on its merits, although such a move might appear to some people to be glib public relations."

Eizenstat asked the president to consider the formation of a fifteen-member commission, to be made up of Jews and non-Jews, that would recommend a national Holocaust memorial. He did this, he later wrote Elie Wiesel, "because of my intense personal interest. . . . I felt that it was important that those six million who died should have a permanent memorial. . . . I had a particularly acute interest in this area because of my own background and because I had numerous relatives who themselves were exterminated in the Holocaust." Joined by White House Counsel Robert Lipshutz, Eizenstat informed the president that "there was now stronger support than ever among many Americans—not just Jewish-Americans—for an official U.S. memorial." He mentioned the impact of NBC's *Holocaust* and the establishment of Holocaust memorials in many nations, and reminded the president that, unless a memorial was begun soon, many survivors would not live to see one. The only necessary government contribution, he thought, would be "a gift of land."

On May 1, 1978, while congressional debate over the weapons package raged, and with Israeli Prime Minister Begin and one thousand rabbis in attendance, President Carter announced the formation of the commission in a White House Rose Garden ceremony celebrating Israel's thirtieth anniversary. The motivation to build a Holocaust memorial was linked with a clear message of the administration's support for the State of Israel. "After I visited Israel in 1963," the president said, "I read Arthur Morse's book 'While Six Million Died,' the tragic account of the ultimate in man's inhumanity to man, the Holocaust," and "out of the ashes was born the State of Israel." United States policy toward Israel, Carter stated, was influenced by these "indelible memories of the past." Switching topics abruptly, the president spoke of the need for a national memorial to "insure that we in the United States never forget"—either the Holocaust or the necessity of support for Israel, apparently—and he announced that a commission would report in six months "on an appropriate memorial . . . to the six million who were killed in the Holocaust."

WHO OWNS THE MEMORY?
THE POLITICS OF REPRESENTATION:
THE PRESIDENT'S COMMISSION ON THE HOLOCAUST

The next day, Ellen Goldstein reminded Eizenstat of the need to move "quickly and wisely," for growing public interest was sparking other public and private efforts to memorialize the Holocaust. For example, Senator Wendell Anderson (D.-Minnesota) introduced legislation in April 1978 to establish a "President's Commission on the Victims of the Holocaust," and called for a national design competition for a memorial in honor of "these eleven million innocent victims." Anderson's resolution designated as Holocaust victims not only six million Jews, but also five million non-Jews. As we will see, these numbers would become the subject of increasingly bitter debates between the White House and members of the Commission and the United States Holocaust Memorial Council, particularly Elie Wiesel.

In addition to Anderson's resolution, Richard Krieger, then executive director of the Jewish Federation of North New Jersey, had written the White House about financial support for a central Holocaust archive and museum in Washington, D.C. And, Goldstein told Eizenstat, "there are no less than eight Holocaust memorial/centers in existence or being planned across the country [and] scores of proposals for programs having to do with Holocaust studies being submitted to the Endowments for grant assistance." Proponents of some of these plans, noted Goldstein, had suggested that their projects become the "national memorial."

Clearly, unless the commission was formed soon, the political capital accumulated by the president's announcement would dissipate as other plans took center stage. Goldstein suggested that Arthur Krim, president of Orion Films, become the commission's chairman. He had, she said, "no particular organizational affiliation," possessed "keen political skills," was an "articulate moderator, Democrat, consummate fundraiser, and he is highly regarded and respected." Goldstein, also worried about control of the project, suggested, "We may want to further influence" the nature of the memorial. It was "accepted," she said, that the memorial would be more than a "marble statue." She thought Washington, D.C., the appropriate city and, significantly, she wondered about whether the boundaries of Holocaust memory should be expanded to include non-Jewish victims: "The President proposed a memorial to the six million who perished; should the Commission consider expanding this to eleven million, as other projects propose?"

Krim declined to serve as chairman, saying, "I prefer to work for something for the future rather than for the past." In June 1978, former Supreme Court Justice Arthur Goldberg recommended Wiesel, because, "in addition to his identification with the Holocaust, he also would be a 'non-political' appointment and virtually free of attack from most sources." Goldstein recommended nine other people, but Wiesel emerged as the strategically sound choice. On June 16, Joyce Starr, a member of the White House staff, told Goldstein that Wiesel was the "one candidate who would be undisputed by the Jewish community," and on July 20, Eizenstat and Lipshutz characterized Wiesel as the "undisputed expert on the Holocaust period" and stated that "his appointment would be without controversy," though stipulating that "his political and fundraising abilities are not clearly established."

Eizenstat reached Wiesel in Israel, was insistent in the face of his resistance, and suggested that he meet with Carter upon his return. Eizenstat needed Wiesel to accept the chairmanship. In late July, Goldstein had informed him that the "Jewish community . . . has heard that the White House is 'not taking this commission seriously' and will be making mostly 'political appointments.' " When they met, Carter quoted Wiesel's own words about the responsibility of memory, and Wiesel gave Carter his conditions for accepting the job: the memorial would have to be educational in nature, commission members would need to travel to Holocaust sites in Europe, and a national Day of Remembrance for Holocaust victims would have to be part of the commission's responsibility. "The work of the commission was crucial," said Wiesel. "We had no tradition, no precedent. This was the period when we decided what this would become."

As discussion with Wiesel was taking place, preliminary commission membership lists were constantly changing. In addition to those from Goldstein's original list who would become commissioners, Eizenstat and Lipshutz received "over a hundred recommendations." Mark Talisman, director of the Council of Jewish Federation and Welfare Funds, was "supportive of the administration and would bring . . . his keen political knowledge and understanding of the government." Sigmund Strochlitz, Auschwitz survivor, businessman, energetic humanitarian, and civic leader, "received the most Congressional support." Benjamin Meed, already well known for his commemoration work in New York, was appointed to the commission's advisory board—created to accommodate people involved in various Holocaust projects—and celebrated civil-rights activist Bayard Rustin gave the commission an interracial character. Already the commission had expanded from fifteen to seventeen, plus ten congressional appointments, five each from the House and the Senate.

Not everyone was pleased with the proposed list of commissioners. Irving Greenberg, a friend of both Eizenstat and Wiesel, informed Eizenstat in August 1978 that the list was "seriously flawed," because it lacked enough people of "perceived moral stature." Greenberg mentioned several people whose appointments were being championed by Wiesel: Robert McAfee Brown, at that time a professor at Union Theological Seminary, whose interest in the Holocaust led to his book *Elie Wiesel: Messenger to All Humanity*; Arthur Goldberg; and Raul Hilberg. Greenberg also recommended Michael Berenbaum, the associate director of Zachor, Greenberg's

Holocaust resource center, and professor of religion at Wesleyan University, whose book, *The Vision of the Void: Theological Reflections on the Works of Elie Wiesel*, would appear in 1979. Wiesel, said Goldstein, was also displeased. He wanted "more scholars and luminaries," did not like the name of the commission, and wanted to enlarge the commission "considerably." Goldstein offered to let Wiesel pick one or two members.

By mid-September, the commission had expanded to twenty-one, and the advisory board numbered twenty-four. Tinkering with the commission's makeup dragged on, and by mid-October a "concerned and anxious" Wiesel told Goldstein "the delay is causing his 'community' to be critical and cynical about the Administration's commitment to the project. . . . Why is there still no Commission?" On October 18, Eizenstat and Lipshutz submitted the membership list to Vice-President Walter Mondale. They called attention to "four Nazi camp survivors; five leading Holocaust historians; four prominent Jewish Community leaders; five Rabbis (orthodox, conservative, and reform), and a number of other nationally distinguished individuals." By October 25, the commission was expanded to twenty-four, in order to redress geographical imbalance, a problem noted by Carter in an earlier handwritten comment, "We also have Jews in the Southeast."

On November 1, 1978, six months after the Rose Garden ceremony, President Carter issued Executive Order 12093, creating the President's Commission on the Holocaust. Its mission was to submit to the president and the secretary of the Department of the Interior "recommendations with respect to the establishment and maintenance of an appropriate memorial to those who perished in the Holocaust," to "examine feasibility of obtaining funds . . . through contributions by the American people," and to "recommend appropriate ways for the nation to commemorate April 28 and 29, 1979, which the Congress has resolved shall be 'Days of Remembrance of Victims of the Holocaust.' "

Greenberg reminded Eizenstat of the commission's potential for either engendering civic enrichment or, if it failed, endangering

Carter's relationship with American Jews. "Properly acted upon [it] can be a strong moral and political contribution to American life." If not, "a large part of the Jewish community . . . will perceive the whole commission as a vacuous and insincere gesture." Eizenstat, too busy to deal with day-to-day commission issues, asked Greenberg to become its director. Greenberg, in turn, would only be able to be in Washington, D.C., part-time, and recommended that Michael Berenbaum be appointed deputy director. He also recommended that some commissioners travel overseas to learn more about various Holocaust memorials. This would not only aid in their planning for a national memorial in the United States, but would "add significantly to the seriousness and solemnity . . . with which the project is seen in Congress, and among the public."

Commission members were sworn in on February 1, 1979, in the White House's Roosevelt Room. The Bible used was one of thousands of books the Germans had looted from the Vilna ghetto. Recovered by American forces, it belonged to Hebrew Union College. Yaffa Eliach recalled that for the survivors present "the story of the survival of this Book of Books was a symbol of their own suffering, survival and determination that the Holocaust will not be forgotten."

In written comments solicited by Greenberg and Berenbaum prior to their first meeting on February 15, 1979, twelve commissioners envisioned a "living memorial" that would soon be seen as a facility housing memorial, museum, archive, and educational institute. It was clear, however, that commissioners were divided about how to balance Jewish victims with others, whether their focus should be solely on the Holocaust, or whether that event should lead as well toward a focus on contemporary genocidal events. On February 6, 1979, Berenbaum told Wiesel that it would be wise "if our memorializing reached out to others in similar difficulty today, even beyond the Jewish realm." Such an approach, Berenbaum argued, would bring "more support than we will have if this is looked upon as a strictly Jewish affair."

The survivors were overwhelmed by the realization that their experiences were to be the basis of a national memorial. Miles Lerman, for example, a member of the commission's advisory board, would play a crucial role in organizing the commission's trip to Europe, and eventually, as a council member, would be largely responsible for agreements with foreign governments that would bring archival materials and artifacts to the museum. He would also become chairman of the council shortly after the museum opened in 1993.

Lerman was born in Tomaszów Lubelski, Poland, a member of a family that for six generations operated a flour mill near the site of what would become the Bełżec death camp. He was working and studying in Lvov, Poland, when he was captured by the Nazis and put to work in a slave-labor camp, breaking up Jewish tombstones for use as pavement. In 1942, he escaped and organized a resistance group consisting mainly of Jews and a few Russians. In April 1944, sitting on a Russian tank, he returned to his hometown and found it a "graveyard." Out of the sixteen thousand Jews who had lived there before the war, eleven were still alive. He and his wife, Chris, an Auschwitz survivor, lived in a displaced-persons camp for eight months, then came to the United States and eventually settled in Vineland, New Jersey. At the commission's first meeting, he told the group that in 1945 he had questioned the reason for his survival. "Today, being part of this august body . . . I feel that there was meaning and purpose to my survival and being here today."

In his opening comments, Wiesel spoke of the challenge of balancing the "purely Jewish aspect of the tragedy, with its inevitable universal connotations." He cautioned that the Holocaust had been possible because the enemy of the "Jewish people and mankind . . . succeeded in dividing, in separating, in splitting the human society. . . . We around this table must see to it that the memory of the Holocaust draws us closer together." And though Wiesel would remain insistent on the Jewish "core" of the Holocaust, he spoke of the expanding boundaries of memory. "Once you remember, you remember everybody. Memory is not something that shrinks but something that enriches. You go deeper, and deeper, you find new layers." Of course, it was just this issue—how expansive could a national memory of the Holocaust become without deviating from the established narrative of the Holocaust—that was up to the commission to consider.

The commission's staff solicited ideas from Jewish and non-Jewish groups. In response to a complaint from the editor of *The Jewish Post and Opinion*, who thought that the Jewish community had been largely ignored in the planning process, Greenberg responded that "letters soliciting advice and judgment" had been sent to the "top lay leadership and the professionals of all the major national Jewish organizations, the presidents and executives of every Jewish Federation; a wide range of community relations, council, professional and/or lay leaders, scholars in the Association for Jewish Studies, selected rabbis ... leaders or professionals in Holocaust Study Centers, as well as survivors and members and/or leaders of survivor organizations." There were also, Greenberg noted, three public hearings (one each in Miami, Manhattan, and Brooklyn), and the commission contacted members of "Armenian, Black, Polish, and other ethnic groups ... whose own history of suffering and persecution we thought would make them responsive and valuable sources of ideas." Certainly one of the most grotesque recommendations came from John Cardinal Krol, archbishop of Philadelphia. His letter spoke about the importance of forgiveness, quoted a former president of the World Jewish Congress who claimed that Jews of the free world were also to blame for the Holocaust, and recommended that "a handy pamphlet, in an interesting and readable style ... would have a far more lasting effect than would any statue or memorial. . . . The purpose of the pamphlet should be to affirm the dignity of every human and the sacredness of every human life."

On April 24, 1979, the commission's first act of national remembrance—the first Days of Remembrance service—took place in the Rotunda of the nation's Capitol, less than a month after Carter had hosted the signing of a peace treaty between Egypt and Israel at the White House, the fruits of the Camp David meetings of September 1978. The idea for this ceremony originated with Senator John

Danforth (R.-Missouri), an Episcopal priest, before he became a member of the commission, and, as Berenbaum and others quickly saw, one way of extending Holocaust memory into American public culture was to have Days of Remembrance become part of the national calendar.

Shortly before the commission's first meeting, Congressman and commission member James Blanchard (who would subsequently become governor of Michigan) suggested that perhaps the Rotunda, rarely used for public ceremonies—except for one involving the Magna Carta during the nation's bicentennial—would be the appropriate site for such an event. Here the Holocaust could lie "in state," at the center of American memory. "This would attract an awful lot of attention," Blanchard said, "and is something that is rarely done." Congress expressed its collective support in a unanimous joint resolution for what Berenbaum characterized as an "unprecedented event." The service consisted of comments from Carter, Mondale, and Wiesel; memorial prayers; songs of the ghetto, sung by the Atlanta Boys Choir; candle-lighting; and kaddish, the traditional Jewish prayer of bereavement.

Carter's comments fueled the simmering debate about who was to be memorialized in the ceremony and, ultimately, in the national memorial. Recalling his trip to Yad Vashem only a few weeks before, Carter spoke of the awesome magnitude of the Holocaust, the "sheer weight of its numbers—11 million innocent victims exterminated—6 million of them Jews." For those concerned about dilution of the Jewish core of the Holocaust through universalization, presidential words were a key, and Carter's various pronouncements sent mixed signals. In the Rose Garden, he spoke only of the "six million"; in the executive order creating the commission, he spoke of "those who perished"; but in the Rotunda, he spoke *first* of eleven million, and then of six million Jews as a part of a larger group of victims. This was, for Wiesel and others, a failure to recognize the distinctive Jewish dimension of the Holocaust, an attack on the uniqueness doctrine which they regarded as the key to proper Holocaust memory. Within this context, they saw Carter's comments as leading, inexorably, to the inappropriate blending of Jewish victims with millions of "others." For them, it was the murder of truth done in the service of memory.

The conviction that insistence upon the uniqueness of the Jewish experience in the Holocaust was essential to prevent effacement of the memory of Jewish victims altogether was strengthened when some commission members and staff, accompanied by family members, invited guests, and several reporters, left on a fact-finding mission to Holocaust memorial sites in Europe and Israel in the summer of 1979, each paying his or her own way. For many it was their first trip back, and, at a time when travel in Eastern Europe was difficult, many believed it would be their last. Michael Berenbaum, who helped organize the trip with Miles Lerman, recalled that it was "designed as 90 percent pilgrimage. Survivors went with the imprimatur of the United States government. They were allowed to go places they would not have been able to go, and they were able to negotiate in Poland and the Soviet Union in ways that they couldn't have otherwise."

The group left New York on July 29, 1979; they traveled first to Warsaw, to lay wreaths at the Warsaw Ghetto monument and the monument for those who died in the Polish uprising against the Germans in 1944, and to attend meetings with Polish officials from the Office of War Veterans' Affairs and from the Main Commission for Investigation of Nazi War Crimes. They then visited the site of the Treblinka death camp; traveled to Auschwitz; and flew to Kiev to visit the ravine at Babi Yar, site of the murder of thirty-three thousand Jews in September 1941, and of thousands of Jews, Gypsies, and Russian prisoners of war in following months. After meetings with Russian officials, the group traveled to Copenhagen to participate with the Danish prime minister, members of the Jewish community, and leaders of the resistance movement during World War II in a ceremony honoring Denmark's successful efforts to save Jews. On August 8, the group arrived in Israel for a trip to Yad Vashem and other Israeli Holocaust-memorial sites before returning to New York on August 14.

Some survivors felt they had been transported back in time, even as they felt the "presence of absence" of Jews in the synagogues and in the towns that some of them remembered—from a different life— as their homes. Cantor Isaac Goodfriend, a commissioner who had sung the national anthem at President Carter's inauguration, visited his birthplace, and could, "for a moment, reflect and hear the same sounds ringing in my ears, a passage of the Talmud or the reviewing of the weekly Torah portion on Friday nights." Even in a city she had known, Dr. Hadassah Rosensaft felt disoriented while standing at the Warsaw Ghetto monument. "Since much of the city had been destroyed and then rebuilt, I did not recognize it. . . . I sensed a painful silence and emptiness. There were no more Jews in Warsaw. The streets that had once teemed with Jewishness now seemed barren. Generations of Jewish life had disappeared."

Many commissioners were troubled and angry about the absence of any effort to memorialize Jewish victims. Benjamin Meed, who arrived in Warsaw three days before the main delegation in order to make final arrangements, was dismayed that even the official schedule was designed to prevent appropriate commemoration. The Polish Foreign Ministry had scheduled first a "large, official wreath-laying" at the monument honoring the Polish resistance movement, and only later a "smaller gathering at the Ghetto Monument." Meed was troubled that there were no plans for the group to visit the Jewish Cemetery or the Jewish Historical Institute. "Our primary objective," he explained to unreceptive officials, "was to honor the *Jewish* victims of the Holocaust."

Immediately upon arriving at the airport, Wiesel, speaking for the delegation, said that the trip would be canceled if it did not begin with a visit to the Warsaw Ghetto monument and Mila 18, the site of the Jewish Fighting Organization's bunker. And it was only after a moving ceremony at the monument and a visit to the bunker that the group agreed to visit the Polish resistance monument. Here, "in contrast to the silence and isolation of the scene at the Ghetto Monument, we were attended with full pomp and splendor, with a military band and a military guard in attendance, with army men assisting us in laying the wreath." Meed recalled that the next day the Polish newspapers and the government's news agency reported the delegation had first visited the Polish monument.

In meetings with Polish officials, "in elegantly appointed offices, with lavish displays of food, drink, and flowers," the Poles would, according to Wiesel, "refer to victims in general," whereas "we speak of Jews. They mention all the victims, of every nationality, of every religion, and they refer to them en masse. We object. . . . The Jews were murdered because they were Jews, not because they were Poles. . . . And so we told our Polish hosts: If you forget the Jews, you will eventually forget the others. One always starts with the Jews."

The Jews of Warsaw, Wiesel observed, "are no longer in Warsaw; they are in Treblinka, two hours away . . . beneath the stones of Treblinka"—the Germans tried to wipe away all evidence of the hundreds of thousands who were murdered at Treblinka. "In the end," wrote Hilberg, "the bodies in the mass graves were exhumed. All the installations were razed, and a Ukrainian farm was established on the site to restore its pastoral appearance. Only a cobblestone path, built by prisoners, was left where Treblinka had existed. After the war, the Polish government laid down concrete ties, arranged as a symbolic railway track, and set up hundreds of jagged stones, each representing a Jewish community, around the stone memorial."

Treblinka evoked strong reaction from the delegation. Meed spoke of its eloquence, its loneliness. Goodfriend characterized it as a "total environment of remembrance." Wiesel wrote of the "austere and simple stones of Treblinka," which from afar "in the twilight . . . can easily be mistaken for Jews, wrapped in their ritual shawls, at prayer." And Raul Hilberg noticed the ease with which physical evidence of the Holocaust emerged from the ground. "After every heavy rain, tiny bone fragments are disgorged by the earth and mix with pebbles on the ground."

The moving, painful silence of Treblinka was, for many, in marked contrast to the vulgarization of the Holocaust at Auschwitz. "Over the years," wrote Meed, "Auschwitz has been transformed into a tourist

Warsaw Ghetto survivor Benjamin Meed, a member of the commission's advisory board. He would eventually become a key figure in the development of the museum, serving as chairman of the museum-content committee and of the Days of Remembrance committee. *(Benjamin Meed/United States Holocaust Memorial Museum)*

mecca, with souvenir stands, shops, refreshment stands, parking lots for excursion buses, and vendors walking among the crowds selling postcards and snacks. . . . At least in Treblinka the memory of the victims has not been trivialized." Lily Edelman, director of the B'nai B'rith Lecture Bureau, who had been invited to join the delegation as a special consultant, heard a survivor remark, "It wasn't enough to give them our parents and grandparents, our brothers and sisters. . . . We also had to leave them a billion dollar tourist industry."

Some were also angered at what they believed was the effacement of Jewish victims from Auschwitz memorials. Except for the "Jewish pavilion," remarked Ben Meed, "nowhere in either of the two Auschwitz compounds [the main camp and the death camp of Birkenau] is to be felt the sense of the unique tragedy of the Jewish people." In contrast to the tourist atmosphere at the main Auschwitz camp, survivors entering Birkenau once again felt time collapse around them. Linking arms, the five survivors walked apart from the others, recalled Rosensaft, "over the railroad tracks, the same ones that had brought us and millions of others to this place. . . . I did not see the empty spots where the crematoria had been. I did not see the ruins of the chimneys. I did not see the people standing near me. I saw myself in Birkenau in 1943. I saw the arrival, the selections . . . flames that consumed millions of Jews, among them my parents, my first husband, my five-year old son. I was standing on ashes, unable to move."

For Wiesel, re-entering what he called the "kingdom of night" was crucial so that he and the other survivors could help others "touch" the event, provide for them the appropriate "feel" of the Holocaust, which would, ideally, inspire and bring integrity to the commission's work. "At that moment," said Wiesel, "it became important to erase all the years, all the words, all the images that separated us from this event, from this place; it became essential to rediscover night in all its nakedness and truth; we had to recapture the unknown before it could become known." And although Wiesel said that "there was no prayer in any book for such places," members of the delegation filled the space of Birkenau with memorial words. Survivors recited the "Shma Israel," and then Bayard Rustin covered Birkenau with American words, words of pain and dignity. Hyman Bookbinder recalled that, "accompanied only by the soft winds of the great expanse," Rustin began singing:

> Oh freedom, oh freedom, oh freedom over me;
> And before I'd be a slave, I'd be buried in my grave
> And go home to my Lord and be free.

The delegation experienced various offenses against memory before and during their trip to the Soviet Union. Irving Greenberg and Miles Lerman, both of whom had long-standing contact with Jewish dissidents, were denied visas. And before visiting Babi Yar, the group was taken on a bus tour of Kiev, stopping last at the monument of Bogdan Chmielnicki, a Ukrainian national hero who, Meed angrily recalled, "distinguished himself by organizing pogroms of Polish and Ukrainian Jews." At the Babi Yar monument, Elie Wiesel angrily protested the failure of the monument to use the word "Jew," and the delegation placed a wreath of flowers commemorating the Jewish tragedy. Immediately afterward, the delegation was driven to a restaurant, where, Meed recalled, an orchestra played "gay Russian tunes for us at lunch." Soviet officials challenged the delegation, claiming that Jews and others were killed as part of the fascist assault on many nations, including the Soviet Union, and that any attempt to "isolate" victim groups falsified history.

After arriving in Copenhagen, Christian theologians Roy and Alice Eckardt, invited on the trip as consultants, were struck by how differently official Danish and Soviet memory expressed the "universal" nature of the Holocaust. The Danes had rescued and remembered Jews because they were neighbors and friends. They did not treat them as "Jews." At Babi Yar, Jews who died became remembered only as citizens of Kiev, victims of a fascist crime. Hence, the Eckardts argued, as it sought to establish the proper balance between the particular and the universal in its work, the commission should ask the question "Does a given form of universalism pay homage to human particularity?" The very mandate of the commission, they argued, "forbids any such sacrifice of the particular to the universal; the people being remembered suffered and died for a singular, highly particular reason." Both the commission and the council would have to struggle, however, with representatives of non-Jewish groups who claimed that *their* "particular" death also belonged within the boundaries of an American national Holocaust memory.

As do so many American Jewish tour groups who travel to Holocaust sites, the delegation concluded its trip in Israel, moving from the world of the Holocaust to a symbol of redemption. They heard an impassioned speech from Gideon Hausner, chairman of the counsel at Yad Vashem, and the former Israeli attorney general who had prosecuted Adolf Eichmann. He warned commissioners that Hitler's heirs were spreading their "concentrated poison" in the Middle East, among those who would deny Jews a "secure and hon-

President Jimmy Carter accepts the *Report to the President* from Elie Wiesel, September 27, 1979. *(Courtesy Jimmy Carter Library)*

orable homeland." And, he argued, "there is no similarity between the Holocaust and other dreadful atrocities in modern history. Any, and every attempt to blur this feature of the Holocaust, is a distortion of an historic truth."

Upon his return, Hyman Bookbinder told a Jewish congregation in Washington, D.C., "If our steps through Auschwitz and Treblinka . . . had not been quite as unbearable as we'd feared, it was because we knew that those steps would ultimately take us to Jerusalem; that in our search for an appropriate memorial to the six million, we understood that the real memorial was already being built and that it must be made a truly permanent, living memorial—and that is Israel itself." As we will see, this troublesome interpretation of the significance of the State of Israel—that it somehow helps make the Holocaust more bearable, that it somehow gives meaning to the Holocaust, that it somehow provides a hopeful ending to the narrative of the Holocaust—would appear again in the latter stages of the development of the museum's permanent exhibition, in the struggle to provide visitors an appropriate and somewhat hopeful ending.

The delegation returned with its sense of the precariousness of Holocaust memory confirmed. Their antennae were alert to the dangers of dilution, effacement, and trivialization inherent in the popularization of Holocaust memory, and many commissioners shared the belief that the memory of the Holocaust as constructed by the State of Israel—itself perceived by some as a memorial to the Holocaust—served as an appropriate corrective to the deficiencies of Eastern European memory.

This trip also became a model for many others who would serve on the council and on the museum's staff. Traveling to these sites would come to be seen as a way to initiate those responsible for the creation of a memorial to an imported event. Eventually, the impact of these sites convinced members of the staff that museum visitors would have to experience such a trip *within* the space of the museum in order to confront the Holocaust viscerally. Trips to Holocaust sites functioned in several ways: they were made in order to collect artifactual material that imported the material reality of the Holocaust into the United States, and allowed museum visitors to touch the Holocaust; and they also functioned as pilgrimages. The excavation of the physical landscape, and the highly publicized trips for the purpose of collecting soil from various sites to bury at the museum site, were designed to provide a spiritual transformation to those who entered the physical remnants of the world of the Holocaust.

On September 27, 1979, the commission presented its *Report*, written by Michael Berenbaum, to the president in the White House's Rose Garden. This emphasized the burden, challenge, and potential of memory: failure to remember the victims would "mean to become accomplices to their murders"; remembrance was important to fulfill the victims' wish to "defeat the conspiracy of silence" and to remind contemporary generations of the dangers of indifference. The *Report* insisted on the Jewish core of the Holocaust. Though it was important to remember "millions of innocent civilians," there was a "moral imperative for special emphasis on the six million Jews." The event, it insisted, "is essentially Jewish, yet its interpretation is universal."

The *Report* defined the Holocaust as the "systematic, bureaucratic extermination of six million Jews by the Nazis and their collaborators as a central act of state during the Second World War. . . . As night descended, millions of other people were swept into this net of death. . . . Never before in human history had genocide been an all-pervasive government policy unaffected by territorial or economic advantage and unchecked by moral constraints." This was actually a combination of Berenbaum and Wiesel's language, and reflected the different sensibilities each brought to the subject. Berenbaum had been a student of Richard Rubenstein, whose *After Auschwitz* was the first frontal assault on the adequacy of Jewish salvation history to accommodate the Holocaust. Rubenstein believed that, after the Holocaust, human beings lived in a functionally godless world. In *The Cunning of History*, Rubenstein characterized the Holocaust as an "expression of some of the most significant political, moral, religious and demographic tendencies of Western civilization in the twentieth century." Rubenstein did not characterize the Holocaust as a transcendent, mysterious event, but as a triumph of bureaucracy, which could organize processes of destruction as easily as any other rational endeavor. The Germans, Rubenstein argued, created a new society in which extermination was merely the endpoint of a society of "total domination."

Clearly, the first part of the definition of the Holocaust reflected Berenbaum's thinking, but the phrase "as night descended" illustrated Wiesel's desire to emphasize the mystery of the Holocaust, and to encode the uniqueness of the Holocaust into an argument for temporal priority. Many of the "other people" to be included within the boundaries of Holocaust victims, however—the handicapped,

Michael Berenbaum, deputy director of the President's Commission on the Holocaust, resigned in January 1980. He rejoined the museum's staff as project director in 1987, and became director of the research institute in 1993. *(Arnold Kramer, United States Holocaust Memorial Museum)*

Russian POWs, Polish intelligentsia, for example—were killed *before* the mass extermination of Jews in killing centers began.

Americans, the *Report* stated, had a "distinct responsibility" to remember the Holocaust. U.S. soldiers had liberated some of the camps, survivors made their homes in this country, and the nation had a legacy of "disastrous" indifference to the Jews of Europe. Through this act of remembrance, Americans would not only memorialize Holocaust victims, but would "instill caution, fortify restraint, and protect against future evil or indifference."

The commission offered four major recommendations. It proposed the creation of a "living memorial" which would include memorial and museum space, an educational foundation, and a committee on conscience, the latter to consist of "distinguished moral leaders in America," who would call governmental and public attention to ongoing instances of genocide. The commission also proposed that "Days of Remembrance of Victims of the Holocaust" should become an annual part of the national calendar. Finally, the commission recommended governmental actions that were "appropriate forms of remembering." It called for the ratification of the Genocide Treaty—which Elie Wiesel would support in testimony before the Senate—asked that Nazi war criminals living in the United States be sought out and prosecuted, and—largely as a result of the delegation's experience in Europe—asked that the State Department bring pressure to bear on foreign governments so that they would appropriately care for Jewish cemeteries, so often left unattended, in ruins.

In response, President Carter said that he hoped this proposed "center" of Holocaust memory would focus renewed attention on the importance of human rights, and hoped that this act of memory would ensure that such events would not be repeated. He also spoke once again of numbers. "In addition to the Jewish people who were engulfed . . . simply because they were Jews, 5 million other human beings were destroyed. About three million Poles, many Hungarians, Gypsies, also need to be remembered."

WHO OWNS THE MEMORY?
THE POLITICS OF REPRESENTATION:
THE UNITED STATES HOLOCAUST MEMORIAL COUNCIL

The commission's attempt to establish the boundaries of the Holocaust through an understanding of the relation between various victims did not end the debates. Indeed, they intensified as the project gained momentum, and advocates of the essentially Jewish nature of the Holocaust engaged in increasingly bitter battles with representatives of various Eastern European ethnic groups and with the White House over representation on the commission's successor body, the United States Holocaust Memorial Council, whose task it would be to implement the commission's recommendations. The stakes were high. The attempt to diversify the membership of the council and broaden the definition of the Holocaust registered in sharply contrasting ways: as an appropriate if belated attempt to memorialize non-Jewish victims of the Holocaust, who had been largely anonymous in the traditional Jewish narrative of the event; or as a cynical political attempt to share in the prestige of a national Holocaust memorial by ethnic groups that had not shown interest in being "counted" as Holocaust victims until the formation of the commission. Those committed to Jewish ownership of Holocaust memory would share it only carefully, and certainly not with representatives of nations who suffered at the hands of Nazis but also killed Jews, nor would those custodians of memory permit the memory of Jewish victims to drown in a sea of politicized inclusiveness.

This storm was gathering well before the president received the *Report*. Pressure for inclusion from the Polish-American community had begun the previous spring. Aloysius Mazewski, president of the Polish American Congress, informed Greenberg that he was worried about lack of non-Jewish Polish representation, and complained, incorrectly, that *all* the proposed members of the commission were Jewish. The three million Polish victims and one million other non-Jewish victims, Mazewski argued, "shared" the Holocaust with the six million Jews. To help Greenberg understand the Polish perspective, he enclosed an article by Kazimierz Lukomski, vice-president of the Polish American Congress, that no doubt fanned the flames of Jewish distrust of the ability of non-Jewish Europeans to come to terms with their past. Lukomski glossed over Eastern European anti-Semitism, and blamed the Jews for their fate. "There might have been excesses here and there," Lukomski stated, "but Poland protected its Jewish citizens." Besides, he argued, "how do you help people who are themselves resigned passively to accept their fate?"

Another letter to Greenberg came from Dr. Eugene L. Slotkowski, who indicated that Mazewski had shared Greenberg's correspondence with him. Slotkowski believed that the numbers of Jewish and non-Jewish victims were equal; consequently, the Holocaust could mean "either the death of six million Jews or twelve million Jews and Gentiles." He informed Greenberg that presidential adviser Edward

Sanders had assured him that the commission would recognize *all* the victims, "including the Poles who suffered the same fate as the six million Jews." Slotkowski did not trust the Jewish survivors born in Poland or elsewhere in Eastern Europe to represent non-Jewish Poles. Even though they were "honorable and fair-minded individuals . . . they are not Christian Poles"—several of whom, he argued, belonged on the commission. In response, Michael Berenbaum said that, since the commission had already been chosen, it would be "impractical" to add members. He informed Slotkowski that the commission's staff had conducted meetings with "leading Polish American intellectuals and scholars."

Concern over Polish resentment at being left off the commission persisted. On September 18, Seymour Bolten, a former CIA operative and former consultant to the Drug Policy staff of Eizenstat's office, who had been chosen to help the project get off to a successful start, notified Sanders that part of the *Report* could be construed as "patronizing and condescending toward the non-Jewish victims of the Holocaust . . . particularly Polish-Americans." Aware of the growing political pressures, Greenberg recommended that an "interim continuation group" be formed to implement the commission's proposals, and that it include several members from the Polish-American community, such as Dr. John Pawlikowski, "priest, distinguished educator and theologian," who had written extensively on Jewish-Christian relations after the Holocaust, and Mazewski.

Some spokesmen for Eastern European nationalities pressing for representation on the council took direct aim at the uniqueness argument. A week before the *Report* was submitted, the director of the Ukrainian National Information Service wrote to the president that Ukrainians also "met Hitler's criteria for extermination . . . [and were] numerically the second largest group to be destroyed in . . . Auschwitz, Treblinka, and Dachau." He proudly declared that Ukrainians had organized the "earliest and most effective resistance in Nazi-occupied Europe" (conveniently forgetting that this resistance movement was violently anti-Semitic and eventually reached a tacit alliance with the Germans). He urged the president to form a group that would "reflect the various nationalities and the numerical proportions of the victims of the Nazi Holocaust."

Pressure from ethnic groups increased after the *Report* was presented, and on October 25, 1979, Eizenstat advised the president to make sure the executive order creating the council "makes clear the memorial is to honor the memory of all victims of the Holocaust—six million Jews and some five million other peoples." Consequently, the next day, Executive Order 12169 offered a definition of the Holocaust different in emphasis from that in the commission's *Report*. The Holocaust was now the "systematic and State-sponsored extermination of six million Jews and some five million other peoples by the Nazis and their collaborators during World War II." In contrast to the *Report*, mention of non-Jewish victims was linked with Jews by an "and," implicitly linking their deaths with those of the Jews. Moreover, there were no longer simply "millions" of others but, rather, *five* million others. Since this was "only" one million fewer than the traditional six million Jewish victims, and since scholars like Gerald Reitlinger and Raul Hilberg thought the number of Jewish victims somewhere *between* five and six million, there was now, both implicitly and explicitly, competition over first place in the Holocaust's body count.

The controversy over *national* representation on the council worried Michael Berenbaum, particularly the possibility that a Ukrainian might be added. Writing to Sanders, Berenbaum quoted from Raul Hilberg's *The Destruction of the European Jews*: "Ukrainians were involved in the fate of Polish Jewry as perpetrators. The S.S. and the Police employed Ukrainian units in ghetto clearing operations, not only in the Galicia district, but also in such places as the Warsaw ghetto and the Lublin ghetto." Berenbaum warned Sanders that "many (not only survivors) would regard representatives of the Ukrainians serving with them on a Holocaust Memorial Council as disturbing, if not offensive. . . . This . . . step goes much too far and threatens to undermine the consensus by which the Commission has operated and by which the Council should operate." Clearly, the White House was hoping to shape a new consensus that would offer Jewish victims their due as primary victims, but also asked them to "share" the Holocaust with various others, needed "on board" the project in order to avoid political trouble for the White House.

Wiesel, who lived in New York, felt that the White House had betrayed him; consequently, communication between him and the White House had broken down. He concluded that he needed a full-time director in Washington, D.C., to deal effectively with the White House and with interest groups concerning council membership and the definition of the Holocaust, to shepherd through Congress the legislation that would establish the council, and to find a site for the building and obtain authorization to establish the museum on that site. He turned to Monroe Freedman, who had previously lived in Washington for fifteen years, served as a legislative consultant to Senator John L. McClellan in 1959, worked as a consultant to the United States Civil Rights Commission, and taught at George Washington University Law School.

In 1973, Freedman assumed the deanship of the law school at Hofstra University. His wife enrolled in one of Wiesel's courses at City College of New York, and the families became friends. Freedman recalled that when Wiesel called upon him he had said yes immediately. "Elie Wiesel and I are the same age. We were both born in 1928. When he was in the camps, I was driving around in a Cadillac in Mount Vernon, New York." Freedman was the son of assimilated second-generation American Jews who moved to Mount Vernon, he said, "to live the American dream." He recalled not even knowing what the seder was until he was in his twenties, and did not hold his Bar Mitzvah until he was forty-two. (His wife, a Presbyterian, converted to Judaism after their marriage and, he said, "pulled me along.")

Freedman met with Wiesel and a group of survivors in New York to talk about the problems and told them that, though the project was a "worthy one, you now appreciate how it gets entangled with the American political process." He warned them about further politicization, about further loss of control, and about increasing conflict with other ethnic groups. "I was talking to them as their lawyer," Freedman said, "and I told them that they were in a position to walk away from this and put the blame squarely on the White House."

The survivors unanimously rejected his advice, and, at Wiesel's direction, Freedman met in late November 1979 with Eizenstat and Sander to talk about both the problem of council membership and what was for Wiesel the unacceptable definition of the Holocaust in the second executive order. Bolten summarized the issues prior to the meeting, revealing his profound philosophical disagreements with and personal disdain for Wiesel. Though agreeing that Jews were the "first and primary subjects for extermination," Bolten argued that "all Slavs of Eastern Europe and Russia were slated for decimation, degradation, and eventual liquidation." It was, he said, "morally repugnant to create a category of second-class victims of the Holocaust as Mr. Wiesel would have us do," and said that Wiesel had "flatly ruled out anyone of Ukrainian ancestry."

Bolten believed that Wiesel's vision was "narrow, parochial, and indeed, ghetto-like." And, he argued, whereas Wiesel accused him of promoting a politicized and unhistorical version of universalism, he had, he believed, done only what was necessary to avoid "open controversy with concerned ethnic groups and their advocates in Congress." Bolten threatened to wash his hands of the project if Wiesel's "philosophy" was adopted, yet he was willing to appease Wiesel in two ways: he recommended deleting reference to a specific number of non-Jewish victims from a definition of the Holocaust in any forthcoming legislation that would create the council on a "statutory basis with its own budget," and he agreed that Wiesel could review nominations for the council. Bolten hoped—rather forlornly, it seems—that the White House and Wiesel could "develop and articulate a mutually acceptable concept of the Holocaust appropriate for the national American Holocaust Memorial."

After the meeting, both Wiesel and Freedman placed the blame for the breakdown in communication with the White House squarely on the shoulders of Michael Berenbaum. Freedman recalled that it was only when he met with Eizenstat that he found out that the second executive order *had* been sent to Wiesel before its release, but that Berenbaum, acting on the advice of Seymour Bolten, had not forwarded it, since he knew Wiesel would object. Eizenstat, in turn, had been operating on the assumption that Wiesel *had* seen the order, and was angered by what he believed was an intentional delay of his criticism in order to put the White House in a bad light. Indeed, in May 1980, Wiesel wrote to Eizenstat, "Nor was I informed until after the Executive Order had been published, when it was too late. Consequently, the new language appeared to me and others to signal a change in attitude and direction in the White House, and that change appeared all the more ominous because of the concurrent pressures to include people on the Council in response to political demands."

Michael Berenbaum recalled the events somewhat differently. "I did forward a copy of the order to Elie Wiesel," Berenbaum said, "but I did not flag the change in language for him so that he would notice it. It was not a significant issue for me, and I did not think it was for him, either." Berenbaum, who believed that inclusion and comparison were essential to a demonstration of the unique situation of Jews in the Holocaust, felt that "this was not an issue to argue about," since the president was "giving us the mandate to create. The order's language certainly has not been influential in the actual creation of the museum. I think we would have been wise to ignore it."

In Wiesel and Freedman's recollection, Berenbaum did not forward Wiesel the draft at all; in Berenbaum's version, he did, but did not bring the crucial change in language to Wiesel's attention because he did not think it either philosophically or politically important. He was quite comfortable with the process he called the "Americanization" of the Holocaust, the process by which memory is assimilated by cultures. "It is just as appropriate to talk about the Americanization of the Holocaust as it is to talk about the Israelification of the Holocaust," Berenbaum said. This process would not require the "dejudaization" of the Holocaust. The story would, however, have to be told in a way that would be meaningful to an American audience; it would have to move *beyond* the boundaries of ethnic memory. For Wiesel, this was more threatening, potentially an assault on the very essence of the Holocaust. Consequently, the significant issues in this controversy are not whether Wiesel saw the draft of the executive order or not, but two others: first, that the president and even Eizenstat felt that political realities demanded a broad-based council and definition; and, second, the serious difference between Wiesel and Berenbaum regarding the significance of an executive order and the importance of the change in language.

This incident, more than anything else, damaged the relationship between Wiesel and Berenbaum, who submitted his resignation on January 31, 1980, only a month after Freedman's arrival. As we will see, Berenbaum returned to the museum in 1987 and eventually became project director, and his understanding of the relationship between Jewish and non-Jewish victims, already articulated during the commission's work, would provide the conceptual guide for this issue in the museum's permanent exhibition.

Wiesel and Freedman's opposition to ethnic membership was more than simply visceral reaction to sharing Holocaust memory with representatives of groups that had also persecuted Jews. They distrusted the motives of the White House, which, they believed, was mistaken in using ethnicity as the sole criterion for membership; and they distrusted the motives of those clamoring for representation. They believed that the real concern was *not* interest in memorializing the Holocaust. Freedman said, for example, that a representative of the Ukrainian Anti-Defamation League had informed him that "membership on the Council would permit him to use political pressure to block any historical references to Ukrainian collaboration with the Nazis which he might consider inappropriate in any Council report on the Holocaust." (His concern was warranted: Ukrainian militia formed the rank-and-file of the personnel of the "Final Solution.")

Adding to Freedman's mistrust of ethnic motives was his perception of their resentment "over any special recognition of Jewish victimization." There were, he said, "pointed allusions to increased anti-Semitism, and threats to obstruct the work of the Council, if certain demands were not met." Freedman reported that a candidate for council membership, a "Ukrainian nationalist" who was also Jewish and therefore acceptable to Wiesel, was rejected by Ukrainian groups solely *because* he was Jewish.

Eventually, Wiesel and Freedman agreed to broad-based membership, insisting upon people "who by virtue of their personal commitments, history, stature, and accomplishments show a deep concern for the Holocaust and its implications." Nevertheless, on December 26, 1979, Bolten told Eizenstat that Wiesel had deleted eleven names from a proposed membership list and added eleven of his own choosing. Wiesel's list, Bolten warned, would "deprive the Council of all ethnic Eastern European and Slavic representation, except for Father Pawlikowski." Bolten particularly noted the deletion of Mazewski, who had "taken a positive interest in the ... project almost since its inception and has kept the Polish-American community from creating a public controversy over the absence of any Polish-American representation on the original Commission."

After an intensive and successful search by Freedman and Berenbaum for a Ukrainian representative acceptable to all sides (chosen was Julian Kulas, an attorney and banker from Chicago, a member of the Chicago Commission on Human Relations, chairman of the Helsinki Monitoring Committee of Chicago, a former president of the Chicago branch of the Ukrainian Congress Committee of America, and chairman of the Interfaith Group of the Jewish Federation of Chicago), Bolten informed Eizenstat on February 5, 1980, that, "at last," a membership list was complete. In order to accommodate not only the demands of balance but Wiesel's preferences, the council had expanded from thirty-five, to forty-seven, and, finally, to fifty, besides the requisite ten congressional members. Three-quarters of the members were Jewish, thirty-one were from the Northeast, ten were women, and included, noted Bolten, were "two blacks, two of Polish ancestry, one each of Ukrainian and Slovenian ancestry." Twenty-six had served on the commission or its advisory board.

The White House staff may have believed, in early February 1980, that membership controversies were resolved, but Wiesel and Freedman still had serious reservations. Eizenstat had assured Wiesel that, though he was committed to recognition of "Nazi atrocities" against others, he had always believed in the "distinctively Jewish nature of the Holocaust," and hoped Wiesel would understand that a broad-based council was necessary for both congressional and popular support. In response, Freedman told Eizenstat that Wiesel was "reassured." Wiesel suggested that *each* nation that claimed Holocaust victims needed to be represented. "What is proposed," Freedman wrote, is "that we begin anew to create [a council] more representative than the group that has evolved over the past months."

After the months of painstaking negotiations, the suggestion to start over did not sit well at the White House, particularly at a time when relations with Israel and American Jews were tense. An angry David Rubenstein—a member of Eizenstat's staff—engaged in speculation with Eizenstat: "I'm not convinced that there has been any real progress. . . . I think they are willing to drag this out forever. Wiesel thinks a postponement until after the election will free us of the political pressures he feels we are responding to now." A "deeply concerned" Eizenstat told Freedman that this would "further drag out a process which should have long since been underway."

Despite White House protests, however, the process dragged on into late spring, as relations between the administration and American Jews continued to deteriorate. On March 1, 1980, the United States voted, with other members of the United Nations Security Council, to rebuke Israel for its settlement policy, and an uproar ensued over the perception that the White House considered Jerusalem to be "occupied territory." Even though the administration backed down, claiming that the vote had been a mistake based on a failure of communication, Secretary of State Cyrus Vance testified before Congress that the administration viewed East Jerusalem in just this manner. On March 5, Carter lost the Massachusetts primary to Senator Edward Kennedy, who also won in New York and

Connecticut, with New York Jews voting four to one for Kennedy.

Despite the pressure of a re-election campaign, and, of course, the ongoing crisis in Iran, which began with the takeover of the United States Embassy in Teheran on November 4, 1979, high-level White House concern with proper ethnic representation on the council was evident from the personal attention given the issue by National Security Adviser Zbigniew Brzezinski and the president himself. In response to a proposed membership list presented by Eizenstat on March 18, 1980, Carter responded, "Delete 3 Jews—work [with] Jack [Watson] & Zbig to add 3 Euro-ethnics." Three days later, Brzezinski was given a list including Jaroslav Drabek, a survivor and prosecutor of Nazi war criminals in postwar Czechoslovakia. By the time the membership of the council was announced in early May, only a few days before their first meeting, Drabek joined others chosen as "ethnic" representatives: Mazewski, Kulas, Pawlikowski, Set Momjian (a first-generation Armenian American whose parents had been orphaned in the genocide and who had served as an adviser to President Carter, a representative to the United Nations, and a White House representative to the United Nations Human Rights Commission), Tibor Baranski (honored by Yad Vashem for saving Hungarian Jews), popular Jewish entertainer Victor Borge (active in foundation work to honor Danes for their help in saving Jews), and Father Constantine N. Dombalis (dean of the Greek Orthodox Cathedral, Richmond, Virginia).

Although Wiesel had been successful in adding several people he trusted to the council, he clearly lost the battle with the White House over a broad-based, ethnically representative council makeup. He understood the political realities that made a broad-based council a necessity, but it remained enduringly offensive to him. In September 1980, a year after the commission's *Report*, and several months into the work of the council, Eizenstat phoned Wiesel and cautioned him that the government of Turkey had warned the White House against any Armenian involvement in the project. Wiesel responded angrily, reminding Eizenstat of the "grim negotiations, in which I and others sought desperately to resist inclusion of Poles, Ukrainians, Hungarians, Croatians, and others who were proposed expressly as representatives of countries that had been Axis powers or that had given substantial aid and comfort to the Nazis in their persecution and annihilation of Jews." Wiesel recalled episodes that, he said, "would be humorous if they were not so disgraceful. A Hungarian was proposed for no other reason than his fund-raising activities on behalf of the Democratic Party in his state. A Ukrainian who had written books about the Nazi occupation, and who is internationally known as an ardent Ukrainian nationalist, was suggested by us on his merits, but was rejected by the White House solely and expressly because he is Jewish and, therefore, would not be acceptable to the Ukrainians. Professor John Roth, a noted Protestant authority on the Holocaust, was rejected because, in the words of a White House staff member, 'We would have to write a whole separate memo to the President just to explain that [despite Roth's name] he's not Jewish.' " Responding somewhat lamely, Eizenstat assured Wiesel that without broad representation "the legislation . . . would have been infinitely more difficult, if not impossible."

The other battle in the two-front war between Wiesel, Freedman, like-minded supporters, and the White House unfolded at the same time as the council-membership controversy and was intimately connected with it: the issue of the definition of the Holocaust. As it became clear that council members would not all share the assumption that the Holocaust was a distinctively Jewish event, all the more important became the decision on an authoritative definition of the Holocaust which, depending on language chosen, could either define the Holocaust as a uniquely Jewish event, or link or even equate Jewish and non-Jewish victims. For Freedman, the second executive order's linking of "six million Jews and some five million other peoples" was "gratuitous," a politically motivated act of dilution. It was a response, he argued, to "complaints from those individuals and ethnic groups who had written to the White House, directly and through Senators and Congressmen, to threaten that any special recognition of Jewish victims would hurt the President politically."

In January 1980, several months after the issuance of the second executive order, Freedman and Wiesel responded to Eizenstat's suggestion that an amendment to the executive order might be possible. They proposed an alteration of language that would separate Jewish and non-Jewish victims *grammatically,* by the use of two dashes. The crucial part of the definition to be used in any executive order or council literature would thus read, "six million Jews—and the millions of other Nazi victims in World War II." This would, in their view, maintain a link between Jewish and non-Jewish victims but not equate them. In March, not having heard whether the White House had agreed to their language, Freedman warned David Rubenstein that "all of our careful work during the past several weeks [regarding changes in council membership] could be destroyed if there is any variation from the phrasing proposed.... *A modification of that language would be perceived, therefore, as a betrayal of a fundamental nature.*" Eizenstat called Freedman and asked if the new language could appear only in letters of invitation to council members and not in a new executive order, and whether the dashes could be replaced by commas. Freedman, emphasizing once again the significance of the issue, informed Eizenstat that section 8.64 of the GPO (General Printing Office) Style Manual "prescribes dashes, instead of commas or parentheses, to clarify meaning."

On March 21, 1980, with the issue still unresolved, Rubenstein finally informed the president of the Freedman-Wiesel "dash solution." Representatives of Eastern Europeans groups, he said, preferred the executive order's language *without* the dashes, "for they believe that the suffering and murders that occurred within their communities have been overshadowed during the past thirty years by the offenses which occurred to Jews." These groups, Rubenstein said, wanted to "redress what they perceive as a failure of the world to recognize the enormous loss that they suffered as well under the Nazis." Rubenstein wrote that Eizenstat thought Wiesel's definition would "best serve" the council in its next executive order and in its letters of appointment, and Eastern European groups could take "solace" in the fact that they had gained representation on the council. Rubenstein also told the president that Eizenstat believed Wiesel "essential" to the project, and that without him "we simply would not be able to get another prominent Jewish leader to serve as Chairman." Rubenstein added, almost as an afterthought, that "on the merits . . . the Jewish experience was different in virtually every respect from that of non-Jewish Eastern Europeans." In his handwritten response to Eizenstat, the president said, "Stu—use the same exact definition as was used in EO 12169 [language without the dashes] delay announcement if you wish or we can simply delay any names." Once again, Carter remained firm in his commitment to a broad definition, and was not amenable to Eizenstat's search for middle ground.

A final expression of White House exasperation was the cancellation of the Days of Remembrance ceremony, which was to be held in the East Room of the White House on April 13, 1980. Thoroughly disgusted with the ongoing battles, the White House simply decided not to hold the event. Eizenstat had proposed it as an appropriate occasion to bring together both Jewish leaders and Eastern European ethnic representatives, to no avail. On May 5, 1980, Wiesel wrote Eizenstat, "In all the discussion with your staff, the emphasis has been on politics, not loyalty to the dead. No assurances regarding the integrity of the project have been kept. We have gone from frustration to frustration, from concession to concession, and why not say it, from humiliation to humiliation." Wiesel stated that Seymour Bolten had "boasted that it was he who inserted a new sentence" in the second executive order, and now not even the memorial ceremony could be held. "What a sad thing it is that such a beautiful idea, announced initially by the President with such apparent conviction, could have come to this."

Summary Reflections:
The Volatility of Holocaust Memory

IN THE BEGINNING, the Carter White House believed that the creation of a national Holocaust memorial would serve as an act of reconciliation between itself and the Jewish community, and serve as an appropriate memorial expression for the victims of the Holocaust. Clearly, those engaged in the project on all sides were stunned, angered, and frustrated by the dilemmas that seemed to erupt in every facet of planning. They quickly learned that memorials do not solve problems or necessarily heal wounds. The more volatile the memory, the more difficult a task to reach a consensual vision of how the memory should be appropriately expressed, and the more intense become the struggles to shape, to "own" the memory's public presence. This was particularly true in the case of a Holocaust memorial that was to be a *national* statement. The stakes were simply much higher than they would be, for example, over disagreements about a Jewish community's Holocaust memorial in any city. The administration's resolve concerning a broad-based council working under an inclusive definition of the Holocaust was matched by Wiesel's fear that this was a step toward the eventual effacement of Jewish victims so graphically evident in European Holocaust memory.

The bitter controversies regarding the makeup of the commission and the council and the definition of the Holocaust must be read in this context. For the White House, and for Seymour Bolten in particular, impatience, anger, and disdain for Wiesel grew, with Eizenstat somewhat desperately seeking to occupy middle ground. For Bolten and others, Wiesel's intransigence bespoke ingratitude over the administration's willingness to create the machinery necessary to plan a memorial. In the midst of a hostage crisis, a difficult reelection campaign, and the complex aftermath of Camp David, Bolten found it inconceivable that Wiesel would want to take up the president's time with disagreements over council appointees, or tinkering with grammar in an executive order defining the Holocaust. Viewing the problem solely through the windows of the White House, the administration believed it had done something for which it asked little in return—not even a political endorsement from Wiesel—and was paying an unfair price. To Bolten, Wiesel was neither holy man nor oracle, but a burdensome presence, engaged in a losing battle with the White House.

To Wiesel and some other survivors, and those sympathetic to them, the symbolic weight of council appointments and the language of Holocaust definition registered differently. Each Eastern European ethnic appointment was at best a political necessity—made only to satisfy White House concerns—and at worst an obscene incursion into the boundaries of Holocaust memory by those whose countrymen had persecuted Jews. Alteration of the relationship between Jewish and non-Jewish victims in the second executive order was perceived as yet another step on the slippery slope toward forgetfulness. Wiesel described this slope in a commission meeting. Survivors, he said, spoke of six million Jewish victims. "Then some friends . . . began reminding us, 'true, but after all, there were others as well.' It's true; there were others as well. So they said 11 million, 6 [million] of whom are Jews. If this goes on, the next step will be 11, including 6, and in a couple of years, they won't even speak of the 6. They will speak only of 11 million. See the progression? 6 million plus 5, then 11 including 6, and then only 11."

"Other" victims would, therefore, be remembered in a national memorial—not because they were in fact *Holocaust* victims, but because Jewish memory would be willing to include non-Jewish others who died at the hands of the Nazis. "Our remembering is an act of generosity," said Wiesel at the commission's first meeting, "a generosity extended to all others." And since others were to be admitted by those who felt they had the right to serve as stewards of national Holocaust memory, the proper conceptual distance between victims was crucial; as council member Hyman Bookbinder cautioned Wiesel several years later, "Careful as we may be . . . the very inclusion of non-Jewish victims will be interpreted by the average viewer or reader as meaning there were Jewish and non-Jewish victims of the Holocaust."

In order to disabuse people of this notion during the formative stages of the project, distance was to be expressed in grammatical separation—the dash formula—and in formal definition. Jews were Holocaust victims, others were victims of Nazi terror; Jews were exterminated, others were murdered. Jews, according to the *Report*, were the first victims; then, "as night descended, millions of other peoples were swept into this net of death." In other words, the *intent* of the Nazis focused on Jews, whereas others were "swept" in. Wiesel's ahistorical reading was aided by historians interested in providing the intellectual underpinning for such distance. In 1978, for example, Israeli historian Yehuda Bauer declared that there was a difference between "forcible, even murderous denationalization, and the wholesale total murder of every one of the members of a community"; total annihilation, he argued, had happened only once, "to the Jews under Nazism." Two years later, in an angry attack on Carter's occasional use of "eleven million," Bauer thought the Holocaust in danger of being "de-Judaized and Americanized." The boundaries of the Holocaust were narrow, concluded Bauer, for it meant the "murder of six million Jews and nothing else." Agreeing with Bauer was Henryk Grynberg, who had spent his childhood years in Poland during the war. The Holocaust, he said, "which was not shared then, cannot be shared now."

The struggle for ownership of Holocaust memory took place on a fundamentally religious level. Invoked were sacred promises made to the dead, blasphemy, and accusations of anti-Semitism expressed in the guise of inclusive memory. Certainly part of the survivors' enthusiasm for the project was their belief that a memorial would fulfill their heartfelt commitment that the dead never be forgotten, a commitment perceived to be at risk as Holocaust memory became public property, as Jewish victims were mixed with others. Also, linking victims together—a basic alteration of the sacred Holocaust narrative operative in much of the Jewish community—registered, predictably, as a religious offense. Irving Greenberg, the chairman of the commission, regarded comparison of the Holocaust with any other form of genocide as "blasphemous," as well as dishonest. Yehuda Bauer and Monroe Freedman perceived different facets of traditional anti-Semitism at work. Bauer believed that the sudden desire among non-Jewish groups for a place in national Holocaust memory revealed an envy of the Jews' "privileged" place as first among victims, an "unconscious reflection of anti-Semitic attitudes." Freedman believed the inappropriate linking of Jewish and non-Jewish victims—"the insistence on referring to six million Jews as an indistinguishable part of eleven million civilians"—was, if not an attempt at religious conversion, definitely one of "posthumous assimilation."

On May 28, 1980, council members representing different interests, approaching from different definitions of the Holocaust, all seeing value in the cultural and political prestige of gaining recognition as Holocaust victims, began their work. They had to respond to those in the Jewish community who were uncomfortable about the continuing fascination with the Holocaust, and to the wider American public, who would need to be convinced that locating a "European" event in national memory was important. And once it was decided that the memorial was to be located not just in the nation's capital but adjacent to the Washington Mall, controversies regarding appropriate location became more intense, as Americans weighed in with various declarations of what did or did not belong "on" the Mall. Even for those convinced that the story belonged in America, and at the physical center of American memorial space, there was still the question of an appropriate physical structure. How could architecture not fall victim to the dangers of trivializing the event? Of course, the struggle to enlarge or constrict the conceptual distance between Jewish victims and others would continue in disagreements over the symbolic ownership of memorial space within the building, and in the nature of the museum's permanent exhibition itself, as forgotten groups made their claim for representation. And, in addition to the politics of representation, those who shaped the permanent exhibition faced the daunting challenge of creating something that would reduce the distance between European event and site, and an American audience in Washington, D.C. These are the issues to which I turn in order to tell the story of the making of the United States Holocaust Memorial Museum.

CHAPTER TWO

The Site of Holocaust Memory

THE OFFICIAL GROUNDBREAKING for the United States Holocaust Memorial Museum in Washington, D.C., located adjacent to the Washington Mall and within the "monumental core" of the nation, took place on October 16, 1985, at ten o'clock in the morning. The nation's most sacred soil—home of the monumental expressions of core national narratives—would now be ceremonially commingled with "holy soils" from European concentration and death camps and venerated cemeteries: Auschwitz, Bergen-Belsen, Dachau, Theresienstadt, Treblinka, and the Warsaw Jewish Cemetery. Elie Wiesel remarked that through the act of groundbreaking "we begin to lend a physical dimension to our relentless quest for remembrance." Mark Talisman, the vice-chairman of the council, called the audience's attention to the significance of the location and the ceremony. "We stand not 1500 yards away from the monument to our first President. We are at the very heart and soul of our beloved country. We gather in this hallowed place to break this earth together, to consecrate this place as a memorial to the victims of the Holocaust."

The commission dealt with the question of whether New York or Washington, D.C., was the most appropriate city for the memorial at their first meeting, on February 15, 1979. Historian Lucy Dawidowicz spoke in favor of New York City, since it was, she said, the "center of the Jewish population in the United States and the cultural crossroads of the modern world. A site facing or near the

United Nations would be particularly suitable." At a meeting of the subcommittee on museum and monument on March 22, 1979, Ben Meed, Warsaw Ghetto survivor and organizer of the annual New York City Holocaust commemoration, and Yaffa Eliach, herself a survivor of the extermination of the Lithuanian town of Ejszyszki, also argued for New York. It was, Eliach said, "a harbor of safety and a cradle of liberty to all coming to America. It was the place where most of the survivors came when they left the Displaced Persons camps." During public hearings held by the commission at Eliach's center, the president of the local senior citizens' club thought that the "perfect" location for a Holocaust memorial would be "in the parking lot next to the aquarium in Coney Island, which would be within walking distance of the old folks in Brighton Beach." There was, not surprisingly, "strong sentiment" among the 720 people who attended the hearing that the memorial should be in the New York area.

Many others—such as Hyman Bookbinder, Washington representative for the American Jewish Committee—thought that, since this was to be a "national" memorial, Washington, D.C., was the proper location. Irving Bernstein, executive vice-chairman of the United Jewish Appeal, agreed that "a Washington site would give this institution a unique character and a special opportunity to contribute to national life. It would make clear that the commemoration of the Holocaust is a concern of the entire American population."

Some commission members voiced concerns about *any* location in the United States. Remoteness from European Holocaust sites could, they argued, make a memorial "something of a non-sequitur, comparable to ancient relics which decorate public parks." Others worried about the danger—a "vulgar tragedy"—were the memorial to become "another 'attraction' on a tourist's itinerary," and spark "considerable resentment on the part of many Americans over the use of public funds for what is perceived as a private and parochial interest." Despite such fears, at their June 7, 1979, meeting the commission accepted the subcommittee's recommendation that a museum be built in Washington. It would have to be, said Michael

Berenbaum, "of symbolic and artistic beauty, visually and emotionally moving in accordance with the solemn character of the Holocaust."

This choice of the nation's capital would prove fortuitous. A museum built in New York, even if national in intent, would clearly be perceived as a Jewish museum built in the heart of the Jewish community in America. Memory of the Holocaust would remain the province of American Jews. A national museum in Washington, on the other hand, made a more expansive—and controversial—claim on memory. Representatives of non-Jewish victim groups felt empowered to claim what they saw as their rightful place in an institution housing *national* memory to the Holocaust in the capital city.

This decision made the commission and the council's work infinitely more difficult. They had to contend not only with the imperatives of American pluralism—that, in this case, many are entitled to make their case for inclusion in the story—but also with the choice of and justification for a particular site; furthermore, they had to decide upon an architectural form aesthetically and politically acceptable in Washington, architecture that would contain and express the enormity of the event to the satisfaction of survivors, many of whom felt that locating the museum in Washington must not dilute the centrality of the Jewish core of the Holocaust.

The commission had not immediately decided that a distinctive building was necessary. Lucy Dawidowicz, for example, envisioned an outdoor monument and an indoor memorial with a permanent exhibition "where basic documents and texts would be on display." This memorial would express "America's abhorrence of anti-Semitism [and] stand in commemoration of the destroyed European Jews and their civilization." Julius Schatz of the American Jewish Congress recommended a park in Washington, with trees, plants, and sculptures contributed by countries whose citizens had been victims of the Holocaust. "In the park I see a place of public gathering, exhibition and performance, where the year around art may be displayed, music, drama and dance performed, and symposia held in memory of those who fell." This park would also serve to soften the impact of the Holocaust, for it offered "affirmation of the human spirit and dignity of the human family."

There were those, such as President Carter, who would have been satisfied with a monument. Commission member Rabbi Juda Glasner suggested that such a monument could be shaped like a "giant Menorah, a candelabrum with six branches, containing a torch, an eternal light . . . a replica of the great Synagogue of Warsaw and the six branches with the torch may represent the six millions of the Holocaust."

It was clear, however, as the commission's work progressed, that official Holocaust memory would be located in a "living" museum. Following the formation of the council in 1980, a subcommittee on site selection considered twelve locations in Washington, among them the cathedrallike Pension Building at Judiciary Square, some vacant land in Georgetown, a school near L'Enfant Plaza, and Sumner School, near the National Geographic Building. Serious attention was paid to Sumner School well into the spring of 1981, a building, one supporter said, "located on one of the choicest areas opposite the National Geographic Building." Named in honor of the nineteenth-century abolitionist Senator Charles Sumner, the school was completed in 1872, and served for a century as an educational center for black students. The council's executive director, Monroe Freedman, noted, "We were very favorably impressed with the potential of the Sumner School as the site for our Memorial/Museum." By the late 1970s, however, there was some movement in the black community in Washington to rehabilitate it, and Freedman expressed concern that there would be "possible repercussions in the black community" if the building were to house the Holocaust museum.

Mark Talisman, who, besides serving as vice-chairman of the council, was also director of the Washington Action Office at the Council of Jewish Federations, was enthusiastic about the possibility of a museum in Washington and eager to locate an appropriate site. It was, he said, "a moment to seize, for we are talking about an issue that transcends Judaism." He obtained a printout from the General Services Administration—the governmental agency that had administrative jurisdiction over federal land—indicating available sites. One place he visited several times was the Auditor's Complex, the current site of the museum, just adjacent to the Washington Mall, next to the Bureau of Printing and Engraving, between 14th and 15th Streets. This complex—the main Auditor's Building and three annexes—was designed around the turn of the century for the Bureau of Agriculture. By 1980, the annexes were unused and in poor repair. The low, crumbling, red brick buildings, however, reminded some council members—survivors and non-survivors alike—of barracks at Auschwitz.

What was most attractive, of course, was the site's location. Not only would there be a national museum to the Holocaust in the nation's capital, but, by virtue of its location just off the Mall, the museum would gain the prestige of a *central* national memorial. Council member Bookbinder, echoing general council sentiment, said, "If we had been told 'select a place' . . . I think we would have chosen that very spot. It is part of what all the tourists go to. . . . There's a feeling about that structure that seems to me to be absolutely ideal for what it's going to be." Elie Wiesel remarked, "I feel it's probably the best that we could get. Really, the best. The possibilities . . . are extraordinary."

Annexes 1 and 2 were transferred to the council on August 12, 1981. Said Freedman, "It's the kind of providential thing that I really still have difficulty believing has happened. One can go to Washington literally with hundreds of millions of dollars . . . and not be able to purchase that building. And there is nothing like it. On the tourist route, next to the Bureau of Printing and Engraving, perhaps the most popular tourist attraction in Washington, right near the Mall, right near the Washington Monument, with space, enormous amounts of usable space." The exact transfer involved .80 acre of land, and annexes 1 and 2. Several members of the National Capital Planning Commission, a governmental agency charged with reviewing development and conservation plans in the District, were bothered, however, by the fact that there was no public announcement of, or public hearing scheduled on, the issue of the land transfer. The

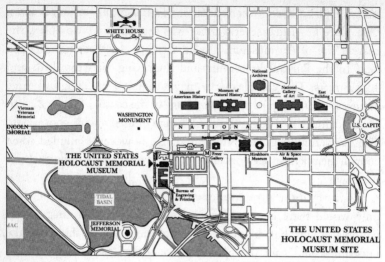

(United States Holocaust Memorial Museum)

The annex buildings as they appeared from the Mall *(Finegold, Alexander & Associates Inc.)*

Washington Post did not announce it until March 3, 1983, and the official transfer did not take place until April 13, 1983, when Vice-President George Bush presented Wiesel the "keys" to the museum in a ceremony in front of the Capitol. All discussions of the transfer took place in executive and not open sessions of Planning Commission meetings. Clearly, the council was wary of what it feared might be mixed public reaction, and one Planning Commission member recalled that the pressure generated from politically well-situated council members to accomplish the transfer privately and swiftly was "enormous."

For survivors, a museum within the monumental core was especially important. It was the logical extension of their desire and need to make Holocaust memory permanent. Nothing less would suffice. Like Civil War soldiers who, at the turn of the century, energetically built monuments to remind future generations of their sacrifice forever, Holocaust survivors saw their ranks thinning, and worried about the preservation of Holocaust memory after their passing, particularly given the threat they perceived from Holocaust deniers, those who claimed that the Holocaust never occurred. Victimized by the Holocaust, survivors believed that, after they were gone, their books and oral histories might not be enough. A museum at the heart of American commemorative space was viewed as an eternal insurance policy. It was proof that the Holocaust took place. According to Council Executive Director Seymour Siegel, the story to be told in a museum "at the most prestigious spot for a museum in the western world, perhaps in the whole world ... puts on a scientific and unshakable basis the truth of our story and the accuracy of the events."

In 1983, when the official announcement was finally made that the government had donated the land, controversy arose among Jews and non-Jews alike regarding the appropriateness of a Holocaust museum located "on the Mall." There was fear that resentment about Jews' "pushing their way onto the Mall" would spark a new wave of anti-Semitism. Others believed that, if the museum was to be in the nation's capital, it had to speak more universally about geno-

cide. "Where are the Native Americans and the black slaves represented?" "First we need a monument to blacks and Indians." Some
argued that the museum would be contaminated by the nation's
hypocrisy during the Holocaust. One respondent to the museum's
direct-mail fund-raising efforts said angrily, "Imagine a Holocaust
museum in the town whose political sages refused to lift a finger
to halt the Holocaust or open our shores to the few survivors!
How offensive to any informed individual!" Likewise, Benjamin
Hirsch, Holocaust survivor and Atlanta architect, worried that
the museum would "subvert history" by honoring President Franklin D. Roosevelt—guilty, said Hirsch, of inaction with regard to
Europe's Jews—since other presidents were traditionally glorified
on the Mall. Others argued, conversely, that any memorial on this
space should celebrate American heroism and sacrifice during the
war. A letter to the *Washington Post* in 1987 called for Holocaust
victims to "build a memorial to the American dead who gave their
lives to free them."

The argument heard most often declared the museum misplaced
because the Holocaust was not an American event. A 1983 letter
to President Ronald Reagan said that the celebratory institutions
on the Mall should not be "confronted by a morbid reminder of
genocidal crime committed by an alien tyranny on another conti-
nent." And as planning for the museum progressed in 1987, a World
War II combat veteran argued, "It is the wrong place, wrong
country, wrong time." Judging it the right museum in the wrong
place, a letter in *Time* declared the building "highly appropriate
in Jerusalem, where it would be more relevant." A member of a
Philadelphia focus group organized by the Peter D. Hart Research
Associates polling firm—hired by the council to analyze public
reaction to the museum and its permanent exhibition in 1992—said,
"It should be in Germany or Austria, where these things happened"—it "doesn't belong" there in Washington, D.C. A response
in *Jewish Week* in August 1987 to Hebrew University Professor
Shlomo Avineri's claim that the museum was misplaced suggested
a novel solution. It called for a portable "Exodus Museum," a ship

that would sail "from port to port, hosting seminars, teaching Jewish history."

Others understood the museum's location as an example of the politicization of the Holocaust. The Kennedy School's Howard Husock perceived it as a regrettable example of the "use of ethnic power politics in the American political system." He was convinced that it would always be viewed as a Jewish museum intruding on American space, functioning as a "surefire way to spotlight day in and day out the historic justification of a Jewish state before Congress and the White House." A Washington, D.C., focus-group member expressed a related, oft-heard fear, that the museum would be "pro-Israel . . . as far as the discussions going on in the Middle East right now."

These arguments were countered by those who believed that the significance of the Holocaust made it a crucially important story to tell within the memorial core. Maintenance of the Holocaust memory was, in this view, a responsibility of the United States, and a centrally located, official Holocaust memorial would function as both warning and lesson. The museum, said Council Executive Director Sara Bloomfield in 1990, belonged in the capital of a nation that is the "standard-bearer of freedom and human rights." Her letter to the *Washington Post* was headlined "A Moral Compass to Keep Us on Course."

Political columnist George Will, a consistent supporter of the museum, said that the Mall told a variety of stories, not all of them pleasant, and, in any case, America had a special responsibility for Holocaust memory. "No other nation has broader, graver responsibilities in the world. . . . No other nation more needs citizens trained to look life in the face." For Will, writing in 1983—the peak year in the "second Cold War," an intense period of nuclear anxiety—the lessons of the Holocaust were Cold War lessons. The museum would teach Americans that the world was dangerous, "a mind-opening reminder of the furies beyond our shores . . . an antidote to our innocence."

For political commentator Tom Braden, who recalled being at

Buchenwald not long after it was liberated, when "the stench still hung," the museum's purpose would be to teach the danger of the brazen misuse of historical analogies—a form of murder of Holocaust memory—practiced, Braden noted, by James Watt, who, ironically, in his role as secretary of the interior, had to "sign off" on the museum project. Watt had written that his own "persecution" as an evangelical Christian motivated him to support the project. The nation needed the museum, Braden declared, because "we wouldn't want our children to grow up to be as ignorant as James Watt."

The museum was seen as a potential storehouse for a whole variety of other lessons. It would remind Americans of the dangers of being bystanders, it would teach Americans where Christian anti-Semitism could lead, and it would impress upon Americans the fragile relationship between technology and human values. Some supporters insisted that the museum would provide a crucial lesson in individual responsibility. Hillel Levine, professor of sociology at Boston University and former deputy director of the council, hoped that Washington bureaucrats, some of whom would see the building every day, would be moved to "reflect on the way bureaucracy fragments responsibility and perspective." He hoped that they would learn from the museum that the Germans who ran the railroads taking millions to their deaths "were not just random workers throwing a switch, but part of a murderous bureaucracy, an organized evil."

Several focus-group members believed that a Mall location would impress upon visitors the need to take personal responsibility for issues usually deemed affairs of state. "It's time we say 'no' to genocide as a country, as a nation. . . . And I'm saying 'Why not start with something that we all know took place?' I don't see it ever really stopping just with the Holocaust of the Jewish people. What about the Cambodian genocide; what about other types of genocide. . . . To me, we have not learned our lesson." Several others in the focus groups also spoke of the need to connect lessons learned from the Holocaust museum to contemporary situations, from the plight of the homeless to the boat people.

The council often emphasized that the museum would have a therapeutic value. Lessons learned would inculcate civic virtue in museum visitors. Ideally, they would emerge from their museum encounter with the Holocaust having a greater appreciation of democracy and a more profound sense of personal commitment to the virtues of pluralism, tolerance, and compromise, and a more sober appreciation of the continuing dangers of anti-Semitism and racism. The implicit message was that the Holocaust clarified the importance of adhering to democratic values, and offered a stark historical example of what happened when such values failed.

The council claimed, moreover, that the Mall was an appropriate place to tell cautionary tales. A space for lessons was also a space for warning about the consequences of not appreciating the lessons. In 1983, *Time*'s Lance Morrow viewed such a museum as the "moral equivalent of impaling heads on spikes by the roadside; it rules the attention of the passers-by and leaves them with a memorable warning." Writing in *The New York Times* in 1984, civil-rights activist Bayard Rustin, a member of both the commission and the council, believed that, from the "center of our democracy," the museum would stand as a "warning against hatred and dehumanization whoever is the victim." An accompanying letter argued that "genocide is a crooked finger . . . pointed at any race or creed." The museum, the writer declared, should remind visitors that "no one is immune from inhumanity."

There have been aesthetic and political controversies regarding other Holocaust memorials and monuments in the United States. In some instances, their message is crafted to their environment. Such is certainly the case with Nathan Rapoport's Pietà-like *Liberation* statue, for example, erected in Liberty State Park, New Jersey, within sight of the Statue of Liberty. It depicts an American GI carrying a Holocaust victim. The image is one of Americans as liberators and America as refuge. Those who argued against the museum's place on the Mall often assumed that the Mall was a place of celebration and the museum would contaminate the cheerful patriotism of visitors, or that the Mall was an unchanging repository of core national stories.

Curiously, however, few supporters of the museum pointed out the dynamic history of the Mall. From the original vision of Major Pierre Charles L'Enfant, hired by George Washington to design the capital city in 1790, to the Mall's current status as a repository of American identity, it has undergone radical change. L'Enfant, who came to America in 1777 as a military engineer, had envisioned an impressive capital city, including a "Grand Avenue, 400 feet in breadth," lined with rows of trees, much like the Champs-Elysées in Paris. Though some of L'Enfant's plan for Washington was realized—the geographical expression of the separation of governmental powers represented by the White House and the Capitol, the street grid and diagonal boulevards which created both private neighborhoods and public spaces—his plan for the Mall would not be recalled until the beginning of the twentieth century.

Before the Civil War, the Mall did not function as memorial space, for much of it was either swamp or commercial land. Pamela Scott noted that "ad hoc private use is recorded as early as 1804 and 1805 when fairs were held near Center Market. Even as late as 1850 the Mall was used for private cultivation of 'grain or vegetables' and for storage of 'lumber or firewood and occasionally for rubbish of an offensive and unsightly kind.' " During the Civil War, volunteers drilled and bivouacked on the Mall, and the grounds of what would become the Washington Monument were used as a cattleyard. At the end of the war, this area became known as "murderer's row . . . the hangout of escapees, deserters, and other flotsam of the war."

The Mall had also been the site of slave pens, and not until 1850, when slave trading in Washington was outlawed, were they removed. Jesse Torrey's *Portraiture of Domestic Slavery in the United States* (1815) described a view from the Capitol of "men, women, and children, resembling that of a funeral . . . bound together in pairs, some with ropes, and some with iron chains."

In 1851, President Millard Fillmore hired New York landscape architect Andrew Jackson Downing to develop a plan for a unified Mall area. He proposed transforming the Mall into a huge public garden "to be traversed in different directions by gravelled walks and carriage drives and planted with specimens properly labelled, of all the varieties of trees and shrubs which flourish in this climate. Downing believed that, if his plan were carried out, the Mall would "undoubtedly become a Public School of Instruction." His plan did not survive his death in 1852, and the Mall was fragmented into seven gardens, administered by different government bureaus.

The Smithsonian castle—whose cornerstone was laid in 1849— was completed in 1855, and the cornerstone of the Washington Monument was laid in 1848. Both projects altered the character of the Mall, although it would be some time before the Washington Monument was completed. Lack of funds delayed construction, and in 1855 the Know-Nothing Party, angry that Pope Pius IX had contributed a monument stone, vandalized the construction site and threw the stone into the Potomac. By the beginning of the Civil War, in 1861, the monumental stump rose only 150 feet. The project would not be completed until 1876, the nation's centennial year.

Each of these events is significant for our story. The location of the Smithsonian Institution helped transform the Mall from a pastoral environment into a place where cultural institutions could help shape an enlightened citizenry. This pedagogical ideal would be associated with the eventual proliferation of museums on the Mall, and provided one of the most popular arguments for the value of a Holocaust museum. The Washington Monument served as the centerpoint for future monumental development of the Mall, and the lengthy controversy that attended its conception and construction foreshadowed future memorial controversies.

The present character of the Mall as a "shrine-like corridor of monumental dimensions" is credited to the McMillan Plan of 1901 and 1902. In the early years of the century, the Mall was still a series of parks and gardens; the Baltimore and Potomac Railroad's depot had been located there since 1872. Beginning in 1898, President McKinley considered various memorial proposals as part of the centennial celebration of the move to the nation's capital from Philadelphia to Washington in 1800. Several of these proposals—the construction of a memorial hall and a memorial bridge across the

Potomac—affected the city's landscape. Senator James McMillan (R.-Michigan) was appointed chair of a joint congressional committee to evaluate these proposals.

The American Institute of Architects, which held its annual meeting in Washington in 1900, was also interested in centennial planning. The Mall, these architects believed, should evoke the "grandeur, power and dignified magnificence [marking] the seat of government and a great and intensely active people." An architects' legislative committee was established to talk with McMillan, who, on March 8, 1901, sponsored a resolution calling for the appointment of a Park Commission to report to the Senate on the state of the city's park system.

McMillan did not have jurisdiction over Washington's public buildings. His Parks Commission, however, was under the direction of Daniel H. Burnham, who played a key role in the construction of the White City in the Chicago World's Columbian Exposition of 1893. He would be joined by another Exposition veteran, architect Charles F. McKim; by Frederick Law Olmsted, Jr., son of the nation's most eminent landscape architect and a distinguished landscape architect in his own right; and by sculptor Augustus Saint-Gaudens. Their report dealt not only with parks, but with a unified vision of the Mall. Even though the commission was dismissed in 1902, its influence remained. Congress passed legislation to remove the railroad depot and relocated the new Union Station off the Mall. Despite bitter objections, the Potomac site of the Lincoln Memorial was approved and construction completed in 1922. This location continued the Mall axis to the Potomac, and the commission's report also extended the White House axis to what would be the site of the Jefferson Memorial. The influence of the commission was felt in architecture as well. "No public building was erected in the capital city that did not conform to the ideals of the plan, and . . . to specific sites and locations. A long generation of artistic dominance extended to the building of the Jefferson Memorial and the National Gallery of Art in the mid-thirties."

Even though the memorial core seems to exude a sense of permanence, the government buildings, national monuments and memorials, and stately museums that inhabit and surround the Mall have been produced in space reshaped to fit various intellectual impulses: the neoclassical ideal of L'Enfant, the pastoral ideal of Andrew Jackson Downing, and the Progressive vision of the McMillan Commission. There are layers of meaning at the ceremonial core, each altering the topography of this space. The widespread contemporary desire to be memorialized on the Mall bears witness to its role as a significant ceremonial center, a place where various groups of Americans now seek to tell particular stories laden, they believe, with universal import.

The National Museum of the American Indian and the National African American Museum, both part of the Smithsonian Institution, will soon join the Holocaust museum as an "ensemble" of new museums that signal another transformation in the construction of American identity on the Mall. Each of these museums is very different from the Holocaust museum, which narrates only that one event. The National Museum of the American Indian seeks to advance the study of "language, literature, history, art, anthropology, and life," and will "collect, preserve, and exhibit" Native American objects. The National African American Museum will "represent the full range and breadth of the experiences of persons of African descent throughout the Diaspora," focusing on "arts and material culture . . . twentieth century history . . . images of African Americans in the media; and African American art."

Just as those responsible for planning the Holocaust museum understood the importance of a Mall location, so too did planners of the other museums. The National Museum of the American Indian will occupy a new building on the Mall near the Capitol, and the National African American Museum will occupy the Smithsonian's Arts and Industries Building. Several supporters of the African-American museum objected to its being placed in an existing building. Representative Gus Savage (D.-Illinois) said angrily that "Jews and Indians" both had their place on the Mall and the Arts and Industries Building was too small. Tom Mack, president of Tourmobile in

Washington, D.C., and an early proponent of an African-American museum, noted, "The two most important prerequisites ... are African-American control and a new world-class museum ... for this precious but sorrowfully neglected history."

As with the Washington Monument, other memorial proposals to follow—particularly the Lincoln Memorial, the Jefferson Memorial, and the Vietnam Veterans Memorial—became the subject of bitter debate over location, style, and meaning. Controversy over the appropriate site and function of the Holocaust museum was not unique. The buildings on the Mall are, as Charles Griswold remarked, a "species of recollective architecture," and the nature and content of national memorial recollection had always been subject to debate, given the malleability of the Mall.

Building Holocaust Memory

JUST AS EARLIER ADVOCATES of monuments and memorials on the Mall struggled with their place on the Mall, so did the council. In 1983 and 1984, while technical studies of the annex buildings were going on, the clock was ticking on what is popularly known as the "sunset clause" of the council's enabling legislation (Public Law 96–388, October 7, 1980). The council had until October 7, 1985, to satisfy Interior's secretary that it was making adequate progress in raising the private funds necessary for construction costs and had satisfied appropriate agencies that the design of the building was acceptable. However, beginning in 1982 and continuing for several years, there was concern that the annexes were too small to serve as home for a permanent exhibition, a research center, an educational-outreach center, and a memorial space. The council faced a problem that council member Raul Hilberg had worried about in 1981: "The size of the building must be large enough to permit us to do the things that we have talked about during the last few years. Our principal theme was that of a 'living' memorial. . . . Above all we must remember that the building will be our statement about the Holocaust. If *it* is too small, so is our memory."

Hilberg expressed an important concern: *any* buildings would be measured against American memories preserved on the Mall that were housed in a monumental obelisk (Washington), temples (Lincoln and Jefferson), and the haunting space of the Vietnam Veterans Memorial. If the building containing this "new" central memory did not measure up, it would not only reduce the impact of the memory, but also be an expression of disrespect for the dead.

The danger of an insufficient building loomed over attempts to fit memorial space, a library and an archive, administrative offices, and the permanent exhibition into the approximately fifty thousand square feet of the two annexes. The job of trying to fit council aspirations into this space fell on Anna Cohn, the first museum professional hired by the council, and the architectural firm Notter Finegold & Alexander, chosen by the council as project architects because they had already been doing restorative work on the Auditor's Building for the Bureau of Agriculture. Cohn had been director of the B'nai B'rith Klutznick Museum in Washington, D.C., for seven years, until she left in 1982 to become project director of the Smithsonian Institution's "Precious Legacy" exhibit, which brought to the United States the rich collection of Judaica housed in the State Jewish Museum in Prague. Cohn gradually became involved in the Holocaust museum's planning, first as a consultant while still at the Klutznick, and eventually as the council's director of museum planning, until her return to the Smithsonian in 1985.

None of the council members had any idea of what it took to build a museum, Cohn recalled, and they talked in grandiose terms of how to concretize appropriately a story of such epic proportions. "They had an endless list of needs, which required an enormous amount of space," she said. "Space for records, artifacts, commemorative space, exhibition space to tell the story, and space for a learning center. Their frustration at not being able to do all of this in the annexes was the first time that their aspirations clashed with the reality of the space available."

After energetic attempts to squeeze council plans into the limited space of the annexes were unsuccessful, it was widely recognized that the annexes were simply too small, and that the council needed to enter into the laborious work of having the buildings "delisted," removed from the National Register of Historic Places—a necessary step toward tearing them down—and then to construct a new building. Cohn recalled that Wiesel and some other survivors did not want to lose the annexes. "These buildings were already perceived by some as essential, as sacred, given their evocation of the feel of Auschwitz barracks." Estimates were that the museum would need at least twice the space—a hundred thousand square feet—and Cohn recommended that the council demolish annex 1, retain annex 2 for offices, acquire annex 3, which had *not* been transferred to the council, and build a "full-fledged museum building."

A climate of uncertainty still pervaded every aspect of the project in 1984. Excitement about a prime location adjacent to the Mall was accompanied by intense fear that fund-raising would be unsuccessful. Consequently, some council members entertained seriously a proposal from Dr. Laszlo Tauber, a survivor who was an orthopedic surgeon from Virginia and chairman of the museum-building steering committee, who offered to provide funding and land in Virginia, largely because he was concerned that a Mall location would engender a wave of anti-Semitism.

Micah Naftalin, who was hired in 1982 as senior deputy director and became acting director when Seymour Siegel fell ill, viewed the Tauber proposal as potentially disastrous for the institution and formed a different building committee to advise the council. One member was Albert (Sonny) Abramson, a prominent Washington developer and president of Tower Construction Company. He was encouraged to supervise the building project by both Naftalin and Anna Cohn, who knew him well from his philanthropic support of the Klutznick Museum. Abramson, a developer who understood square footage, became the moving force in the delisting process. In November 1984, the council designated him "its full and general agent to superintend all aspects of the planning and building processes through final construction . . . specifically including the option of clearing the site." From that day on, Naftalin said, "the project was on the right track. Abramson had made a judgment that he needed *all* the power to do the building or it wouldn't get done." In retrospect, Naftalin thought, "he was probably right."

By December 1984, the council had received permission from the Advisory Council for Historic Preservation to tear down the two annex buildings. Naftalin commented, "Whatever symbolic significance was first seen in the buildings has always been secondary to the site [near] the Mall and what we want to do. Now we have an option of making an architectural statement about the Holocaust, starting from scratch." The way was paved for deliberation on an architectural design appropriate for national memory of the Holocaust.

There was intense pressure to jump-start the building project: fund-raising was slow, the council needed a substantive building plan to make the project "real" to potential donors, and there was a desperate urgency among some survivors on the council. Cohn recalled how each new delay, each complication, evoked comments from survivors—"You know, in five years, some of us will not be here." They knew their time was running out, and they wanted to see the museum built in their lifetime. There was pressure of a practical sort as well, for the sunset clause was fast approaching, and until December 1984 there was no assurance that the council would get permission to raze the annexes and start anew. Abramson was insistent, recalled Maurice Finegold, of Notter Finegold & Alexander, that "I show him a new building soon," yet there had been no discussion about what a new building should look like, no discussion with the council, only the directive from Abramson. "I felt," said Finegold, "like there was a gun at my head." Abramson, he believed, was *only* interested in the façade of the memorial space, the Hall of Remembrance, which would face the Mall. What was important to Abramson was to have something for fund-raising purposes.

After their selection as architects for the project, Finegold's firm prepared a building model for presentation to the council in December 1984. Shortly before this, Abramson brought Finegold to

ABOVE: The Finegold
building proposal
*(Finegold, Alexander &
Associates Inc.)*

RIGHT: The Enav
building proposal
*(Zalman & Ruth Enav
Architects Ltd.)*

BELOW: The revised
Kaufman building
proposal *(Finegold,
Alexander & Associates
Inc.)*

Washington to comment on a sketch design done by a staff architect of Abramson's Tower Construction Company, Karl Kaufman, in which the Hall of Remembrance was suspended over an open plaza space. Abramson liked it, because it had a sculptured façade that faced the Mall. Finegold told him he thought the plaza would be an "unpleasant space." After presentations of both designs to the council, Abramson told Finegold, "We like elements of both; work it out with Karl."

Finegold's graceful and evocative building was designed to draw visitors into a vortex in which the Hall of Remembrance was shaped like a large oval. This form, the design concept stated, was "reminiscent of formal Washington architecture," and partook of Jewish symbolism as well, the oval/egg being a part of a meal after a funeral. Its shape was to remind visitors of the "fullness and continuity of life, even in the face of death." The oval, however was not whole, "symbolizing that the Holocaust fractured the wholeness of life." The exterior of the building was to be dark-red and gray stone.

Some time after the December meeting, Israeli architect Zalmon Enav submitted a design concept at the invitation of Elie Wiesel. His building was designed to move visitors from ordinary space to the world of the Holocaust as they descended underground into a "deportation court," leading to a "dark and misty" basement in which visitors would move on caged platforms through exhibit areas grouped around the "Kaddish Hall." The exterior was black granite, designed to contrast "dramatically with any surrounding buildings, parks, or any other element of the 'normal present.' " Finegold recalled that the model was widely viewed as "disruptive, inappropriate for the area, and it was quickly dismissed."

Though not fond of the Kaufman design, Finegold worked to help pass it through two advisory groups: the Commission of Fine Arts, directed to rule on the aesthetic appropriateness of public buildings in Washington, and the National Capital Planning Commission. Each had the power to recommend design modification or recommend to the secretary of the interior that a design be rejected.

Consequently, on May 10, 1985, the council presented to Fine

Arts its building design, in which the Hall of Remembrance was suspended twenty feet above the main entrance. Benjamin Forgey, the influential architectural critic for the *Washington Post*, was already worried about the intrusion of the museum on the Mall. The building, he thought, must take a "distinctly secondary position" to other memorials on the Mall. He called for a smaller building, a change from dark red to a color matching neighboring buildings, and an alignment on the site line of the Bureau of Printing and Engraving. Echoing Forgey's concerns was the Planning Commission, which on July 3, 1985, said that a Holocaust memorial presented as "difficult, although different, a problem as that of the design of the nearby Vietnam Veterans Memorial." While functioning as memorial and museum, the building would "have to play a clearly subordinate role to the major symbols of the nation in its immediate vicinity."

The design ran into trouble at the Commission of Fine Arts meeting. Several commissioners spoke of it as too "massive," noting that the Vietnam Veterans Memorial proved that "simplicity and delicacy are more provocative." Commissioner Edward Stone remarked that the building exuded "foreboding, almost so severe that it may not welcome you with open arms." Also worried about the building's "feel" was commissioner John Chase, who argued that the function of memorial architecture was to provide an "emotional backdrop." This museum, he said, needed "some real feeling . . . some love and understanding."

The Kaufman sketch depicted a strident and ostentatious building. Expressing the view of some commissioners that the building looked more like a monument to the perpetrators than to the victims, Fine Arts Chairman J. Carter Brown wrote Secretary of the Interior Donald P. Hodel, "The Commission has serious concerns. . . . The sheer massiveness of the elements . . . tends toward an inhuman scale and an overstated emphasis on physical strength, both questionable characteristics in a memorial that is to reflect the human dimensions of the Holocaust." An angry letter to the *Washington Post* on June 6, 1985, put the matter more bluntly: "From the front, the building looks like a huge oven. From the side it looks like a huge coffin.

Apart from that, it is pompous—the last sentiment I would associate with a proper memorial to Hitler's civilian victims."

After the meeting, Abramson considered starting over but decided that the plan could be "fixed." The Hall of Remembrance was lowered, and a colonnade was added from 14th to 15th Street. On June 28, 1985, Fine Arts unenthusiastically approved the revised concept for the 15th Street façade, but wanted more work done on the 14th Street side. They were willing to approve the design conditionally in order to give the council more time to raise funds and improve the building—in short, to save the project.

There were also revealing disagreements over symbolic ownership of interior space. The President's Commission had already envisioned a three-part institution: museum, monument, and educational center. The "monument" was soon understood as a clearly distinct memorial space for victims of the Holocaust. In 1984, Anna Cohn, David Altshuler (professor of Judaic studies at George Washington University, who came to the museum with Cohn as interim director of education), and Elie Wiesel met regularly in New York, envisioning both the thematic content and the spatial layout of the institution: a Hall of Witness to tell the story, a Hall of Learning to confront the contemporary implications of the Holocaust through education, and the Hall of Remembrance to mourn those who were murdered. However, just as the relationship of Jews and non-Jews in council membership, in Holocaust definitions, and in exhibit plans was unsettled, so too was the function of memorial space. Who was to be remembered here? Just Jews, or all victims of the Nazis? During the work of the President's Commission, there was a suggestion that those of different religions—belonging to different victim groups— should have *separate* chapels, distinct memorial "homelands." "While the Holocaust should be depicted in a manner which certainly emphasizes its particular significance for our Jewish people, it should also reflect the destruction of . . . non-Jews. . . . There may be chapels where one can pray and seek solace and they would represent different faiths."

The Hall of Remembrance remained contested space even during planning for the annex buildings, and the issues endured into planning for the new building. At a museum-content committee meeting in 1985, the issue came to a head, revealing not only the continuing tension regarding the appropriate representation of various victim groups—for any resolution of the dilemma would by definition make a statement about the issue of Jewish uniqueness—but also the fragility of relationships among council members, relationships that endured only because of the importance of the project, or in some cases because of personal allegiance to Elie Wiesel. Despite the attention devoted to this issue by the commission and the council, the issue had been resolved, Hyman Bookbinder remarked, only in a "general philosophical, good will way."

As he had done and would continue to do in other meetings, Father John Pawlikowski, professor of social ethics at the Catholic Theological Union in Chicago and longtime council member, tried to allay his Jewish colleagues' fears that non-Jewish representation in the museum or in memorial space would threaten the centrality of Jewish victimization, which he strongly affirmed. He objected, however, to including various groups in the permanent exhibition but leaving them out of the Hall of Remembrance. "I just don't think you can bring people along a path and include them now as you have done . . . and then have absolutely nothing." He wondered if "creative use" of some triangles that prisoners had worn might solve the problem. Pawlikowski emphasized that there had to be a place where those who came to commemorate non-Jewish victims would "feel comfortable"—a place, perhaps, where they would be able to "organize a small commemoration."

When Albert Abramson reminded people of the hexagonal shape of the hall, and said he believed the agreement had been that this was "essentially a memorial for the six million Jews," Pawlikowski disagreed: "I think it's very crucial that the non-Jews who visit the museum feel impelled to go there and remember too, after having seen this and contemplate not only what happened, but perhaps even more importantly why it happened and . . . since the overwhelming majority of them would be Christian—why the Christian churches had a pivotal role in the process." Holocaust survivor Sam Bloch countered, "We . . . have no intention of creating the Jewish ghetto. Don't look at this that way. But we are entitled in this museum to one area that should be specifically Jewish. We owe it to the memory of our six million people."

Council member and Holocaust survivor Kalman Sultanik, vice-president of the World Jewish Congress, also made it clear that the memorial space was only for commemoration of the six million, and that there were bitter feelings about treating those whose country-men might have been killers as victims worthy of commemorative respect. "Jews," he said, were "killed not only by Germans." Ideas were again floated for separate rooms—a room with a Jewish center, a commemorative hall of national patriots. Council member Franklin Littell asked Sultanik if Daniel Trocmé could be remembered in the Hall of Remembrance. (Trocmé was the second cousin of André Trocmé, the heroic pastor of the French village of Le Chambon, which, under the leadership of André Trocmé and his wife, Magda, saved many Jews. Captured by the Gestapo in a raid, Daniel Trocmé was murdered in the gas chamber at Majdanek on April 4, 1944. Israel declared him a "Righteous Gentile" in 1976 and planted a tree for him, as they had done for Pastor Trocmé, at Yad Vashem.) "No," said Sultanik, he couldn't be honored there, because "he didn't die as a Jew. . . . The six million Jews . . . died differently."

Mark Talisman, chairing the meeting, sensed how tenuous were the bonds of civility, and said, somewhat desperately, "No need to get angry over this because we are friends. We have come too far to have this dissolve." Attempting to resolve the situation, Abramson, obviously thinking out loud, said, "I think we will specify that it is a non-religious memorial; that we want no religious symbol; it's a place for creative design." Of course, the problem was not "reli-gion" but, rather, once again, the issue of inclusion, exclusion, and the clash of victim-group memories. For some survivors, claiming symbolic ownership of space near the Mall was not enough. Memory was first to be legitimated through emplacement of the museum in the monumental core; then boundaries had to be defined and hierarchies clearly constructed in its interior space. This was a way of rooting in place the centrality of Jewish memory of the Holocaust. Here the issue was not who got "wall space" in the permanent exhibition, but what space was appropriately "owned" by what group, who was at home in certain space, and who was to be merely a visitor—or perhaps not welcome at all—in another person's memorial place.

Questions of ownership of interior space were accompanied by bitter remarks about potential defilement of such space. The council's 1982 fund-raising plan recognized the need to honor donors in a "dignified way consistent with . . . practice in the great museums of the world." The plan envisioned naming for generous donors facilities within the museum: "a theatre, kosher dining pavilion, library . . . education, research, and archival center." In the late 1980s, as the fund-raising arm of the council, "A Campaign to Remember," moved into high gear, an elegant brochure described space in the museum which would honor donors. Givers of $1 million or more would have their names engraved on a "Founders Wall" near the elevators that carried visitors to the permanent exhibition. Near the 15th Street entrance there would be a "Donors Lounge" with dark granite panels listing donors on four separate levels, according to the amount of their gifts. There would also be two leather-bound books with names of those making more modest donations, and a computerized "Scroll of Remembrance," listing all who gave smaller amounts. Joseph M. Brodecki, national director of the campaign and son of a survivor, said that these names would all be placed in "nonsacred" places; Michael Berenbaum said, "No amount of money would get your name on the Hall of Remembrance."

For some, however, the whole museum building was a sacred environment, and it was inconceivable to them that any part of a building devoted to Holocaust memory could be characterized as nonsacred. Naming facilities and honoring donors in such a manner was, in this view, a form of defilement. At Fine Arts meetings in 1987, for example, Warner Hausenberg, a survivor of Westerbork and Bergen-

Belsen, voiced his opposition to "the notion of permitting generous donors to . . . have parts of the monument named after themselves or their designees." This would, he said, "desecrate the memory of millions of nameless persons who were victimized by the Holocaust." Emma Andrea Kolodny, a founding member of a group of Jewish child survivors, objected, telling Fine Arts commissioners, "The idea is inappropriate, because a Holocaust Museum should commemorate the fate of the millions of nameless Holocaust victims."

By early 1986, Albert Abramson was getting the message from a number of people that the Kaufman design, born of the desire to jump-start the project, was simply not appropriate. Finegold, deeply troubled, characterized it as "neo-classicism worthy of Albert Speer." Wiesel had also expressed his ambivalence: "Ideally I would have preferred a different building. I would have preferred a building that would evoke content also. . . . However, this is a compromise." Wiesel and Abramson were told that a new architect would better design what the council wanted, a "world-class" museum building. Each received advice to approach the prestigious architectural firm of I. M. Pei and Partners in New York, and Abramson was also advised by J. Carter Brown that it would be wise for the council to hire a museum director who might then serve as an intermediary between the architect and the council. Brown suggested Arthur Rosenblatt, in the midst of a distinguished career as vice-president of architecture and planning at the Metropolitan Museum of Art in New York. Though not eager to leave the Metropolitan, Rosenblatt said he was willing to become the museum director, because of what he characterized as a Jewish "Pavlovian response" to Holocaust issues, and because of a deep sense of social responsibility inherited from the Yiddish socialist tradition of his father.

When Rosenblatt arrived in Washington in April 1986, Abramson was still convinced that the Kaufman design could be modified. Rosenblatt thought that, at best, it needed "major surgery," and convinced Abramson to consider proposals for a new building. Rosenblatt met with the distinguished architect Kevin Roche, who, based on his understanding that the Kaufman building was to be modified, decided he was not interested. It was at this point that Rosenblatt turned to I. M. Pei, who said that he was too busy with an addition to the Louvre in Paris. Then Rosenblatt met with one of Pei's associates, James Ingo Freed, in New York's Plaza Hotel. Rosenblatt was initially interested in having Freed become a consultant and work with the existing design. Freed, however, already convinced that a new design was needed, told Rosenblatt that if the council was interested in talking to him about coming on board as a new architect he would be interested, but he was not interested in working with the old design. Freed was introduced to council members at a meeting in December 1986.

Rosenblatt would leave the museum on September 30, 1988, largely because of disagreements over his authority to shape the permanent exhibition in addition to the building project. He remained proud of what he believed was his lasting legacy to the museum, the selection of Freed. At a time when planning for the permanent exhibition was moving in quicksand, and fund-raising was sporadic, the selection of a prominent architect was a major coup for the council. It gave the project a legitimacy that it badly needed, and paved the way for Freed to design what museum supporters—and many architectural critics—proudly referred to as a "world-class" building. Rosenblatt was clearly pleased to have had a role in this. "Survivors and developers," he said, "are people who are not visual. We taught them that architecture is a more profound experience than they could dream of. I helped bring about what they should be proud of."

Freed was born in Essen, Germany, in 1930, and emigrated to Chicago in 1939. He attended the Illinois Institute of Technology, whose school of architecture was directed by Ludwig Mies van der Rohe. After he graduated, he joined Mies van der Rohe in New York in 1955, and Pei the following year. Freed, who designed the Jacob Javits Convention Center in New York and the Los Angeles Convention Center, struggled with early drawings for a building with little success. He began to recall his childhood years as a German Jew, particularly Kristallnacht, the "Night of Broken Glass," which

James Ingo Freed *(Barbara Bordnick)*

he spent riding the streetcars with his father to avoid the violence. Freed escaped with his sister when he was nine and went first to France, then to Switzerland, and finally to the United States. His father and mother arrived in 1941 on one of the last refugee ships. In 1945, Freed's mother learned that most of her family—parents, brothers, sisters—had been murdered. His family stopped speaking German at home. "There was a conspiracy of silence about the Holocaust and about our being Jewish," Freed recalled. "Only since I've been working on this project have I really thought about my childhood. I did what a lot of people, a lot of my friends did—we just forgot about it, took it out of our minds."

Freed, who had grown up completely uninterested in the Holocaust, recalled seeing a drawing of the Kaufman design in a magazine and thinking to himself, "Gee, they could do better than that." After accepting Rosenblatt's offer in 1986, he proposed a three-month trial period to see what design would emerge. Intrigued by the "seeming impossibility of making something . . . more than just a box for artifacts," he immersed himself in Holocaust literature and documentary films, but every time he began a design, "I just froze."

He soon realized that he had to visit Holocaust sites before he could create a satisfactory design, and in October 1986 Freed, Rosenblatt, and Finegold left for Europe. Finegold spoke of walking with Freed through Auschwitz. They had arrived on All Hallows' Eve, at a camp shimmering in candlelight and full of people. They walked through the Auschwitz Museum's permanent exhibition—barracks containing displays made brutal by their sheer mass—of victims' hair, eyeglasses, shoes, and personal belongings—walked to the ruins of the crematoria in Birkenau, and went upstairs into a guard tower that overlooked the massive city of extermination that was Birkenau, where, Finegold said, "the enormity of the Holocaust became apparent." Freed recalled being grasped by the power of the place. "When I walked into this, some archaic memories must have been stirred, because emotionally this was a turning point for me. As we walked to the crematorium, there were scuffed-up little bones everywhere that had never turned to dust. I stood in a time warp, realizing that, except for good fortune, I would have been brought to such a place to die." He also remembered struggling to detach himself from the place. "I retreated into a more analytic [mode] where I look[ed] at things and I began to speculate how one would do a building that might . . . incorporate some of these techniques of construction." He started to sketch his building that evening.

Freed decided that this could not be a neutral container, a "black box" that "had nothing to tell you, neither outside nor inside." Such a building, Freed believed, would say, "I give up," ceding that there could be no adequate architectural statement about the Holocaust. Nor could he envision a high-tech building "that would not fit into Washington, would not fit into this subject matter." His building, he

RIGHT: Freed in
Auschwitz *(Finegold,
Alexander & Associates
Inc.)*

BELOW: Freed in Hall
of Witness during
construction
(© 1992 Alan Gilbert)

Detail of construction in Hall of Witness *(Jou Min Lin of Pei Cobb Freed & Partners)*

thought, had to be "expressive of the event." It would have to communicate through raw materials and organization of space the feel of inexorable, forced movement: disruption, alienation, constriction, observation, selection.

Freed paid attention to the tectonics of the camps, the way buildings were put together. His use of steel, brick, and glass evoked what architectural critic Herbert Muschamp called the "hard industrial forms" of the Holocaust. The museum, he observed, "is a place quarried from the memory of other places." For example, at Auschwitz, Freed studied the banded steel that had been strapped around the crematoria because brick was exploding from the intense heat of burning bodies. And though this steel strapping is evident in the museum, Freed insisted that such symbols be "sufficiently ambiguous and open-ended so that others can inhabit the space, can imbue the forms with their own memories." Discussing his formidable towers, read often as camp watch towers, Freed declared, "I don't want to [tell] anybody these are towers and towers are bad. Towers may be good. . . . I wanted to do this . . . so that you are forced to acknowledge your separation from . . . Washington, from the world that you're in."

Freed's building, from its outward appearance to its interior mood and insistence on certain ways visitors inhabit and move through space, is designed as a place of disorientation, a building that will force visitors to "leave" Washington, D.C. Ironically, then, though the location of the museum in the monumental core was deemed crucial for those who believed that Holocaust memory should be an integral part of the nation's memory, Freed's building has as its object the removal of visitors from Washington, so that they may be receptive to the story told in the permanent exhibition. The location of the museum asked visitors to "pay attention" to a crucial memory, and the attributes of the building informed visitors that they must, in order to pay attention, leave Washington. "I don't think you just ever walk into the door and there is the Holocaust," Freed remarked. "You can't do it. You have to prepare yourself psychologically for it." Evocative architecture and the manipulation of interior space served as Freed's agent of spiritual preparation for a journey into the Holocaust.

This reorientation of priorities began even before visitors entered the building. No longer was the 15th Street side of the museum merely a city street. On October 8, 1986, it was renamed Raoul Wallenberg Place, and a plaque was dedicated to the Swedish diplomat credited with saving thousands of Hungarian Jews in 1944–45. (Wallenberg was captured by the Russians, and his fate has remained a mystery ever since.) Visitors encounter the redeeming memory of Raoul Wallenberg, and walk into General Dwight D. Eisenhower Plaza on their way into a story in which acts of resistance and rescue are minor, albeit important, themes. And even as Freed's building seeks to take visitors out of American space, they are reminded that during this symbolic journey their purpose is to remain firmly rooted in American ideals.

On outside walls of the Hall of Remembrance appear statements by Presidents Carter, Reagan, and Bush, and the eyewitness account

Fourteenth Street entrance (©1993 Norman McGrath)

of the horrors General Eisenhower encountered in Ohrdruf. In the hallway of the 15th Street entrance is George Washington's famous statement that the government of the United States "gives to bigotry no sanction, to persecution no assistance," and a statement from the Declaration of Independence about the "unalienable rights" of man; inside the 14th Street entrance is a statement by President Clinton.

Visitors enter the building on either 14th Street or Raoul Wallenberg Place. The *Washington Post*'s Benjamin Forgey and *The New York Times*'s Herbert Muschamp described their entrance at the museum's opening. Forgey wrote, "The entry sequences themselves are disorienting. Directions are not clearly labeled. The visitor must choose—go left, go right, go down, up, forward. Passing through the revolving door of the monumental west facade [Raoul Wallenberg Place] one confronts a slablike wall of black granite with a single, square window that opens onto a cavernous atrium, a space one can get to only by going down and then up again." And Muschamp, entering on 14th Street: "Visitors walk toward a monumental portico, a turret-shaped bulge of limestone that provides a frame for three tall rectangular arches. . . . The arches do not welcome. They gape."

Having made the initiatory journey, visitors enter the Hall of Witness, a dense and cold space. "It's like a railroad station," said Freed, "a place of comings and goings, and from here, there is no way into the exhibition except through the mechanical means of elevators." Once again, Freed wanted his raw materials to create appropriate space in which to negotiate the museum: "Brick walls, exposed beams, boarded windows and metal fences and gates will let visitors know they are in a different place—that the Holocaust is an event that should disturb and be felt as well as perceived." Visitors may have an uncanny sense of being watched, as people move on glass-bottom walkways on the floors above, hinting, architectural critic Joseph Giovannini remarked, "at inaccessible, anonymous presences in control." The walkways themselves call into question what Freed understood as a misplaced confidence in the beneficence of technol-

RIGHT: Detail of the twisted skylight *(Jou Min Lin of Pei Cobb Freed & Partners)*

BELOW: Hall of Witness *(© 1993 Norman McGrath)*

RIGHT: Hall of
Witness *(Jou Min
Lin of Pei Cobb
Freed & Partners)*

BELOW: Hall of
Witness, looking
toward 14th Street
entrance *(© 1993
Alan Gilbert)*

ogy. "It failed us once," he said, "yet we have more faith in it than anything else."

The Hall of Witness is not a comfortable space to inhabit. From the skylight cutting across diagonally, held in a warped, twisted metal truss, to the cold and inhuman cross-bracing under the skylight and the steel bands that seemingly hold the brick walls together, there is a sense of a space that is twisted and tortured in the effort to contain the story of the Holocaust, a space that screams as it seemingly strains to rip itself apart. It is also a space perceived from various vantage points as visitors work their way from the beginning of the permanent exhibition on the fourth floor, across bridges to tower exhibits, to the end of the exhibit on the second floor. "You circle down," Freed remarked, "gathering information as you come." And from bridges on the fourth and third floors, visitors glimpse the Hall of Witness through glass panes etched with names of destroyed communities, and first names of murdered people.

How people view the Hall of Witness very much depends on the evocative play of light in the museum, for Freed designed the building so that at certain times of day the names on the bridge's glass sides "just disintegrate," and the Hall of Witness itself can be fractured by a grid of shadows. The Hall of Remembrance, on the other hand, has an enduring smooth and soothing light, like the "interior of a lantern."

Freed intended that before visitors returned to the Mall, they would linger in the Hall of Remembrance, containing an eternal flame under which is buried soil from Holocaust sites and American military cemeteries. Freed insisted that no traditional memorial form could penetrate the Holocaust, and felt "completely unequipped to do sculpture." He was willing to try to accommodate Abramson's desire for a hexagonal memorial space, which he characterized as "contemplative space," and which survivors could, of course, read as a Star of David, thereby consecrating the area as Jewish memorial space.

OPPOSITE: Hall of Remembrance (© *Timothy Hursley*)

While occupying this space, visitors would have the opportunity to reflect on moving inscriptions engraved on the walls of the Hall of Remembrance. Over these too there was disagreement. Should they be biblical, or testimony from victims and survivors of the Holocaust? Should they inspire hope in visitors? There was vigorous resistance to a suggestion that New Testament inscriptions appear with those from the Hebrew Bible, and to a suggestion that an inscription from Anne Frank would be appropriate. Michael Berenbaum wanted the traditional Jewish invocation of memory to appear over the entrance to the Hall of Remembrance—"May their memory serve as a blessing"—and he wanted to add "a warning," because, he said, in "dealing with the Shoah, such an invocation is dialectical—memory is not only a blessing, but must also be a warning." There was debate over whether Holocaust deaths could be considered "blessings," and appearing instead is Elie Wiesel's motto for the council, "For the living and the dead we must bear witness."

Berenbaum felt strongly that the central quote in the Hall of Remembrance should be testimonial, "from the 'testament' of the Kingdom of Night to our world." Suggestions included:

> Letters torn by living hands
> Into the walls of prisons, ghettoes,
> Death-camps, in every tongue and every
> Shade of human agony:
> I beheld my name in you, and forever
> Hear your holy song in me. . . .
>
> Abraham Sutzkever

> I have told you this story
> not to weaken you
> but to strengthen you.
> Now it is up to you!
>
> inmate of Sachsenhausen
> orienting new arrivals

OPPOSITE: Skylight and bridges viewed through window with first names of victims (© Timothy Hursley)

After it was decided that only biblical quotations were to be used, Berenbaum argued for Micah 6:8 as the central quote:

> He has showed you, O Man, what is good,
> And what the Lord requires of you:
> Only to do justly
> to love mercy
> And to walk humbly with your God.

This, said Berenbaum, "speaks not of death but of life and of the task of those who survive. It speaks of simple, basic values, of the reaffirmation, the revelation of these values." Some objected that this was too "religious," however, so chosen instead was Deuteronomy 4:9:

> Only guard yourself and guard your soul
> carefully, lest you forget the things
> your eyes saw, and lest these things
> depart your heart all the days of your life.
> And you shall make them known to your children
> and to your children's children.

The inscription on one side panel deals with the primal murder, recorded in Genesis 4:10, "What have you done? Hark, thy brother's blood cries out to me from the ground!" The inscription on the other side panel is from Deuteronomy 30:19:

> I call heaven and earth to witness this day:
> I have put before you life and death, blessing and curse.
> Choose life—that you and your offspring shall live.

Albert Abramson and others liked this because it was "hopeful." Berenbaum disliked it because, he said, "it spoke of choice that the victims did not have." Also left out because it did not convey hope was a quotation from Job 16:18, "Earth do not cover my blood; Let there be no resting place for my outcry!"

The exterior of the Hall of Remembrance, facing the Washington Mall, would prove to be the most contentious exterior space in the museum, as Rosenblatt and Freed were to discover when they began their journey through Washington's bureaucracy. On May 22, 1987, they took the new building design back to Fine Arts. Freed said that his building had to be a "good neighbor" to the limestone building of the Bureau of Printing and Engraving and the brick Auditor's Building, and he agreed that the Hall of Remembrance would have to be modestly sized so as "not to compromise the other institutions or monuments." He also noted, however, that it needed to protrude beyond the site line of the Bureau of Printing and Engraving, because, when lined up, his building was swallowed by the other's monumental size. "There is a complex, spiritual side to this," said Freed. "Set back in line with the other buildings, this could never be a monument; it will always be a building." At a June meeting, Fine Arts gave approval to the design, although it made Freed pull back the Hall of Remembrance five feet eight inches, to the exact site line of Printing and Engraving. This reduced the building by about twenty-six thousand square feet, or almost 10 percent, and the height was cut by five feet, to seventy feet.

During a period reserved for public comment, a member of the Exhorters, a religious group, objected to the Hall of Witness, calling it a "synagogue." "Just imagine," Stan Rittenhouse declared, "if a Ukrainian group were to propose the building . . . of a memorial to the victims of Stalin's purges and genocide . . . in the form of a Christian cross." He also declared that the "essence" of the design was "offensive to Americans of German descent . . . and to the Bible-believing Christian community, for Christianity teaches forgiveness and love while Zionism and this museum . . . will emphasize and represent revenge . . . and an unforgiving spirit." Freed recalled with a smile that, after this presentation, it was hard for any of the Fine Arts commissioners to oppose the design.

Impressed yet still ambivalent was the *Washington Post*'s Benjamin Forgey, who characterized Freed's design as "difficult and uncompromising." Forgey was at first "deeply troubled" by the building's relationship to the Mall, since, in his opinion, the Holocaust was not an "American story." He walked around it a good deal, realized it had an oblique relationship to the Mall, and decided, in his words, "not to take it on." He agreed, however, that the Hall of Remembrance had to be moved back to avoid competition with other memorials.

Forgey *was* willing to join with Washington preservation forces to oppose the council's latest request that annex 3 be torn down. Whereas some argued for the architectural value of this building, Forgey was more direct, and probably more honest about his reasons for opposing its demolition. He argued that, by removing the annex, the council was "insisting that the museum building be more a part of the Mall, less a part of the city. . . . If Annex 3 is destroyed to make a plaza-park, the . . . Museum and its striking Hall of Remembrance will forevermore exist in direct sightline with the Washington Monument as well as the Jefferson Memorial, and will rival both. This, I submit, is wrong." (The council withdrew its request, and in December 1990 the annex was transferred to the council and now houses its administrative offices.)

Embedded in these discussions is an important disagreement regarding the status of the museum. Was it merely a museum building occupying a prime location in downtown Washington near the Mall, its primary architectural mission that of a "good urban neighbor"? In this case, annex 3 served well as a shield, protecting a portion of the Mall from the disruptive aesthetic presence of Holocaust memory, represented by the Hall of Remembrance. Or was the museum, as the council understood it, a new national monument whose presence in the monumental core was essential to the civic health of the nation? If so, its architectural mission was not primarily to be a good neighbor; rather, it was to evoke the "indigestibility" of the Holocaust through a building steeped in Nazi methodologies of construction, and by means of its unsettling presence, to proclaim the importance of this story for the Mall.

Whether urban building or integral part of the monumental core, the museum's aesthetic impact bothered some on the Commission of Fine Arts. In 1988, Freed faced calls for minor building alterations that appeared to be merely aesthetic concerns but were in essence requests that he create a preferred architectural narrative to soften and dilute the building's strong visual statement. "When we write of martyrs instead of victims; focus on resistance instead of mass murder; celebrate the human spirit and bypass the human body; invoke the dignity of the self and ignore its humiliation—we are," said Holocaust literary analyst Lawrence Langer, "initiating the evolution of preferred narratives that use embattled words to build buffers of insulation against the terrors of the Holocaust, without bringing us any closer to its complex and elusive truths." The desire for such "buffers of insulation" was certainly at work in reaction to Freed's design.

Meeting on February 18, 1988, several commissioners declared that Freed's building should somehow resolve or redeem the Holocaust. Vice-Chair Neil Porterfield asked, "Is there any part of this memorial that gives hope and gives joy about the future? Commissioner Diane Wolf said, "With a gate and a forbidding entrance I doubt whether people will want to enter and the whole idea of a Holocaust Memorial is to teach people so it doesn't happen again." Also conflicted about how—or if—a message of hope should emerge from the building was Robert Mendelsohn, vice-chairman of the council's building committee, who wondered aloud whether or not the Hall of Remembrance *should* provide "an uplifting experience?"

At a March 17, 1988, meeting, Commissioner Wolf announced that she was bothered by the bricked-up windows in the Hall of Remembrance. These had been characterized by Benjamin Forgey as an "eloquent, understated suggestion of the extraordinary tragedy that is being memorialized within." "You have done," Wolf said, "an awfully persuasive job of showing us that humanity has been awful. . . . I would like to ask my fellow Commissioners if they don't feel that perhaps those windows, which are now blocked up . . . shouldn't be opened to reflect some light and to reflect some hope. Af-

Exterior of the Hall of Remembrance viewed from the Mall *(Jou Min Lin of Pei Cobb Freed & Partners)*

ter all, the western facade faces our nation's greatest memorials . . . four of them." Freed noted that at each corner of the free-standing walls there were slits of glass to let in sun as a sign of hope, but this was not enough for Wolf, who said the windows "were blocking those symbols of America. Don't block the symbols. Incorporate them in your building." Hope, she said, "means open arms, it doesn't mean closed, blind windows."

These closed, blind windows served a particular purpose: they kept American space from contaminating memorial space. Freed worried that visitors would have a full view of the Mall anywhere in the museum. In the Hall of Witness, for example, he altered a window at the top of a set of narrowing stairs—reminding some of receding train tracks—because he did not want the Mall to be a "player" in the museum. It was there, partially visible, however, and served a crucial function. "Why," asked Freed, "do you consciously make openings where you can see the various American icons on the Mall? Because these are the things that save you." It is, he said, "very important to bring into play these monuments, not to be seen as an equal to them, but to glimpse them, just barely glimpse them." Freed's architectural strategies were designed to alter the way in which visitors perceived the Mall, just as the permanent exhibition was designed to alter perception of citizenship in a modern state.

In response to Wolf's call for further "study" of the bricked-up windows, Freed spoke of the Hall of Remembrance as space betwixt and between the story of the Holocaust told in the Hall of Witness and the Mall. Visitors *must* go through the Hall of Remembrance before emerging from the museum, he argued. "I think that memorials are not gazebos. . . . I am fanatically convinced that we don't want people walking to a window looking out on the Mall. . . . We want people to have a moment of concentration, because after you have seen all of this, I don't think you are ready to go out." Commissioner Roy Goodman was also troubled by those who wanted the building to provide a redemptive ending to Holocaust memory. "There really are a substantial number of people in the world," he said, "who believe that the lessons of the Holocaust are not lessons which involve the vanquish[ing] of evil and the emergence of hope. . . . The returns, in the view of some of us, are not yet in." Fine Arts Chairman J. Carter Brown asked that, in the interest of collegiality, Freed think about the issue, but, he said, he could not imagine a design improvement. "It has," Brown remarked, "a kind of indescribable poetry . . . which you could easily destroy by fussing with it." Freed remarked that he found the discussion "very disturbing." He did not know, he said, how to "design hope."

At the next meeting, on April 21, 1988, Freed brought a modified plan, in which brick had been removed from the windows and limestone inserted, making them match the rest of the building. He sacrificed brick, and with it the resonance of the ghetto, but remained adamant in his refusal to transform the Hall of Remembrance into American space. He argued, "If we made the interiors visible from outside, that would dissipate energy and sacrifice discovery. We need to help people make the transition from official Washington into a world of shifted values unlike anything they have ever perceived."

Visitors would, he hoped, occupy the mediating space of the Hall of Remembrance before returning, albeit in altered condition, to the Mall.

After the museum opened, Michael Berenbaum observed that the Hall of Remembrance had not functioned as meditative space. For this reason, said Berenbaum, architectural alterations were under way. Freed understood the reasons for these changes differently. "The success of a place," he said, "creates new meanings." Originally designed to be a place for solitary contemplation and private remembrance, the Hall of Remembrance has become a place for public ceremonies and shared remembrance, a space now defined, said Freed, "not by vacant space, but by people." To accommodate the change in function, Freed designed a new entryway that directs people toward a ceremonial entrance and focuses their attention straight across the Hall of Remembrance to an eternal flame under which is buried soil from thirty-nine different Holocaust sites, as well as soil from Arlington National Cemetery, commemorating the Americans who liberated the camps.

Clearing of the site began on September 12, 1988, and Blake Construction Company, awarded the building contract on July 17, 1989, began work on August 2, 1989. This would not be a normal construction project for Blake's president, Stanley Prill; for the project manager, Adam Prill; or for the construction workers. In addition to problems normally associated with any building project, they had to work with a restricted site, an intricate design, and a building that went together, Stanley Prill said, "like a jigsaw puzzle." What the building *was,* Prill remarked, added another dimension. Seemingly intractable problems registered differently because this was the Holocaust museum. Workers, said Adam Prill, were willing to go "way beyond the extra mile. The museum got everything out of us that we had to give."

The building itself changed as plans for the permanent exhibition changed, and the impact of what the building represented struck many of the workmen when installation of exhibits began during the latter months of construction. Part of the building, for example, had

Freed's building offers a somber contrast to the Washington Monument, only a few hundred yards away. *(Jou Min Lin of Pei Cobb Freed & Partners)*

to be constructed around a German railcar, of the type used to transport Jews to death camps. The decision to include Yaffa Eliach's photographs of the murdered Jews of Ejszyszki in a tower of faces stretching from the third through the fifth floor necessitated removal of slabs of cement flooring. Indeed, said Stanley Prill, "the building evolved as it was being constructed."

Freed's building "means" in a number of important ways. Its very location and existence—quite apart from its architectural attributes—were a triumph for those who believed the Holocaust an event apart, deserving of a prestigious location in American memory. The building itself can be perceived as a "code," a collection of Holocaust symbols that need to be identified and "read." In 1992, for example, museum staff taking donors and other VIPs on tours of the unfinished building occasionally used a four-page guide to the building which decoded architectural symbols in a straightforward manner: "The curved entranceways leading off the [Hall of Witness] are reminiscent of the shape of the crematoria doors, while the massive brick towers on the north side . . . represent chimneys." The building also means as a part of "official Washington," especially in the way its outer skin of limestone and brick relates to its neighbors. In this way, Herbert Muschamp stated, the building's outside "vocabulary," its civilized connection to other buildings, existed in contrast with its interior vocabulary, the world of ghettos and death camps. "We see," Muschamp wrote, "that these faces are not cleanly separated from each other, but . . . dissolve into one another, as though the official body of the State were slowly revolving to face us with a gun. We see that the brick that seems to harmonize so happily with [Printing and Engraving] is in fact derived from the barracks at Auschwitz."

The building means in at least one other way. Just as the Lincoln Memorial is associated with the advancement of civil rights, and has been the site of famous protest gatherings, so too is the Holocaust museum associated with American democratic tradition, albeit in complex ways. For some, the story it expresses and contains can be seen as so radically different, so alien to American life, that the museum and its story become an anomalous place housing an anomalous event. In this case, the museum reinforces American identity by graphically revealing what America is not. For others, more willing to recall genocidal impulses in this nation's history, the museum may serve as a warning beacon, a contemporary commentary on the ever-present dangers of racism and anti-Semitism. Finally, whether visitors understand the Holocaust to be an alien story or expressive of tendencies found in every culture and individual, the museum aimed to be associated with faith in the so-called lessons of the Holocaust. It sought to function, as we have seen, as space for civil enlightenment, contributing to the wisdom of the body politic.

Freed's own articulate discussions of the building have, ironically, provided a canonical reading of the building, his desire for independent readings notwithstanding. He bristled, however, at any suggestion that the building and the permanent exhibition would not work well together, and thought, accurately, that one reason there had been so much attention directed at the building was that it was impossible to write much about the rest of the museum prior to its opening. Though Freed's building has continued to attract thoughtful attention and quite often rich praise—bordering at times on veneration—from architectural critics, after the opening not everyone was comfortable with the architectural expression of Holocaust memory, even if such criticism did not often appear in print. English filmmaker Martin Smith, the former director of the museum's permanent exhibition, considered the building too positive. Just the fact that it was *new* was problematic for him, for he believed that the very act of building such an edifice could glorify what should not be glorified. In his view, the building was monumental, and it concretized evil in an unfortunate way. "For me," Smith said, "there would be no building, because I don't believe in any architectural solution to the Holocaust. If I built anything, I would build it underground."

For many observers, however, Freed's building successfully negotiates the maze of taboos and imperatives that govern Holocaust representation. For Raul Hilberg, the building itself was more significant than the permanent exhibition. Freed, Hilberg said, had accomplished something quite extraordinary: he had "built a concentration

On April 17, 1990, two milk cans containing a scroll of remembrance signed by Holocaust survivors were buried under the basement level of the Hall of Remembrance. The act was reminiscent of the burial of milk cans containing records of ghetto life in Warsaw collected by the Oneg Shabbos group, organized by historian Emmanuel Ringelblum. *(© 1990 Alan Gilbert)*

camp on the Mall," evoking the world of the perpetrators. The museum, Hilberg thought, "rewrites the ground rules about what Americans should be concerned about," allowing Americans to incorporate something done to Europeans into "the fabric of our national memory."

CHAPTER THREE

Embryonic Thoughts:
The Commission's Museum

THE BURDEN OF MEMORY loomed largest as the commission solicited ideas for an appropriate permanent exhibition, viewed as the heart of the museum, where the Holocaust story would be told, while around it, like planets around the sun, would whirl other systems: archive, library, learning center, temporary exhibits, and educational outreach.

In his opening comments at the commission's first meeting on February 15, 1979, Elie Wiesel spoke of this burden. "We have been entrusted with an awesome legacy, and we are being judged by invisible friends, brothers, teachers, parents and they are all dead. And they all had but one wish, to be remembered. As we begin our proceedings, we hear the Kaddish of a community somewhere in the Ukraine, a community that did not live long enough to complete the prayer. We hear the whispers of thousands and thousands of human beings, walking in nocturnal processions toward the flames. . . . We hear the battle orders of ghetto fighters. We hear the mute laments of abandoned children. We hear Bergen-Belsen. We hear Treblinka, and we hear Chelmno. And we are seized by Maidanek. We shiver because of Auschwitz and we burn because of Auschwitz."

From the beginning, then, creating the museum was understood as partially fulfilling the debt of remembrance. Any failure of historical or aesthetic representation would resonate as not just a "mistake," but as a desecration of the memory of Holocaust victims. Menachem

Rosensaft, founding chairman of the International Network of Children of Jewish Holocaust Survivors, and son of commission and council member Dr. Hadassah Rosensaft, herself an Auschwitz survivor, cautioned the commission, "Anyone who casts aspersions on their [Holocaust victims'] memory somehow participates retroactively in their murder." Those responsible for the creation of the exhibit would have to walk the razor's edge, for "aspersions" could be cast, inadvertently, through display of a particular artifact or a particular interpretation of historical material. Failure to carry satisfactorily the burden of survivor memory would be tantamount to spitting on a grave and then removing the gravestone so that memory of the dead was effaced.

The general character of the museum took shape early in the commission's work. Many commissioners liked the phrase "living memorial," and for two-thirds of them this meant educational programs created in a Holocaust resource center. Only historian Lucy Dawidowicz thought a traditional monument would be adequate—"Now, I'm in the minority, one of the few people who would like bronze," she said. Yaffa Eliach explained that to her a living memorial would consist of a "library, archives and reference files relating to all existing Holocaust material which will serve ongoing research, and a museum, memorial section and an outdoor memorial park."

Other commissioners spoke about the functions of a living memorial: it would "expose" the crime of the Holocaust; Americans would "learn" from it; it needed to be something "visible and tangible" that people "will want to visit"; it must "mean something to the young"; its educational component must serve as an "early warning system" about potential genocidal conditions—"It is precisely the immensity of the fires of Auschwitz that so illumine our moral landscape that in the ghastly light we may see things that would otherwise escape detection," one commissioner wrote—it must be a testament to the "living and not the dead ... leave the replicas of skeletons and charred bones far away"; and it would provide physical evidence in the ongoing battle with Holocaust deniers, for "the proposed memorial center presenting authentic material will effectively counteract . . . endeavors to falsify history."

In February 1979 appeared the first of many interpretive dilemmas that would bedevil those entrusted with telling the story. After delivering his caution to the commission about the murder of memory through aspersions cast on the dead, Menachem Rosensaft touched on the enduringly sensitive issue of resistance during the Holocaust. He, like many others, thought that perceiving victims as "sheep being led to the slaughter" was one of these aspersions, and told the commission that "all 6 million victims resisted, whether physically, spiritually, morally." For him, as well as for some survivors, this was not interpretation, but a fact that protected the integrity of the victim and provided a less problematic memory for future generations. Such facts, he said, should be presented in a "national memorial" that would present an "objective" view of the Holocaust, encompassing "all that happened, the way it happened, without embellishment, without emotion, without distortions."

Elements of a "preferred narrative" of the Holocaust, attempts to soften the harshness of the story, were also evident in early conversations. Some commissioners believed that the memorial should emphasize the "extraordinary efforts to preserve human dignity and life," and that such efforts "offer a measure of consolation and hope for humanity." Museum visitors would learn not only about the "shattering tragedy" but the "tenacity of the human spirit." Several commissioners used the term "martyrs" to describe Holocaust victims, particularly problematic given that, even for Jewish martyrs during the Maccabean revolt against Antiochus IV (175–164 B.C.E.), martyrdom involved choice: Hellenization through renunciation of faith, or death through allegiance to faith. The Nazis offered no such options to Holocaust victims. "These millions were slaughtered for an idea," wrote Bruno Bettelheim; "they did not die for one." Occasionally, the term "martyr" was linked with the vision of a redemptive ending to the Holocaust story. "Israel, rising out of the ashes of the Six Million, is in itself, a living memorial to the martyrs," wrote one commissioner in March 1979.

Some commissioners turned their attention to artifacts and the emotional power that they would convey. "I would like to recommend," wrote one, "a recreation of some of the realities of those monstrous days. Perhaps there can be a large chamber or floor devoted to a train through which people would walk reflecting the box car confinement for those destined to death, the platform onto which they embarked and the gates of hell that confronted them. Let them walk into the barracks and trace the footsteps of their fathers and mothers to the showers, the gas chambers, the crematoria and the burial pits. I firmly believe that pictures are inadequate and stories have their limitations. Let there be a physical experience realized by all who enter the portals of this museum and let them derive a personal feeling of what the process of life, death and survival was like." In addition to providing lessons, the permanent exhibition was to "inflict" the Holocaust on the visitor. The commissioners assumed that it was important to arouse strong emotion in the visitor in order to bring about a moral transformation; their unspoken assumption was that enlightened attitudes toward others and wise public-policy decisions would emerge from emotional encounter with the museum's Holocaust. Some believed that the encounter with American indifference to the plight of Nazi victims would force museum visitors to weigh the cost of being a bystander, past or present, for one of the "lessons" was that "the indifference of the bystanders was critical to the success of the aggressors."

The commission understood itself, then, as a kind of public-health worker, responding to the dangerous pathology of anti-Semitism and racism that lay at the heart of modern civilization. The museum, commissioners hoped, would provide a cure, leaving those healed to work for a "deepening of [the] quality of American civil and political life and a strengthening and enrichment of the moral fiber of this country."

Early discussions began to probe the boundaries of the Holocaust regarding representation of "non-Jewish" victims. In his comments at the commission's first meeting, Raul Hilberg, willing to characterize the Holocaust as "unique," also pointed out that it was not "without its precedents and not without its implications. . . . It would not be a fulfillment of the overall task to ignore the fates of other people, be they Armenians, or be they, during the events, the Soviet prisoners of war that died during captivity, or . . . other victims." Hilberg wanted to stretch the boundaries of memory back to include the Armenians, victims of Turkish genocide in 1915, and he wanted to stretch the boundaries outward, to include non-Jews murdered by the Nazis. Others cautioned that the "unique" situation of the Jews in the Holocaust—"Never before had one people denied another people the fundamental right to live," argued Lucy Dawidowicz—made it crucial to maintain the Jewish core of the Holocaust, although "others" could perhaps be allowed to penetrate the outer edge of the boundaries in a carefully managed hierarchy of victims. As we will see in chapter four, no other issue—particularly with regard to Armenians and Gypsies—would so consistently engage the attention of those responsible for the creation of the permanent exhibition.

In his concluding remarks at the commission's meeting on April 24, 1979, Wiesel argued: "The universality of the Holocaust lies in its uniqueness. If I speak as a Jew about Jews, of course, I speak about others as well. If I were to stop speaking about Jews, I would betray both the others and my own people. . . . I was terribly moved by our Armenian friends [who had spoken at the meeting about the importance of their being included in this story]. I cannot tell you how much. I understand therefore, the initial impulse to extend and to elaborate and to enlarge. . . . What I am afraid of is if you go too far, we will do neither you . . . nor ourselves any good." Wiesel emphasized the difficulty of the issue. "If I were to tell you that I have an answer how to solve [this] I would lie. I do not know how."

By the time the *Report* was issued in September 1979, the commission had decided upon broad themes for the museum. An exhibition would have to present the story of life as well as death—"the existence and culture of the Jews of Europe before and during the war"—and it would have to deal with the dilemma of non-Jewish victims through insistence on the Jewish core—for failure to recognize this would be falsification in the "name of misguided universalism"—and through representation of "Poles, the Gypsies, and other exterminated groups." The museum would have to deal with the role of Americans as bystanders and liberators, and America as postwar home to many survivors. Finally, the museum would have to lead visitors to an "understanding" of the Holocaust through an examination of the world of the perpetrators.

Several weeks after the *Report* was submitted, Michael Berenbaum wrote Wiesel about the function of the commission's successor body—the council—as yet unformed by the president. Planning for the museum was, he thought, the "problematic area," for, he said, "we have not yet articulated what we want the visitor to undergo. Aside from the words emotive or intellectual, we have not named the spectrum of the visitor's experience. . . . Since this will be perceived as the central focus of our activity and will be the visible center of the living memorial, it is imperative that we act with due and deliberate speed." After a seven-year absence from the museum, Michael Berenbaum would return to play a major role in the formation of the permanent exhibition that awaited visitors in April 1993.

Beginnings: 1980–87

BERNARD RASKAS SERVED AS A RABBI in St. Paul, Minnesota's Temple of Aaron Congregation. Active in community affairs, the first Jewish chaplain to the Minnesota state legislature, Raskas was a member of the council and in the summer of 1980 was already at work with a twenty-four-member museum/memorial committee to develop themes for the permanent exhibition. The themes developed by this committee were proudly presented to the council for discussion in December 1980 and April 1981 as products of consultation with "scholars, museum designers, historians and architects, plus visitations to Holocaust memorials, sites of former concentration camps, and centers of Holocaust research in Western and Eastern Europe, and Israel."

Elie Wiesel was himself deeply committed to the need for a "pure" process through which the museum would be built, with a sacred institution the end result. Not surprisingly, he had a strong sense of ambivalence regarding the adequacy of physical representation. Wiesel recalled that President Carter wanted a monument, he himself wanted an educational/archival center, and his "heart was not in" the idea of a museum. "By showing, you exclude what you can't show, the mystery was gone," he said. "When we decided on a museum, then the troubles began."

During their April 30, 1981, meeting, council members suggested that visitors could enter a "darkened chamber in which Elie Wiesel's words found in *Night* could be amplified as individuals stand silently." After exhibits focusing on the destruction of the Jews, there would be an "exposition of the gypsies, political prisoners, etc. who were killed." After discussion of the Righteous Gentiles—non-Jews who risked their lives to save Jews throughout Europe—the museum "could proceed to end in an uplifting manner." (One suggestion was to engrave uplifting words by Anne Frank as the museum's epitaph.) In order to impress the story on visitors, simulation of Holocaust experience seemed an attractive option. "A room might be constructed like a railroad car and as individuals are in this rocking chamber, views would pass them." There would be a series of "conversations" that visitors could listen to in various languages: "Hitler speaking to Eichmann, Eichmann issuing orders to his underlings . . . A family of German Jews deciding whether to flee Germany . . . A parent trying to explain to a child the meaning of the Holocaust . . . A conversation between American soldiers when they first enter the camps." To impress the visitors further with the magnitude of the Holocaust, there would be a "large digital clock ticking [with] every second representing a life lost." There would be a full-scale model Auschwitz, a room with "the ashes of some of the martyrs," and, as emotional climax, a "large room with just shower heads. A metal door is clanged shut and then a voice says, 'This is the last thing millions of Jews heard.' "

These ideas left a number of council members uncomfortable.

Hilberg, for example, believed, "We should avoid the obvious. Too many Stars of David, too much barbed wire, too many flashing lights will leave nothing to the imagination. Too much teaching or explaining will leave nothing to reflection." In his desire for historical accuracy in the museum—he characterized himself as a "footnote writer. . . . And when I read that we should represent a conversation of Hitler and Eichmann that never took place then I must protest"— Hilberg offered a minimalist view of an exhibition. "We should have on permanent display, in total silence, a few relics of the Holocaust; an original German poster, ghetto money, a canister of Zyklon B, a real possession of a victim (even if only a suitcase)." He proposed a series of "rotating exhibits," including "fate of the Armenians," and "Gypsies under Nazi rule." These would deal substantively with people or issues only mentioned in the permanent exhibition and because they were *temporary* exhibits, they would maintain the accepted hierarchy of victims. The "others" would occupy a location connected with but separate from the Jewish core.

Council members Irving Greenberg and Robert McAfee Brown, the latter now professor emeritus of theology and ethics at the Pacific School of Religion and author of *Elie Wiesel: Messenger to All Humanity*, worried about visitors' reaction to gruesome exhibits. "How," said Brown, "are we going to get people to come back and back and back? Because the one thing that could be destructive would be that it would be labeled as a horror museum; people would stay away from that." Greenberg thought that a room with shower heads or a railroad car could be either an "overwhelming experience or a total disaster," and he strongly objected to softening the ending with phrases from Anne Frank. Amid this cacophony of contending voices, Wiesel responded, "I believe that we are dealing here with something so sensitive, something . . . so sober, so austere as an ancient prayer. Now how do you translate ancient prayers into something visual? I think everything must be pure."

No doubt Wiesel's desire for purity—of process and result— depended in part on a consensus regarding the politics and aesthetics of museum representation: who should be represented and how.

From the beginning of the project, of course, there had been no such consensus on even who should be empowered to *tell* the story. Purity, if it meant a reverential deference to survivors' visions of the museum, was not often in evidence. Indeed, it was often difficult enough to maintain civility. In 1981, for example, Aloysius Mazewski, council member and president of the Polish American Congress, was highly critical of emerging plans for the museum. They were, he wrote Raskas, "highly prejudicial," since they did not show that in addition to six million Jewish victims there were "three million Poles and four million other Christians who suffered the same . . . death from the Germans." (Note that Mazewski posits superior numbers of non-Jewish victims.) His ideas for the museum revealed a strikingly different reading of the Holocaust: exhibits about Polish non-Jewish victims, the murder of Polish officers in Katyn Forest by the Russians, Polish actions to save Jews, the history of fourteenth-century Poland's welcome of Jews.

In response, Raskas agreed that the "full story" of Polish involvement should be told, but his Holocaust consisted of quite different events. In a bitterly sarcastic response, he told Mazewski that he agreed that the history of Jews in Poland should be told. "I would hope that this would include the long, sad and documented history of Polish anti-Semitism. Specifically, it should include the pogrom in Kielce . . . on July 4, 1946 when a mob stormed the Jewish Community Center and murdered forty-one Jewish survivors. . . . One might also philosophically reflect as to why it was that the Germans selected Poland as the site of the Auschwitz-Birkenau death complex." Not surprisingly, Mazewski responded angrily that Raskas was "irresponsible," and that these "remarks of hatred are imbedded in your nature."

By 1981, the council had succeeded in establishing Days of Remembrance as a yearly tradition held throughout the nation, under the direction of survivor and council member Sigmund Strochlitz, with the central services in the nation's capital. In October of that year, the council's international-relations committee, under the leadership of Miles Lerman, sponsored the International

Liberators Conference, held at the State Department. Soldiers from fourteen nations gathered with survivors whom they had encountered in the camps, historians, war correspondents, chaplains, and medical personnel for two days of moving testimony. The burden of memory hung heavy over the gathering. Survivors—Miles Lerman, for example—expressed a sense of awe. "Little did I dream in the dark days . . . that some day I would stand in the assembly hall of the State Department of the United States . . . the symbol of freedom and hope, and fulfill the most fervent wish of those who perished—a wish to be remembered." In his opening remarks, Wiesel reminded the gathered of the rise of neo-Nazism in Europe, and that their testimony would be further evidence against "groups all over the world that simply deny that it [the Holocaust] had ever taken place." Testimony would come from those who had seen the face of war, and would express "our concerns and our hopes not for our own sake, but for the sake of humankind."

Planning for the permanent exhibition had stalled, and on March 30, 1982, a new committee was formed to bring plans to fruition. The committee introduced a group that would develop themes: Seymour Siegel, Anna Cohn, Micah Naftalin, and Hillel Levine. Shortly before the December 2, 1982, council meeting, Siegel and Naftalin were optimistic, declaring, "This is the year we go operational [with] a substantial increase and acceleration of museum planning activities." At the council meeting, Mark Talisman announced that the museum would be named the Museum Memorial Education Center, and that after the official transfer of the red brick buildings in April 1983, it would be important to have a "temporary ongoing exhibition while the museum is being done, so that we have, not only an address, but a door to walk through."

Wiesel continued to express his ambivalence about the project. He compared the museum to the invisible temple of a Talmudic story. "I'm always afraid," he said, that "because of bureaucracy, because of the nature of things, because of the fact that we deal with prosaic matters, meetings, budgets, human relations, positions, honors, telephones . . . somehow this vision of the temple . . . occupying a space that is between one world and another ... will disappear." And, Wiesel reminded council members, "it is this temple that we are trying to bring down in Washington."

In April 1983, Talisman, concerned that exhibition-planning initiatives lacked a professional museum focus, urged the creation of a new planning team, led by Anna Cohn, David Altshuler, and exhibition designer Chris White. Together with architect Maurice Finegold, they struggled to adapt exhibition plans to the limited space of the annexes. By that fall, there was clear frustration with the pace of planning and the awkward, ever-changing committee structure. At the August 4, 1983, council meeting, attention turned once again to the issue of representation of victims in the museum. In response to continuing concern about non-Jewish inclusion, Miles Lerman expressed once again the slippery-slope argument: "As long as you're being philosophical about inclusiveness, who could be against it? But when you come down to practicality, you cannot be totally inclusive and have an institution left. ... I'm just pointing out to you that there are people [who] feel that if we step away from the basic concept that this museum is dedicated to the memorialization of the victims of the Holocaust and the other victims of Nazi brutality, we are exposing ourselves to a very dangerous open field." And yet, Lerman remarked, he was not even sure that the council had defined the Holocaust to everyone's satisfaction. "I think it's important that we define in unmovable terms what was the Holocaust."

Taking direct issue with a basic principle of Jewish uniqueness which was supposed to guide the council—that Jews were killed for who they "were," and others were killed because of what they "did"—was council member Jaroslav Drabek. A lawyer before the war, Drabek joined the Czech underground, then was captured in 1942 and sent to Auschwitz. He survived Nazi prisons and an insane asylum. He became a chief prosecutor of Nazi war criminals in postwar trials, and escaped the communist takeover of Czechoslovakia in 1947, fleeing with his family on skis. "I remember thousands and thousands of Poles, Russians, Czechs and many other nationals. ... They were killed not for what they did," he said, "but because of what they were." Drabek informed the council of his opinion that "Czechs, just like other nations, races, members of religious groups or simply groups of people who were being exposed to mass destruction at the hands of the Nazis, should be entitled to be considered as victims of the Holocaust."

In response to a question from Wiesel about the general problem of non-Jewish representation and Drabek's comments in particular, Hilberg responded that "there was no blanket decision to annihilate the Slavs by physical means. . . . That is why there is basic truth in the statement that Jews were killed for what they were and others for what they did, so long as we keep in mind that (in the German definition) 'doing' was a wide category." Of Drabek's assertions, Hilberg noted that Czech labor was used by Germans in production of "tanks, aircraft, and other heavy equipment. These policies alone precluded drastic action against Czechs even vaguely reminiscent of the destruction of the Jews. . . . To put it simply, the fate of Jews and Gypsies was unique, but it cannot be isolated from history."

Other non-Jewish members of the council also argued for partial ownership of the story. Ukrainian-American Julian Kulas noted that non-Jewish members were, in effect, advocates of various ethnic communities, present on the council to "make sure that the atrocities committed against that particular community are . . . depicted in this Holocaust memorial." Though willing to acknowledge the uniqueness of the "Jewish problem," he insisted that the suffering of non-Jews, "those people who [also] carry that ugly number on their arms from Auschwitz and other camps, cannot be a post scriptum in the museum."

Some Jewish council members, particularly survivors, grew uncomfortable during this exchange. They were clearly uneasy about honoring members of Eastern European countries that had been in a position, during the war, both to fight the Nazis and to kill Jews. Sigmund Stochlitz—originally from Poland, imprisoned in Auschwitz in 1943 and liberated from Buchenwald in 1945, a successful businessman in New London, Connecticut, and a close friend of Wiesel's—said, "I am not really sure how Holocaust survivors will feel when they enter a museum and see some of their oppressors being part of the [museum]." Civility was usually maintained, for all realized the stakes were too great to risk excessive frankness. Yet it was obvious that—particularly for survivors—allowing Poles and Ukrainians to inhabit space in the core narrative was almost too much to bear.

Perhaps only the official commitment to inclusiveness prevented an irreparable breach, which would have doomed a project already struggling to put into motion plans for building, fund-raising, and exhibition. Several attempts were made to bridge the gap. Hilberg, who considered the research facility and archive a much more enduring legacy than a museum exhibition, thought that archival inclusion and publications could resolve the issue. "I cannot imagine a journal or a publishing series . . . that does not cover the fates of many peoples because these fates are interconnected." A thoughtful attempt to bridge the gap was offered by council member Arthur Davis, a Des Moines, Iowa, attorney, and chairman of the community-relations committee of the Jewish Federation in Des Moines. "We as Jews," said Davis, "have a tendency to encircle the Holocaust, as if, if we can capture it as our own some wondrous thing will happen. . . . I think that's wrong. . . . If we capture the Holocaust we will exclude the support of many other groups." Davis argued that, if the boundaries of the Holocaust were widened, other groups "will feel that the museum is partly theirs." Certainly, he said, the Jewish core should exist; it could be done, however, in a "historically honest way with many others who deserve it."

Painful and impassioned position statements—which seems a more apt characterization than "discussions"—would often begin with a single comment on the issue, often a non-Jewish member of the council reminding colleagues that, soothing rhetoric to the contrary, the issue was still alive. The intensity of the debate would grow as memories were protected, positions staked out, ethnic communities defended, principles honored, and strategic gains sought. There would be no resolution. Participants hoped that the problem would work itself out in the process of bringing the museum into being, that conceptual clarity would emerge from the intellectual construction of the exhibition rather than provide an underpinning for such construction.

During this council meeting, Wiesel offered a vision of the opening of the permanent exhibition that was an expression of his minimalist tendencies, his suspicion of any aesthetic form that would, almost by definition, trivialize the story. "I'll give you the beginning," he said. "I see . . . first of all a kind of hall and we enter that hall and it seems endless. And I would like that hall to be covered with photos . . . of Treblinka. . . . From all the far corners of exile and memory people have come there, to die there. . . . And then I would like maybe a voice or a guide to speak softly, to whisper . . . 'look at the faces, look at them well. You don't understand, don't try. Just remember.' This is the way I would begin." And, offering a distinctive view of the transformative function of the museum, he said, "I want those people who go there to come out 2,000 years old." The museum existed, in this view, not to provide proof to counter Holocaust deniers, or as an agent of civic revitalization, or as institutional prescription for the pathology of modern culture, but as an initiatory center. Here the sacred mystery that was the Holocaust would stamp itself on individual psyches, and visitors would, ideally, emerge with a renewed appreciation of its mystery. For Wiesel, the museum needed to be a place where the impossibility of knowing existed alongside the traditional ways of "knowing" in a museum.

A team of consultants led by Anna Cohn and David Altshuler worked on the first full plan for the museum—building and permanent exhibition—which was contained in what was called the "Red Book." One of the distinctive elements of the plan was the idea of a "reverse chronology." Visitors would move from the Holocaust, from mass murder, to the world before. Cohn and Altshuler had met often with Wiesel in 1983, and worked with Eli Pfefferkorn, who had survived concentration camps and death marches from 1939 to 1945 and became a journalist in Israel, where he came to know Wiesel. He eventually came to the United States and earned a Ph.D. at Brown University. In 1982, when the council hired him as a consultant,

Pfefferkorn had just written a Holocaust education curriculum for Jewish schools in the Washington, D.C., area. He was determined to shape the museum in ways acceptable to Wiesel and other survivors. In 1982, for example, he informed Micah Naftalin that, although he understood Wiesel could not be an "active presence" in planning, "to make his spiritual presence felt, a manual containing excerpts from his works should be developed. [These will] help shape a vision and also give some direction."

Pfefferkorn was not pleased with the plan documented in the "Red Book." He favored a thematic approach, which would explore, for example, "hunger, alienation, entrapment, and bearing witness," for he wanted visitors to appreciate the slow loss of power, the constriction of the world of the victims, that preceded destruction. Despite his resistance, however, after a year of planning, the report, entitled "To Bear Witness, to Remember, and to Learn," was presented to a council education meeting on February 28, 1984, and to the full council on March 14, 1984. Recall that Cohn and Altshuler were, at this time, planning within the confines of the annexes. Altshuler had labeled the three distinct architectural components the Hall of Witness, the Hall of Remembrance, and the Hall of Learning. Together they would fulfill the council's mandate of witness, remembrance, and education.

There was as yet no architectural entry as dramatic as Freed's design, but the plan did recognize the need for visitors to separate from the "business of the street," and called for a "long, narrow, quiet passageway" from 14th or 15th Street to serve that purpose. Visitors would enter a spiral-shaped space in the Hall of Witness and listen to the testimonies of "survivors, liberators, righteous people interspersed with documentary footage." The main exhibit would be housed in six discrete spaces.

The first space would have six artifacts, standing alone, examples of the "last vestiges of the lives of individual victims . . . a pair of glasses from Bergen-Belsen, a tin cup from Belzec . . . a child's drawing from Theresienstadt." Visitors would confront a life-size photo of the electrified fences of Majdanek. Moving toward the apex of this triangular space, visitors would find a can of Zyklon-B gas, a crematorium, and a *New York Times* article from 1942 reporting on the extermination of Jews. "These artifacts would speak to the impersonal viciousness of the perpetrators and the shame of a world that knew but failed to rescue." Before visitors left, they would see, on a wall, engraved identification numbers that were tattooed on inmates' arms.

The next space, a seventy-foot-long rectangular area, would dramatize deportation through the presence of one artifact, a suitcase, an expanse of wall with names of victims, another wall with film footage of deportations, and a railcar. Visitors would then move to a third space with various exhibits on ghetto life, each with one artifact and one face, a "human image to continue the sequence of numbers and names from previous galleries." The fourth exhibit space would depict eviction from homes to ghettos, including a wall with names of "ravaged" communities, and the fifth space would detail the deprivation of human and civil rights, and Nazi Party rallies, with the base of each exhibit case to be set in the floor "configured with jagged edges to symbolize the shattered glass of Kristallnacht."

The final and largest gallery would illustrate the world before, the "pre-war lives" of various Jewish and non-Jewish groups, and would open into the Hall of Remembrance. In this reverse journey, visitors would travel through "paths of memory, retracing and recovering the sparks of life, until the worlds that were, and are no more come into view. . . . From ashes to numbers, numbers to names, names to faces, faces to communities." The exhibit would not "mourn the human capacity to do evil, but the terrible theft of precious souls and all the holy acts our world lost with them." This exhibit plan was primarily, although not entirely, devoted to Jewish victims. The Hall of Learning was envisioned as the place where permanent and changing displays on contemporary victims of genocide—Biafra and Cambodia, for example—would join exhibits on the Armenian genocide, and exhibits on Holocaust "themes," such as resistance and rescue. There were intense discussions about connecting the Holocaust so directly with issues of contemporary strife and genocide. Many survivors did not object as long as the permanent exhibition and memorial space was devoted to Jewish victims. Boundaries could be permeable in the learning center, but not elsewhere.

Reaction was quick and mixed. Survivors were, with few exceptions, uneasy about the reverse chronology, the movement from death to life, which seemed to them to deny the survivors their rightful place in the story. They wanted visitors to feel the inexorable progression of the construction of life in the Nazis' world. Raul Hilberg agreed with them. "You all remember the Via Dolorosa," he said, "and the stations of the cross. They are not in reverse order." Menachem Rosensaft thought this approach gave too much emphasis to Jews as passive victims. Mark Talisman worried about presenting such an unpalatable beginning to tourists coming fresh from the Mall. Council member Franklin H. Littell, one of the first Protestant theologians to struggle with the implications of the Holocaust (in his book *The Crucifixion of the Jews*), reacted more positively, arguing that the reverse chronology presented an ending that expressed a "much more life affirming note. . . . It doesn't end in total defeat. . . . It ends with the beauty and integrity of a culture which was destroyed." John Pawlikowski remarked that the six exhibit spaces, symbolizing the six million Jewish victims, seemed to exclude non-Jews through the very logic of the exhibit. Elie Wiesel objected to crematoria or railcars: "I would not show ovens. I think it vulgar. I would not show a cattlecar. We don't need it."

Having already heard Pfefferkorn's strong objections, as well as those of many survivors on the council, Wiesel did not want to proceed with this plan, even though it represented a year's labor and was the first full-scale plan presented to the council. "If we say that this is the concept," Wiesel remarked, "we cannot go back. And, therefore, I hesitate." Soon hesitation was followed by a decision to go back to the drawing board. In November 1984, Wiesel rejected the museum plans that were being directed by Anna Cohn and planned a retreat with "internationally renowned Holocaust scholars and museum specialists" to be held in January 1985 to begin, once again, the planning of the museum.

He remained unconvinced, however, that a museum could accommodate this story, and readily admitted that thinking conceptually about museum exhibits was foreign to him. Wiesel wrote, in the invitation letter to prospective retreat attendees, that the Holocaust "defies attempts at representation. . . . Hidden in the witness accounts lies a terrifying tale, sanctified by the suffering of the dead and those still living. Can this sanctity be retained on public display. . . . My world . . . is that of words and verbal images, not of lenses and visual images." Wiesel offered another partial vision of the exhibit in which the convergence of Jews from the far corners of Europe unfolds in a relentless process of destruction; "the journey moves from life's fullness to ashes." He offered a sober vision of an ending, a final gallery where "ruin and revival mirror each other. . . . Despite the vitality manifested in establishing new families . . . the rent cannot be mended." The retreat never took place, and despite the appointment of yet another planning committee, Museum Project Review, a workable plan for an exhibition seemed as unattainable as—perhaps even more so than—during the work of the commission in 1979.

Though Anna Cohn remained at the museum for almost another year after the rejection of the "Red Book," her position and relationship with Wiesel were irreparably weakened. She would eventually return to the Smithsonian Institution. When we spoke, she reflected thoughtfully on her tenure at the museum, and why, in her opinion, she and her colleagues had been unsuccessful in moving the museum forward. She recalled that, when she was hired by the museum, first as a consultant and then as museum director in 1984, the council was desperate to engage someone knowledgeable in museum planning. Greeted with enthusiasm, she thought she would be at the museum for some years. In retrospect, she believes that she was the wrong person for the survivors' needs at the time. "They needed someone who came out of the historical experience of the Holocaust," Cohn said, "someone who spoke their language, and could translate their sentiments and pain into a museum." She arrived speaking the language of a museum professional, working with survivors desperately searching for ways to express the pain of their past. It became, she said, "an issue of trust."

Most of the survivors trusted only Elie Wiesel to safeguard the passage of their stories into a public forum. He had, said Cohn, a "trust covenant" with them, with other council members, and with crucial members of Congress. Yet, by the time Cohn arrived, she knew that museum planning had to move beyond the "rhetorical shaping of the museum" evident in commemorative activity—Days of Remembrance ceremonies and conferences—and council discussions. Cohn came to ask different questions. She knew full well that, in addition to the conceptual issues that had demanded attention, the "prosaic matters" that Wiesel worried would somehow contaminate the planning were, in fact, an essential part of the planning. Work had to be done on site studies, land surveys, staff planning, fundraising, archival planning, and exhibition and learning-center development. She asked questions about where pipes would go, what problems were posed by zoning regulations, what it meant to be in a historic-site area, where rest rooms and coat rooms should be placed, where bus dropoffs would be located, how accommodations for elderly and disabled visitors would be handled, and how humidity, lighting, and storage would affect potential artifacts. She introduced the "language" of collection: accessions, customs regulations, transfers with other museums, identifications of artifacts, and cataloguing. This was, she believes, the first time the enterprise had not been framed in reverential language, and in her opinion it registered among many as a language of defilement. Perhaps, subconsciously, survivors viewed the various plans that came before them, and the various museum professionals who would present these plans, not as allies, but as challengers. The problem may have lain not with the conceptual dimensions of the plans, but with the fact that the survivors on the council were not yet able to cede their stories to *any* plan. Anna Cohn, at least, would agree with this. "Between my time at the museum and Shaike Weinberg's coming on board in 1988 as director," she said, "museum people and survivors learned about each other."

In the summer of 1984, Wiesel went to Israel, where he met with Shaike Weinberg, the acclaimed creator of Beth Hatefutsoth—the "Museum of the Jewish Diaspora"—located on the campus of Tel Aviv University. Weinberg declined to become director, but agreed to come to Washington in the spring of 1985 as a consultant. Cohn and Weinberg traveled throughout the country, talking with various developers and designers in considering different conceptual plans. In Washington, Cohn and Weinberg also met with Albert Abramson, upon whom Beth Hatefutsoth had made a profound impression, and who had met Weinberg when the latter brought a traveling exhibition from his museum to the Klutznick in the late 1970s. In 1985, already in charge of the building project, Abramson would soon have the authority to hire a museum director, and he wanted Shaike Weinberg. In May 1985, Weinberg presented a "concept outline" that he and Cohn had developed featuring a "story-telling" approach to the museum. This was the way, he said, to trigger an "emotional identification with the victim," which, he believed, was crucial for a Holocaust museum.

The heart of his exhibit was a one-hour film on the history of the Holocaust. There would be complementary exhibit halls, and a Holocaust information center which was one of the places where non-Jewish victims would appear. This, Weinberg recognized, was a major challenge—"how to reconcile contradictory attitudes and aspirations of various religious, ethnic and political groups that have a close relationship with the museum. In these and many other respects, planning . . . the Washington museum involves problems that do not pertain to any 'normal' museum."

Micah Naftalin told Wiesel that the seeds for "the most powerful museum yet conceived" were present in this plan, but, lacking museum planning professionals able to command the respect and confidence of the Council," he feared it would be stillborn. We are, he said during the summer of 1985, "fairly close to ground zero." He noted that there was a "tricky political sensitivity issue." The museum had to "keep faith absolutely with the Jewish character of the subject," but also to "keep in mind that others were victims and that this is an

American and not a strictly Jewish institution." Albert Abramson was also impatient. He wanted one committee that would take over decision-making for the building and the exhibit, and believed that the big question was "how . . . do we tell the story of the Holocaust to the American public. . . . In four years' time, nobody has even come up with a concept of what . . . the museum is all about."

Naftalin was enthusiastic about another consultant, Stuart Silver, a former chief of design at the Metropolitan Museum of Art in New York, and Barry Braverman, a design-management consultant and former project officer at the Walt Disney organization's Epcot Center. Wiesel disliked the idea of Weinberg's film, and had little enthusiasm for hiring someone from Disney; in the fall of 1985, he prepared, with the assistance of Eli Pfefferkorn, a document entitled "Chairman's Guidelines for the Content Committee."

The "Chairman's Guidelines" combined a chronological approach to the Holocaust with Wieselian mystery. Straightforward presentations would be preceded by "a guide or voice-over [explaining] that the visitor had entered a world which is the negation of all worlds, a time which is the negation of all times; for here creation was destroyed; a new creation was invented by the killers." The main narrative, perhaps using survivors as guides, would end with liberators as guides, showing renewed life in the displaced-persons camps, but reflecting a "sensibility that holds, within every promise of the future, the shadows of the past." Wiesel thought that perhaps loneliness would be an apt closing theme, "the loneliness of the dead . . . matched by the loneliness of the survivor who is alone also, alone with the dead, the invisible shadows." These guidelines would provide the framework for the exhibition plan produced by Stuart Silver in 1986, the last plan presented to the council during the chairmanship of Elie Wiesel.

This was not an auspicious time for a museum professional to ask survivors to trust the integrity of public memory. On April 11, 1985, the White House announced that President Reagan had decided not to visit a concentration camp on his upcoming trip to West Germany, but would join West German Chancellor Helmut Kohl in a visit to the Bitburg military cemetery, in which, it was soon discovered, were buried members of the Waffen-SS. There was a firestorm of protest from Jewish groups and American veterans' groups, an appeal from fifty-three United States senators and 253 members of the House of Representatives, and an eloquent appeal from Elie Wiesel. At the White House to receive the Congressional Gold Medal, he turned to the president and implored him not to go to Bitburg. "That place, Mr. President, is not your place. Your place is with the victims of the SS." The president remained firm, however, and made matters worse by adding a visit to the concentration camp of Bergen-Belsen as a concession. This was considered an act of desecration by many. Menachem Rosensaft led a group intending to "reconsecrate" the camp shortly after Reagan and Kohl had joined on what Rosensaft characterized as "a macabre tour, an obscene package deal, of Bergen-Belsen and Bitburg." President Reagan had, before leaving the United States, violated the integrity of Holocaust memory even more by characterizing the SS dead and those murdered in the Holocaust as equivalent victims of war. "They were victims," he said of the SS, "just as surely as the victims in the concentration camps."

Coming from a president who had been strongly supportive of the council, had spoken at several public events sponsored by the council, and had talked openly of the need to learn from the Holocaust so that "it" would not happen again, the Bitburg affair stunned council members, and contributed to a feeling—present since the first council meeting—that their work was taking place in an environment in which Holocaust memory was besieged from all directions. Synagogues had been burned in France, Jewish cemeteries were still in ruins throughout Europe, and deniers grew more sophisticated in their methods of Holocaust denial. Even the council's museum planning was plagued, if not with attacks on Holocaust memory, with the unsettling stretching of boundaries, given the imperative of inclusion and the problem of Holocaust representation. So the council faced a crisis. Would mass resignation be an act of integrity? Could they continue to serve a president who equated Nazis and victims of the Holocaust? Could their commitment to honor the memory of the dead be sustained if they continued to serve on the council? In an emergency meeting on April 15, 1985, and in several subsequent meetings, the council anguished over the issue. Wiesel asked, "How can I speak on behalf of memory and the sacredness of memory [when] the highest official in the land is honoring the memory of those who killed our people and killed people, Jews or non-Jews." Robert McAfee Brown offered a passionate case for resignation: "To continue . . . is to give passive approval of his denial of the need to remember, his equation of victims with victimizers, his honoring the killers and his claims that these things are done in the name of morality."

There was, however, little enthusiasm for resignation. Some saw the issue as evidence of the need for the museum. Others were comfortable with Hyman Bookbinder's proposed statement that "our determination is now stronger than ever to move ahead." Raul Hilberg suggested, "We should not go back to the White House for three years. We should not meet under the auspices of the White House or of that State Department. We should not say anything more about the President." He also noted that the council antedated this particular president. Hilberg has since recalled that his suggestion did not please either "those who enjoyed having their picture taken with a president or those who wanted to resign." The council decided not to resign, although subsequently Wiesel said, "For the record, I wanted the Council to resign. I supported a resolution calling for resignation. And when it was rejected, by the overwhelming majority of the Council, of course I accepted the decision . . . and remained. I could have resigned alone, but I didn't want to do it alone. I didn't want to repudiate my colleagues." Years later, Hilberg recalled, with a sardonic smile, the vicissitudes of memory when he said, "We didn't resign. We went back to the White House, and we talked to the president."

Beginning in the summer of 1985, Stuart Silver chaired a design-concept development committee which presented its plan to the council on January 31, 1986. Visitors, Silver argued, should leave the museum understanding that the Holocaust was the "worst case of genocide in history." They would move through a controlled, chronological story that was designed to "transform self aware-ness . . . to bring about the realization that everyday ordinary human beings can become both victims and victimizers." Jews were present-ed as the "first and worst" victims. Methods of repression, Silver argued, were tested against Jews, then against others. Therefore, though "other" victims were also part of the exhibit, they would appear only after presentation of Jewish victims. Stories would tell of the "murder of Polish intellectuals, euthanasia of the elderly, the Gypsies, the homosexuals, religious dissenters. . . . At least one non-Jewish witness should be seen on video commenting on Nazi actions against the other victim groups."

The exhibit contained stark contrasts. For example, in the "cold and constricted" exhibition space devoted to the death camps, one space would be "dark and dramatically lit," with victims' "shoes, eyeglasses, valises, gas canisters." This would be juxtaposed with a "light and clean" space displaying evidence of courage: diaries, let-ters, the "legacy of the possibilities of the human spirit." And the exhibit's ending was substantially more uplifting than that presented in the "Chairman's Guidelines." Entitled "1946–Today: Renewal, Summary," it would deal with postwar trials; then visitors would witness "families resuming their place in the world." This renewal of life was characterized as a "triumph of the human spirit." Thus, the plan stated, "the circle is closed; those ordinary humans who became victims are once again among the community of life. . . . Bright images in a bright environment, and perhaps simple music will con-vey a tone of celebration." Here, perhaps more than in any other plan before or any yet to follow, appears a ponderous attempt to shape a Holocaust narrative in an insidiously redemptive manner. Yes, the plan declared, terrible things happened, and we must remember them, but, it insisted, there is an emotionally satisfying ending to the narrative. The Holocaust is resolved, because life went on. One wonders if visitors would have felt the need to recall any-thing but the warm ending.

The Silver plan was not accepted. Meanwhile, though 1986 would bring Arthur Rosenblatt and James Freed on board to create what would become an acclaimed building, the year would see no further progress in planning for the permanent exhibition.

The End of the Wiesel Era and Beyond

ON DECEMBER 4, 1986, Elie Wiesel announced to the council that he was resigning the chairmanship. "I feel the time has come. . . . We are entering now into a very important phase. And here, I can be of no help. I don't know anything about finances. I know nothing about building. I know nothing about management. I know absolutely nothing about all the hundreds of possibilities that will arise day after day when we deal with the building of a museum." Many members of the council implored, pleaded, for Wiesel to remain. He was asked to be at least the "spiritual leader of the project." In response, he reminded members that he was not resigning from the council. Yet many seemed to understand tacitly that Wiesel was, with his resignation, withdrawing from the project. He would not take part in an official council activity until his speech at the museum's opening in 1993.

After Wiesel had left the meeting, Harvey "Bud" Meyerhoff, who would be appointed chairman of the council in February 1987, spoke bluntly to the council about their precarious situation. Meyerhoff had become involved in the project through his wife, Lynne, who had helped the council raise almost a million dollars at one meeting in 1985. She had wanted him to "get involved," but Meyerhoff, president of Magna Properties in Baltimore, active in many civic organizations, including service as chairman of the board of the Johns Hopkins Hospital, resisted. He recalled that he had never had a "passionate interest" in the Holocaust, even though he had visited Mauthausen in 1969 on his way to Israel. At his wife's urging, he began sitting in on some meetings about the building in the latter part of 1985, eventually worked closely with Albert Abramson on the building project, was appointed to the council that same year, and agreed to help raise funds. After his wife was diagnosed with stomach cancer in 1986—she died in 1988—he promised her he would continue. He had the right "credentials" to be appointed chairman: he was Jewish, had contributed a million dollars from his own foundation—and would eventually give five million more—he was a builder of national reputation, and he was identified with various Jewish philanthropies. Michael Berenbaum credited Meyerhoff with "bringing the financial house into order," and Meyerhoff himself took pride in the success of the fund-raising efforts, which began to show real progress in 1987.

Speaking after Wiesel offered his resignation, Meyerhoff impressed upon the council how important it was to delegate decision-making power for museum construction to the museum-development committee, formed largely out of frustration with the snail's pace of the project, and chaired by Albert Abramson.

Throughout the summer of 1986, Abramson also argued that the committee had to control content as well. This, not surprisingly, was more controversial. Meyerhoff then summarized the problem of paralysis "in the areas of content, design, selection of experts and consultants." There had been "delays of weeks," he said, "occasioned by the absence of the Chairman and the inability to make a decision in his absence. The issue hangs, ladies and gentlemen, because the Chairman de facto has been happily for us . . . Albert Abramson." Meyerhoff argued that the museum-development committee could "comprehend, translate, and execute the mission of the Council." He noted that its members had "contributed nearly 25 percent of all the pledges and commitments made to date, nearly 8.5 million. These members are weary, disappointed, somewhat disenchanted, yet remain committed." And, lest anyone protest, Meyerhoff said, "This Council must today acknowledge that past efforts have failed, and they have. And someone ought to tell you so, and I will. And it must commit itself unequivocally to delegate this task with its concomitant responsibility and accountability, to a relatively small group of the Council." The council voted twenty to six, with one abstention, so to empower the new committee.

Journalists who have written about the development of the museum have focused their attention on tensions in the council between Wiesel and the "developers"—Abramson and Meyerhoff, particularly—and have portrayed Wiesel's departure as the end of an era, when "dreamers" gave way to "builders." For example, writes Robert Greenberger, Wiesel's resignation represented a "clash between headstrong men burning with ideas and those who were called to translate their ideas into reality." The *Washington Jewish Week*'s Larry Cohler believed that this marked the "ascension of the contractors, developers and technical experts . . . after years of leadership by scholars, historians and survivors." Here the break is framed too sharply. There were, after all, survivors serving on the museum-development committee. And in order to safeguard the boundaries of living memory in response to survivors who *did* worry that they were losing control, the content committee, organized as the institutional safeguard of survivor memory, was formed in early 1987. Sigmund Strochlitz declined to serve as chair of this committee, for he thought that Wiesel's resignation would "force us to uncomfortable compromises." Despite a unanimous resolution from the museum-development committee asking him to reconsider, Strochlitz refused, and Ben Meed accepted the chairmanship. The content committee would play a significant role in the intense negotiations with the museum's staff regarding the shaping of the permanent exhibition.

Popular fixation on Wiesel's resignation, and newsworthy stories about controversy on the council, as well as the desire to contrast Wiesel with those who followed, obscured much. Even the council's many frustrations through the Wiesel years were part of the process of creation. The Commission of Fine Arts pushed the council to think long and hard about what kind of building it had—in 1985—and what kind of building it really wanted. Could the permanent exhibition have been built without the wrenching debates over the appropriate building to house the exhibit, the appropriate display of horror, crucial decisions about various artifactual evidence that might be used, or the most appropriate means of representing various victim groups? The Wiesel years and those that followed are complementary. The intellectual seeds of the museum, after all, had been planted in the commission's *Report*. Those who worked with Wiesel were hardly "dreamers," as any examination of their activities quickly reveals.

Elie Wiesel's long-standing public ambivalence regarding the museum has led to speculation that he really did not want it built. This is both mean-spirited and incorrect. He was ambivalent for many reasons. For Wiesel, whose instincts emerge out of Hasidic Judaism, the Holocaust remains a mystery, and only certain words spoken in certain ways by certain people allow the proper balance between revelation and concealment, between speech and silence. He was asked to envision a museum that would have to translate the Holocaust into architecture, into a museum exhibition, expressed through the American ideal of inclusion. And for Wiesel, as for other survivors, failure either to bring the project to fruition or to control the story being told and ensure the integrity of memory would be not simply the end of a project, but a broken promise to the dead, a failure to commemorate them properly. The endless discussions in council meetings about victim groups, the endless parade of exhibit plans were part of what Wiesel viewed as a process of purification. The pure exhibit, the sacred exhibit, would emerge from a lengthy winnowing. That Abramson, Meyerhoff, and even some survivors grew impatient was also not surprising. For Wiesel, bureaucratic deadlines were less important than the purity of the project. "I was not in a hurry. So what if it takes another year? We're dealing with a monument for centuries. We have to be sure of what we are doing rather than go fast in the wrong direction. We could build something that would be the wrong statement, and then history would never forgive us." For those concerned with "secular" schedules, and worried about tangible results in what to them was a reasonable period of time, not to mention Department of Interior sunset-clause deadlines looming in 1985, purity did not register as a major concern.

The end of Wiesel's chairmanship did not bring instant results with regard to the permanent exhibition. Several exhibit designers would fail to impress the council during Arthur Rosenblatt's tenure as museum director. During this time, responding in part to the still-unresolved issue of representation, the council sponsored a conference entitled "The Other Victims: Non-Jews Persecuted and Murdered by the Nazis," at the State Department on February 23–25, 1987. Organized by Carol Rittner, director of the Elie Wiesel Foundation for Humanity in New York, and convened under the chairmanship of Elie Wiesel, it was designed to point the way, Michael Berenbaum noted, toward "solving the dilemma . . . [of] how to memorialize all of the Nazis' victims while remaining faithful to history and mindful of the unique state-sponsored policy of annihilation directed with particular fury against the Jews."

In January 1987, the museum-development committee voted unanimously to hire museum designer Herb Rosenthal & Associates from among twenty-seven firms competing for the job. His plan was presented to the council in April 1987. Once again, the intent was to prove the Holocaust unique, for, if it was not, Rosenthal believed it would be "reduced to just another minor thread in the complex tapestry of the Twentieth Century." He planned to use four techniques. "Time Capsules" would be collections of documents, films, and photos, which would offer "slices of history." "Tributes" would offer emotional memorials to individuals and places throughout the exhibition. For example, in memory of those murdered by the mobile killing squads, "we might print huge, ghostly images of victims directly on a photo-sensitized wall of bullet-pocked concrete." "Narrative voices" would personalize the story through observations by war correspondents, readings from Holocaust literature, and interpretation by scholars. Finally, "Words Writ Large" would feature "boldly inscribed" words like those in the Lincoln Memorial. However, according to one member of the content committee, Rosenthal tried to shape a design without sufficient interaction with the survivors. In April 1987, after his plan failed to generate enthusiasm, Rosenthal resigned.

Though yet another exhibit designer had been found wanting,

the council took a major step toward reestablishing trust with the survivors by hiring Michael Berenbaum as a consultant in April 1987. He would become project director in June 1988 and, after the museum opened, director of its Research Institute. Both Ben Meed and Miles Lerman, perhaps the two most influential survivors on the council, had remained close to Berenbaum since he had been dismissed by Elie Wiesel in 1980. "All of us," said Lerman, "held on to Michael in those years." Even before Rosenthal's failure, they had begun to increase the pressure on Meyerhoff and Abramson to hire Berenbaum. Their words carried weight, for the project could not afford to lose the support of the survivors. Berenbaum brought what no museum designer could: a clear vision of the conceptual underpinnings of the museum set forth in the commission's *Report*, and the trust of the survivors, even more important now that Elie Wiesel was no longer chairman. "I had a profound respect for their experience and a deep sense of compassion for them. I understood them, because I grew up in the transitional generation, the first after the Holocaust and the last to be in the presence of the survivors," he said.

Berenbaum directed a design team including historians Sybil Milton and Brewster Chamberlin, curator Susan Morgenstein, and Alice Greenwald—who eventually wrote the exhibition script—whose task it was to develop an acceptable story line. At a content-committee meeting on January 20, 1988, Susan Morgenstein reported that the team had been "composed of those who know the story . . . and know how to shape the story so that it may be experienced by an American visitor." She said that the story would focus on the "history and centrality of the Jewish experience," and would be told from the point of view of "those who suffered, those who died, those who rescued and those who stood idly by." Though the story line paid attention to victims and bystanders, it left out the perpetrators. As we will see in the next chapter, appropriate representation of the German architects of extermination and their collaborators would become a significant issue for those shaping the exhibition.

In 1988, at long last, a story line was quickly approved. Berenbaum recalled that only two defining project statements had been approved without opposition—the *Report to the President* and the concept team's story line. The design team decided that the exhibtion, meant to "inform the visitor's moral imagination," would begin in April 1945, with a segment to be called "Encountering the Camps," and then return to a focus on Jewish life before the Holocaust, after which it would develop the exhibit chronologically: "The Assault—1933–1939; The Holocaust—1939–1945; The Aftermath—1945 to the Present; and Conclusion—Bearing Witness." Berenbaum emphasized the innovative elements of the plan: a careful inclusion of non-Jewish victims, a balance between Jewish life before the Holocaust, the extermination, and the return to life after; and emphasis on Americans, characterized as bystanders and liberators.

The team, already working within the terms of Freed's design, envisioned the exhibit beginning on the fourth floor and descending to the second. Housed in exhibit space on all three floors, it would also make use of the "intense" exhibit space in Freed's towers. For example, one third-floor tower, "The Gas Chamber," would be constructed of "concrete walls, floors and ceilings and steel doors." This room would be designed to "evoke the hideous functionalism of the space; a peep-hole in the wall will convey the equally horrific inhumanity of the Nazi murderers." A subsequent tower room was originally designed as space evocative of the crematorium, "which will interpret the Nazi efforts to obliterate the victims and to erase the material evidence of their crimes." A final third-floor tower room, "Faces of the Dead," would consist of photos "gathered from survivors and their families."

The story line also sought to moderate the impulse for redemptive endings so popular in some other plans. Second-floor exhibits would deal with death marches, liberation, and return to life, and would tell the story of "Poles, Czechs, Ukrainians . . . Jews." The primary focus of a segment called "New Lives/New Homes" was to express the experiences of Jewish survivors, but would also "explore the lives and achievements of diverse survivors in countries throughout the world." After examining the shattered remnants of European Judaism—"the synagogues and study halls now in secular use, the cemeteries vandalized, desecrated and abandoned, the aging, despairing populations"—the exhibit's conclusion would remind visitors of various lessons of the Holocaust. At the end of years of failed exhibit proposals, Berenbaum's seven-minute presentation was followed by a few questions, and unanimous approval.

As the design team developed the story line, exhibit designer Rudolph de Harak was hired in September 1987. By July 1988, however, both Rosenblatt and de Harak had resigned. At a museum-development committee meeting on July 27, Abramson reported, "Mr. Rosenblatt and Rudy de Harak could not get a handle on the permanent exhibition and it was going nowhere." Abramson had proposed that Rosenblatt continue direction of the building project but not the permanent exhibition; however, "Mr. Rosenblatt did not agree to these conditions."

Jeshajahu "Shaike" Weinberg and the Changing Nature of the Permanent Exhibition

IN JUNE 1988, Albert Abramson finally succeeded in bringing Shaike Weinberg to the museum as a consultant. He would become the museum's director in April 1989. Weinberg brought to the project a record of innovative success and a conviction that the museum could and would be done, and he pushed hard to have the museum ready for opening, which, in the two years leading up to it, seemed quite impossible. "Without Shaike pushing hard," recalled former Director of the Permanent Exhibition Martin Smith, "the museum never would have opened in April 1993."

Weinberg was familiar with the history of the project, having served as an occasional consultant since 1982. After he and Anna

Museum Director
Jeshajahu (Shaike)
Weinberg *(Arnold
Kramer, United States
Holocaust Memorial
Museum)*

Cohn had made recommendations to the council regarding exhibition designers in 1985, Weinberg had commuted from Washington, D.C., to New York to help David Altshuler plan the permanent exhibition at the Museum of Jewish Heritage in New York.

Born in Warsaw, Poland, Weinberg moved to Berlin, Germany, with his family at the age of two. He was raised in a Zionist home, with a Hebrew teacher at home before he entered grammar school. Shortly after Hitler came to power, having been told that political symbols were forbidden in schools, Weinberg asked the director of his school to have students remove their swastikas. Soon he was informed that his life was in danger, and his father took him on the train to Warsaw that same night. His family emigrated to Palestine in 1933, when Weinberg was almost fifteen. He lived on a kibbutz, joined the Haganah, and volunteered to fight in the European theater with the Jewish Brigade in 1942. After the war, he helped smuggle Jews from displaced-persons camps in Italy and Austria to Palestine. Weinberg left kibbutz life in 1955, became proficient in data processing, and eventually introduced computers to the Israeli prime minister's office. He disliked civil service, however, and left to become director of the Cameri Theater in Tel Aviv for fifteen years. He recalls that he "slid" into museum work when friends directing Beth Hatefutsoth asked him for help. After eight years of planning and six years as director, Weinberg retired. However, Teddy Kollek, mayor of Jerusalem, asked him to come and plan another museum, the Tower of David Museum of the History of Jerusalem.

Both museums bear the imprint of Weinberg's unique sensibility. They were, as he likes to call them, "story-telling museums," not dependent on artifacts, as are collection-based museums. In Beth Hatefutsoth, for example, there is a replica of a relief from the Arch of Titus in Rome showing Roman soldiers carrying the candelabrum from the Temple of Jerusalem in 70 C.E. There are slides of contemporary Jewish life projected onto multiple screens, and films on different Jewish communities. At the Tower of David Museum, the history of the Church of the Holy Sepulchre was "told with the aid of computer graphics, and a nine-screen video [conveyed] what it was like in Jerusalem under the British Mandate." Weinberg also emphasized interactive computer terminals in learning centers, available to visitors in various languages.

At the Holocaust museum, Weinberg wanted to create an "exercise in visual historiography," admittedly, he said, a "crude method of expression," in which "one cannot be subtle." The museum would tell, through the "meaningful arrangement of artifacts, photographs, audiovisual displays, and interactive information retrieval facilities . . . the story of the Holocaust." His museum would be, in essence, a primer on the Holocaust for an American audience. He wanted it to be a "hot" museum that would "trigger in the visitor's heart feelings of emotional identification with the victims." These feelings, Weinberg believed, would lead visitors to consider the "moral implications of the absorbed historical information."

Abramson's decision to hire Weinberg as a consultant in 1988 did not please some members of the content committee, who felt that their authority was being usurped. Though Ben Meed offered his strong support during discussions on June 28, 1988, others raised questions. Was Weinberg still devoted to a film as the centerpiece of the exhibit, as he had been in 1985? Were rumors that he considered research and collections unimportant accurate? Would his recommendations make the museum too "Disneylike"? Did he, as an Israeli, understand the United States well enough to direct the museum successfully? Weinberg's responses satisfied the committee. When asked why he thought other designers had failed, Weinberg said that there were few who had experience in storytelling museums. "There should be a search ... with the goal of finding somebody with an unconventional approach. Modern audiovisual technology will be indispensable: we must speak the language of 1990 and 2000."

From Jeremy Isaacs, head of Channel Four in London, who had been executive producer of the *World at War* series, Weinberg learned about the work of British documentary filmmaker Martin Smith, who had received an Emmy Award for a segment in PBS's *Vietnam—A Television History*, produced two segments in *The World at War*, and produced the series *The Struggles for Poland*. Smith met with Weinberg and Berenbaum in London, and though ambivalent about taking the job—besides having no experience in museum work, he thought it an "intrinsically impossible task"—he agreed to direct the formation of the permanent exhibition for two years beginning in the fall of 1988. Smith recalled that the Holocaust had been only another "part of history" for him until his film editing on the *World at War* series. "On a flickering viewing table I saw unedited images of the British Army advancing through northern Germany. Within minutes I was appalled, nauseated and horrified. A world of corpses stretched before me, naked men, women and children piled high like cordwood being literally bulldozed into mass graves. The location was Bergen-Belsen. . . . Thereafter I perceived the Holocaust as *the* event of history." One of the segments in his series *The Struggles for Poland* was done by American filmmaker

Martin Smith, director of
the exhibition department
*(Arnold Kramer, United
States Holocaust Memorial
Museum)*

Raye Farr, who would become director of the permanent exhibition at the Holocaust museum after Smith returned to England. Smith recalled being haunted by the images of Farr's film *A Different World: Poland's Jews.* "Each time I viewed it during the editing process I became haunted with fear. 'They' hadn't realized what was about to happen; 'we' didn't care. Were similar tragedies awaiting our world?"

After arriving in Washington, Smith met with several exhibit designers, none of whom excited him. His last appointment was with Ralph Appelbaum, who had been a runner-up to de Harak in 1987. Smith recalls, "Those 45 minutes with . . . Appelbaum changed my working life." Appelbaum, from a secular Jewish family, trained as an industrial designer at the Pratt Institute of Art. He then joined the Peace Corps and worked in Peru with museums intent on preserving traditional Peruvian material culture. In New York, he was involved in Project Earning Power, whereby designers created projects that handicapped people could participate in: deaf people working in noisy environments, for example. Appelbaum's firm created the Living History Center for the national bicentennial at Independence Hall in Philadelphia, and a permanent exhibition at Monticello, yet he recalled that he very much wanted to design a Holocaust museum, and was devastated when, in 1987, his firm was not chosen. Of his first meeting with Smith, Appelbaum recalled, "Martin and I saw the world the same way . . . visually, pictorially . . . as storytellers."

Joining Appelbaum as project director was Cindy Miller, who had approached him about working on the project. Miller, who had studied Jewish history at Columbia and Brown, had worked in television as a newswriter, and as an assistant editor at the publishing house Alfred A. Knopf. "The thing I do best is to communicate complicated issues to people," Miller said. "I worked on the edge between content and design. It's one thing to say, 'We need to have an exhibit on what happened in the ghettos,' for example. It's another thing to turn that into a design. We started in 1988 with the story line, blank floor plans, and a list of small artifacts, and we had to decide what parts of these larger topics could fit into an exhibition."

Smith and Appelbaum had six months to convince the content committee that they could bring the story line to life, and they recalled the general feeling among museum staff that they would not make it past the first meeting, and a general fear that Smith's background as a filmmaker would mean the "Disneyification" of the Holocaust. Smith was asked, for example, "So what's to be done, 'Roger Rabbit goes to the Holocaust museum'?" Both of them were comfortable with the story line. Smith found it "sufficiently elastic and sufficiently right. It was a map of the territory to be explored." They were uncomfortable, however, with the nature of the artifacts the museum had obtained. As a result of a worldwide plea in 1988 calling for donations of "documents, letters, diaries, original works of art, articles of clothing, photographs and other objects that were created in the camps, in ghettos or in hiding," over ten thousand items—called "object survivors" by the curatorial staff—were donated to the museum. These were not only to be evidence of Nazi crimes or American responses, but would illustrate "armed and spiritual resistance . . . rescue . . . [and] reestablishing life anew." The collection did not impress Appelbaum, who characterized it as "the contents of what survivors brought out in their pockets," or Smith, who called the collection "pitiful and tragic. To my eyes there were fewer than a dozen tiny artifacts worth displaying and a photographic collection that seemed a motley of happenstance and cast offs. Yet it was vouchsafed as the basis for a major national exhibit."

Smith and Appelbaum were convinced that film, photographs, and small artifacts alone could not carry the story line. Traveling in Europe in 1988 with Michael Berenbaum, who had made several trips to the camps since the commission trip in 1979, and again in 1989, they were struck by the impact of the material world of the Holocaust that littered the European landscape. They went to Mauthausen, to Auschwitz, Treblinka, Łódź, Warsaw. At Majdanek, they met with the enthusiastic support of the director, Edward Dziadosz. After telling him that they could be the "window into Majdanek's story," they asked, "What if we could get this for the museum?" and were stunned by how much material evidence of the Holocaust remained, often in unexpected places. Appelbaum recalled that, while walking in Warsaw, he glanced at an area excavated for phone lines and saw, clearly, a layer of rubble of the ghetto. "We found what we didn't expect. . . . We found shoemaker's tools. . . . We found a cart that was used to pull people's belongings in, to bring bread in, and to take bodies out. That was the vehicle of the ghetto. It seemed critical to have that somehow." The "scars" of the Holocaust were everywhere, Appelbaum said, "and we were struck by how simple things took on another quality. A hook on a wall became something more when you learned that people were hung on it. A field became something more when, after a rain, you saw bits of human bone on the ground." After the trip, Smith argued successfully that his design team needed two full-time staff members to travel through Europe searching for more substantial artifacts, even though this sparked tension with staff members who believed that a traditional collection-based museum represented the most appropriate way to tell the story of the Holocaust.

Smith and Appelbaum had to convince Weinberg that large artifacts were crucial to the story, for his approach to exhibitions did not rely on them. He did, however, believe that there had to be a "terrible immensity" in the museum in order to tell the story of the Holocaust adequately: "blow-ups of photographs and other strong means of expression." In this museum, he said, they needed a "Grand Canyon of memory, not just valleys." He was willing, recalled Smith, to change the museum's collection process abruptly, giving the design team authority to begin searching for the large artifacts that would dramatically alter the nature of the exhibition. Joining the design team were Charlotte Hebebrand and Jacek Nowakowski. Their search—Hebebrand in East and West Germany, Yugoslavia, and Czechoslovakia, and Nowakowski in Poland and the Soviet Union—would not only lead to the acquisition of significant artifacts, but would be for each of them a personal encounter with the Holocaust.

The immense task of collection was carried out at different levels. Remembering negotiations with camps in Poland, for example, Berenbaum recalled, "Once we knew Auschwitz had dismantled barracks, we asked for one. Once we knew that Majdanek had hundreds of thousands of shoes, we could ask for four thousand." The final stage was a series of intergovernmental agreements negotiated by Miles Lerman, who, readers will recall, survived the war as a partisan, helped plan the commission's 1979 trip, and became an influential member of the council. In this period, Lerman was chairman of the international-relations committee, and took advantage of the political changes sweeping Eastern Europe. By 1992, he had signed official agreements with every Eastern European country except Albania, not only paving the way for artifact collection, but allowing the museum to copy massive amounts of archival material heretofore inaccessible to scholars. Lerman remembered signing the first of these agreements in Poland with the Main Commission for the

Front row, far right: Miles Lerman, during ceremony with Polish government representatives at the site of the Bełżéc death camp, where members of his family were murdered. Next to him is Professor Kazimierz Kąkol, chairman of the Main Commission for the Investigation of Nazi War Crimes. *(Miles Lerman)*

Investigation of Nazi War Crimes, and, at the recommendation of the Polish government, the signing took place on the site of the former death camp in Bełżec, near his hometown, with over three thousand people in attendance, some of whom had known Lerman's family before the war.

"I represented the United States government," said Lerman, and explained how he had focused the discussion on the need to remember and the need for preservation. "We all know the Nazi period was brutal," he would say; "we need your help." Lerman would point out, "Your documents are old, they'll be nothing but powder soon. We can make microfilm copies for you and for us." After agreements on archives, Lerman focused on agreements regarding artifacts. Michael Berenbaum would join Lerman, according to Martin Smith, in "begging, pleading, demanding . . . of the authorities in Poland and Germany that we had to have some of these artifacts."

Charlotte Hebebrand had met Michael Berenbaum while she was

studying at Georgetown University, and worked as an assistant research curator with council historian Sybil Milton before joining the permanent-exhibition department. Because she grew up in Germany, her search for artifacts led her to learn about the Holocaust anew. "I was aware of it. . . . My parents told me what happened. . . . I learned about it in school. But I think it was very easy to really not think about it much. I think the best way for Germans to really learn more about the Holocaust is to look at the past of their particular community rather than learning about the Third Reich's top twenty Nazis." She looked for material from the years 1933–39. "This is a very significant part of the story . . . Jewish children kicked out of their schools, all of the ways that people were excluded. . . . It's not something we think very much about when we contemplate the history of the Holocaust. We usually focus only on the annihilation in the death camps of the later years, without studying the period leading up to it."

Hebebrand was responsible for locating numerous items for the museum. Aided by a German Gypsy (Sinti) filmmaker, she acquired materials from that community of victims, including clothing, jewelry, and a musical instrument. She found triangles from prisoners' uniforms in Buchenwald, anti-Nazi clandestine booklets, a Torah Ark defaced on Kristallnacht, prayer books saved from destruction, a sign—quite popular in Nazi society but difficult to find in recent times—that read "Jews are unwanted here," and items displayed in the "Murder of the Handicapped" exhibit: a bed, blankets, restraints, and a doctor's coat.

With Martin Smith, she traveled to Theresienstadt and acquired children's toys and paintings, and a ghetto cart which, she said, transported anything "from loaves of bread to corpses." In Prague, she was able to obtain photographs of Theresienstadt taken by a filmmaker forced to make a propaganda film on the camp by the Nazis. Since his attempts to publish the photographs after the war had been futile, "he was very glad to give us the photographs and just seemed really relieved that people would actually see these after all these years." With the help of a computer-science professor in East

Jacek Nowakowski and Martin Smith in the Remuh cemetery, Cracow, Poland *(United States Holocaust Memorial Museum)*

Germany, Hebebrand obtained a Hollerith machine, a punch-card apparatus which was the forerunner of the computer, used by the Nazis to tabulate racial data from census forms and identify "enemies of the state." She was also able to obtain anthropological measurement tools used by Nazi doctors in the practice of "racial science."

Jacek Nowakowski, who had been curator of the Polish Museum in Chicago, came to the Holocaust museum as an associate curator in 1988 and eventually became director of collections. When he first came to the museum, he worked for Susan Morgenstein, the museum's curator, searching the photographic archives at the Main Commission for the Investigation of Nazi War Crimes offices in Warsaw (whose director, Kazimierz Kąkol, was one of the most outspoken anti-Semites during Poland's anti-Jewish campaigns in 1968, and repented in the 1980s). Eventually, Nowakowski joined the design team, and was a central figure in the museum's acquisitions plan in Eastern Europe. Nowakowski had grown up in Poland, but it was not until he began his explorations for the museum that he learned from his mother, a survivor who lives in Cracow, the details of her experience. "Each trip brought me an appreciation of a different dimension of the Holocaust," Nowakowski said, "and allowed me to explore my family's story as well."

Mindful of the museum's "shopping list," Nowakowski searched through Warsaw for evidence of everyday life—a street sign with a bullet hole, for example. Since ghettos made use of Jews as a labor force, he looked for tools; he obtained a sewer cover as a symbol of a means of escape. For the floor of the museum's display on the ghetto, he was able to negotiate with the city of Warsaw for two thousand square feet of cobblestone, and, in a discovery that had reverberations far beyond the museum's permanent exhibition, he was taken in 1989 to one of the only remaining sections of the infamous wall that surrounded the ghetto.

During a three-week trip with Martin Smith, Nowakowski met with Stanisław Soszyński, Warsaw's deputy city architect. Nowakowski had mentioned the museum's interest in finding a remnant of the wall to help visitors appreciate ghettos as places of exclusion, confinement, and, inevitably, way stations to the death camps. Soszyński said he could help. "I was a witness to the death of this city," he said, and first took Nowakowski and Smith to his home, where he showed them relics of the ghetto: a flattened baby-carriage, a piece of a bullet-ridden windowsill, and exploded artillery shells. Then he took them to the wall, still standing between two apartment buildings in a rather nondescript part of the city. "When we got here," Nowakowski recalled, "no one knew about this wall. No one really paid any attention to this piece of history, with the exception of one person who lives here in the neighborhood, who was trying to impress on the city authorities that this is a memorial place and it should be treated this way."

He visited this one-man preservation squad, Mieczysław M. Jędruszczak, who, after fighting against the Germans with the Polish Home Army, was imprisoned by the Soviets, and returned to Warsaw in 1950, to rent the apartment that looks out on the ghetto wall. The city, he said, wanted to paint the wall, but he had been able to muster enough support to preserve it in its original condition. In August

1989, as part of a major agreement with the Polish government, as well as with the state museums of Auschwitz and Majdanek, a council delegation—including former U.S. Ambassador to the United Nations Jeane J. Kirkpatrick and columnist George Will—arrived in Poland to accept numerous artifacts. While in Warsaw, they joined in a ceremony at the wall, where the council was presented with two of the original bricks and was allowed to make a casting of dental latex—an exact replica—for the museum's permanent exhibition. A plaque now commemorates the site and the event. In his spirited defense of the wall, Jędruszczak had kept it "alive," so, when Nowakowski came, he—and the interest of the council—could bring a forgotten place to life. The 1989 ceremony attracted interest, and now this segment of the wall, and another nearby, have become recognized as places of memory where the work of commemoration can proceed. Jędruszczak proudly showed Nowakowski his scrapbooks with notes and cards from visitors—tourists, official delegations from Israel, the United States, and many European countries who now visit this place.

Nowakowski also played a crucial role in negotiations with officials at Auschwitz and Majdanek, who agreed to loan artifacts that the museum used as graphic evidence of the world of the death camps: thousands of pairs of shoes, a casting of a crematorium, a casting of a dissecting table, the chassis of a truck on which bodies were burned, fence posts—which hauntingly dominate the landscape of Auschwitz-Birkenau and other camps like concrete vultures—cans of Zyklon-B gas, women's hair, part of an Auschwitz inmate barracks, suitcases, cooking utensils, razors, toothbrushes, mirrors, and artificial limbs. The museum made a point of not buying artifacts, partly in fear of creating what Martin Smith characterized as an "obscene market." Consequently, Nowakowski often fashioned creative arrangements with the camps to be formalized in Lerman's agreements, since the camps were unable simply to deaccess artifacts and give them to the Washington museum. Instead, long-term loans were worked out, with the artifacts not expected to be returned. There was close cooperation between institutions. At Majdanek, for

Casting a remnant of the Warsaw Ghetto wall *(Edward Lawrence Associates for the United States Holocaust Memorial Museum)*

example, the council donated video equipment to aid in the collection of oral history. But some interesting problems arose, such as when officials at Auschwitz wanted to write the labels that would accompany display of their artifacts in the museum, a request unacceptable to the Washington museum's staff.

Majdanek's current director, Edward Balawajder; his deputy, Dr. Czesław Rajca; and the curator, Tomasz Kranz, spoke of the wisdom of exhibiting these artifacts in a museum in Washington, D.C., so far from the original site. Balawajder said, "Most people in the United States will not see Treblinka, Auschwitz, or Majdanek. While nothing can replace the site where an event happened, the museum in Washington will bring the story closer." Perhaps, he went on, "after visiting the museum, some Americans will want to come to Poland and visit the camps." Similar thoughts were voiced by Krystyna Oleksy, the deputy director of the Auschwitz Museum. From the perspective of these sites, the museum in Washington, D.C., is not a center of Holocaust remembrance, but an extension of the fabric of the center: the original sites. Through the artifacts, the museum could connect to the center, so that Americans could feel the "shiver of contact," could "touch" the Holocaust at an outpost of memory.

In order to locate artifactual material that would help tell the story of the murder of thousands of non-Jewish Poles, Nowakowski had walked around the mass graves of Polish intelligentsia murdered between 1939 and 1943, located in the beautiful Palmiry Forest, near Warsaw. "I was looking for an artifact to show the activity of a firing squad, and that is difficult. I thought perhaps there would be some bullets in trees. The Nazis attempted to keep the executions secret, but a local ranger was watching the executions, and marking the graves with bullet shells, left by the Germans after the executions. He was nailing the bullet shells into the tree stumps." After two days in the forest with no success, Nowakowski was about to give up. He recalled walking with the director of Palmiry's museum, who found "a very teeny bullet shell inside of the tree trunk, right next to a place which marked a mass grave from the execution in 1940." The tree stump with the embedded bullet is on display in the exhibition.

Polish women taken by German soldiers into the Palmiry Forest for execution. *(Archives of Mechanical Documentation, Warsaw, courtesy of the United States Holocaust Memorial Museum)*

Men and women awaiting execution in the Palmiry Forest *(Main Commission for the Investigation of Nazi War Crimes, Warsaw, courtesy of the United States Holocaust Memorial Museum)*

These beautiful woods, with the sound of the wind rustling through the trees, made it difficult to visualize the horror that had occurred. Nature softened the impact of the site, and awareness of the tension between beautiful site and historical event heightens consciousness of the precarious nature of the context in which memory works. Not only had the Nazis murdered people, and attempted to erase the physical traces of that murder, they chose places that made it difficult for those who came after to visualize in the mind's eye what had happened, to feel the horror that was appropriate to the place. Instinctively, I expected, perhaps needed, horrific deeds to have taken place in an ugly, foreboding landscape. I felt close to and removed from the power of the Holocaust in the Palmiry Forest, for we were both at the site and at the memory of a site at the same time, hoping to grasp some "truth" through our presence.

Nowakowski described his own sense of the elusive significance of the site. "The thing is that, if you are in places like that, you realize that, at the time when it happened, it was the same sky, the same sun . . . and it's still here. . . . And you look at the birds and you look at the trees, and you feel it's like nothing happened, it is still running, it still is going, and that, I think, says our museum is very much needed, because everything is still going, still running, and we have to stop it somehow and say . . . this is something which you should remember always. Try not to repeat that same mistake. Being in places like that makes you very, very humble."

Nowakowski helped obtain other artifacts: trees from a Lithuanian forest that sheltered resistance fighters, the cemetery gate from the town of Tarnów, where thousands of Jews were killed, and the door from the Łódź ghetto hospital, whose patients were brutally deported by the Nazis. By August 1992, the museum had collected approximately thirty-two thousand objects, and Shaike Weinberg announced that the museum had "reached its objective in obtaining all of the objects now planned for inclusion in the permanent exhibition."

Most of the artifacts were housed in a museum storage facility in Maryland, under the direction of Emily Dyer, who came to the museum from her position as registrar at the Smithsonian Institution's Arthur M. Sackler Gallery of Asian Art in 1988. "Some of my colleagues at the Sackler thought I was crazy to come here," she said, "but the Holocaust museum needed everything that I loved doing, and I was dealing with elements of the human condition that are rarely documented, preserved, or displayed." She was, she recalled, "revolted" when material started arriving. "There were shoes, a Gypsy wagon, part of a V-2 rocket that was a hunk of rust." The shoes, on loan from Majdanek, arrived in large bags, with a strong smell of decaying leather, and some of them fell apart in the staff's hands. Dyer recalled her own professional and personal reactions. "Professionally, I had been used to dealing with beautiful things. These things were not beautiful, except for some of the small artifacts. They were dirty. My first thoughts were about treatment and stabilization." Everything had to be fumigated, cleaned. She also recalled, however, how difficult it was to work with such diverse material, instruments of murder alongside relics of the victims' lives. "We had to try to steel ourselves from becoming emotionally involved," she said, "but, of course, it was not always possible." She spoke softly about seeing a pair of baby's pajamas, crying, then forcing herself to return to work. "The most evil things for me," Dyer recalled, "were the Zyklon-B canisters and the Nazi banners." The Zyklon-B arrived in a box lined with plastic, but the containers "looked too healthy, as if the evil was not dead."

Other staff members also reacted strongly to the canisters of Zyklon-B as a powerful symbol of evil. Some feared that their power could reach into the present. Michael Berenbaum recalled that, when the canisters arrived, someone called the Environmental Protection Agency for advice on how to store them, and, he said, "they hit the ceiling." Even though the canisters had been exposed to the air for over forty years, one of the collection staff threatened to sue the museum over potential health hazards from the canisters. Berenbaum wrote a letter absolving the staff of responsibility for the canisters, and one night, he put them in his garage, and eventually had them tested, whereby they were judged safe. "It was not," said

Berenbaum, "the canisters that people were scared of, it was what they represented."

One of Dyer's most vivid memories was the arrival of the women's hair from Auschwitz. She had to unpack the hair and freeze it without damaging it. During an exhibit staging, at which time artifacts are selected for use, Dyer had to arrange the hair on two tables; she went to wash her hands, and when she returned the pile of hair, which had quickly absorbed the humidity of the room, had grown immensely and taken on color. "That hair," she said, "seemingly had a life of its own. This is an image I will never forget."

Many of the artifacts posed particular preservation problems. Conservation consultant Steven Weintraub, hired by the museum in 1990 to supervise the conservation program at the museum, faced some unusual challenges. His job was not cosmetic—to make old, decaying artifacts look more beautiful—but, rather, to stabilize them, so that they would endure. For example, should suitcases, movingly displayed near the railcar, battered and scarred now, but perhaps new when they were used, be cleaned up? And how best to preserve the mud that clings to one of the most affecting artifacts in the museum, a milk can, excavated under the streets in Warsaw in 1950, in which was buried the archives of the Oneg Shabbos group, organized by historian Emmanuel Ringelblum, detailing the life of the Warsaw Ghetto? Weintraub developed an intricate process to preserve the mud, considered an important part of the milk can's history. "The mud is almost symbolic of the fact that they were trying to hide this information from the Nazis to preserve it. . . . We're trying to maintain that look, just as it came out of the ground."

Large artifacts posed particular preservation problems as well. Nowakowski, Smith, and Appelbaum saw a German railcar in a depot in Warsaw. It had been used as a prop in a film, and struck them as "real." They were able to determine that it was a railcar of the type used to transport victims to death camps. It arrived in Baltimore on July 6, 1989, but could not be installed until February 1991. Since there was no room for it in the Maryland warehouse, it was stored in a small metal shack in Hanover, Maryland. "When it arrived," Dyer said, "the paint was still wet." The Polish government had painted the car just before shipment, to the consternation of Nowakowski and others. When he asked Polish officials why, they responded, "How could we send such an ugly car to America?" Despite what seemed to be good intentions, Dyer's response, like that of many others in the museum, was "They wanted to hide its past, and we wanted to reveal it." Dyer recalled growing attached to the railcar, "in ways I didn't know one could be attached to such things, even though I was revolted by minds that would put a piece of equipment to such use." While in its shack, it was subjected to rats, raccoons, leaks in the roof, and workers who left food on the car. Finally, the museum shipped the railcar by flatbed truck to Asheville, North Carolina, where a preservation specialist working with a medical scalpel and an X-ray machine peeled away nine layers of paint and managed to restore the railcar to its wartime appearance.

Dyer also remembered the arrival of a Danish rescue boat which carried Jews to safety in Sweden. "It had just been lifted out of the water and then shipped. We had a flood when we opened the container, and we had no place to put it. The caulking was weak, and because of severe warping the boat literally changed shape." Dyer said, "Despite our best intentions, we did more damage to that railcar and boat than had been done in their natural environments."

These artifacts affected people in a number of ways. One of Dyer's most valued staff people quit after several years, saying he "just couldn't take it anymore." Some staff members found it overwhelmingly painful to handle clothing of victims. Once, she recalled, a group was invited to the warehouse to see the Auschwitz barracks standing as it would in the exhibition. "I will never forget one woman, a survivor, who, after being near the barracks, reverted to a shuffle as she walked back to the bus. She reverted to the way she moved in the camps, triggered by the barracks. I will never forget that."

I had three quite distinct experiences with Holocaust artifacts. In the summer of 1991, I visited the Maryland warehouse and saw many of the items for the first time. It was painful to see suitcases,

ABOVE: Installation of Danish rescue boat in September 1989. It alone saved approximately 1,400 Danes, including 700 Jews, during October and November 1943.
(© 1992 Alan Gilbert)

RIGHT: Museum conservator Steven Weintraub observes treatment of the Ringelblum milk can.
(Sam Eskenazi, United States Holocaust Memorial Museum)

ABOVE: Textile conservator Anna Fine treats a prisoner's uniform in preparation for its display. "There was not a conscious attempt to improve the visuals. . . . We just wanted to stabilize these things long enough to be on display. The condition they're in tells the story," she said. *(United States Holocaust Memorial Museum)*

BELOW: Railcar and casting of the entrance sign at Auschwitz on the third floor of the permanent exhibition *(© Jeff Goldberg/Esto)*

and various other small items that I could imagine a person using. I was both attracted to and repelled by such items as the cans of Zyklon-B, and I was bothered by my reaction. Was it impossible not to fall victim to some ghoulish desire to "see" one of these cans? What was the purpose of seeing it? Of displaying it in a museum? Would it really be simply part of the physical evidence that the Holocaust "happened"; would it serve to teach visitors about the process of destruction; or was it precisely because these canisters had been used to kill millions of people that they carried a power, a fascination that made it impossible *not* to include them in a museum display, a different kind of artifact in a terrible cabinet of curiosities?

My next encounter with artifacts, with the physical memory of the Holocaust, was during my 1993 trip to Poland. Here the artifacts carried a terrible immediacy. They were "at home" in these places, framed certainly by the interpretive lenses of each museum and site, but more in context nonetheless. Out of so many vivid memories, I recall stepping into the barracks at Majdanek with curator Tomasz Kranz, a barracks that held thousands of pairs of shoes. I had, moments before, stood in Majdanek's gas chamber, watching Jeff Bieber's film crew work, feeling quite strongly that this was not a place where people should stand. It was not holy ground, but it was the site of monstrous death, and the evil that created Majdanek was still palpable: Kranz pointed out to me that the walls of the gas chamber were still changing color from the effects of the gas. It, and what it represented, were still alive. I felt very much the same way at certain places in Birkenau, at the mass graves at Chełmno, and on the field of Bełżec—numbness, anger, fear, horror, disbelief, grotesque attraction, and the slumbering presence of evil. They were completely unlike any other historic site I had visited, for the demands they made on a visitor were overwhelming. In the barracks of shoes at Majdanek, I could only go in a few feet. The smell and the impact were overpowering, suffocating. I was stunned by the power of the ruins and artifacts at Majdanek and Auschwitz, and the mass graves—artifacts of a kind—at Chełmno. All these spoke bluntly of the enormity of the Holocaust, and I understood well, in a way that

I could not otherwise have, that it was this enormity, this sense of realness, the sense that the Holocaust was more than images in black-and-white photographs and text in a history book, that Smith, Appelbaum, and others wanted to capture for the museum, to create patches of Holocaust space within a building that has removed people from American space and placed them in the artificial world of exhibition space.

They were under no illusions, however, that they were involved in an act of re-creation. For Appelbaum, the artifacts were "icons along the passageway" of the museum. "They stop and hold you for a while so that you have a little time to think." Martin Smith, who joined Nowakowski and Appelbaum in Cracow, Poland, in January 1993 for a two-day visit to Auschwitz, walked through the ruins of the gas chambers and crematoria, stood in a barracks in Birkenau, and said of the museum, "You're going to walk through bits and pieces of a barracks. You're not walking through a Holocaust barracks. We're not making any pretense you're walking through.... You get a semblance of shape.... Auschwitz is here and the museum is in D.C. It's something altogether different. And we didn't try to recreate that. What we tried to do was to convey facts using physical evidence as well as copied evidence, which is essentially what books and photographs are.... We wanted to try and take back as much of the physicality as we could possibly convey in the pitiful amount of space that's available for it."

Smith also passionately defended the museum against charges that these artifacts—particularly the Auschwitz barracks—belonged only at the site. His greatest fear, he said, was that someday every site would be like Bełżec, where approximately six hundred thousand Jews died. Now the site is merely a field in the small Polish town, with only a monument to mark the site. Sweeping his arm across the field of the Birkenau barracks, both standing and in ruins, he said, "The evidence is disintegrating.... Everything is rotting away. Somehow or other these things have to be seized."

I next encountered these "seized" objects in my initial visit to the completed permanent exhibition in April 1993. Seeing and smelling the shoes, on either side of the visitor in a tower room on the third floor of the exhibit, I was, rather jarringly, taken back to Majdanek. And yet it was easier somehow to view these in the museum. The shoes were "visitors," and there was the sanctuary of recognizable space just outside. Even though they—and other artifacts—were skillfully woven into the fabric of an intense Holocaust narrative, their raw power and seemingly unmediated presence in the barracks at Majdanek was moderated. In both places, of course, the shoes served as props in a larger story. In Majdanek, however, the story was told within the total environment of the camp, an environment that seemed to collapse the distance between event and recollection of event, an environment in which the shoes were actually worn, taken off, left behind, and collected. They were less selected arti-fact—by definition something out of place, put on display—than remnant, at home in the camp. In Washington, the shoes clearly had the status of artifact, and for me, at least, their presence as part of a narrative in the controlled environment of the museum domesticated them, made them "safer" to view.

The impressive work of collection not only altered the character of Holocaust memory in the permanent exhibition, but forced costly alterations in the home of that memory, Freed's building. Floors had to be strengthened in order to display granite blocks from the Nazi concentration-camp quarry at Mauthausen, where thousands were worked to death. And since numerous artifacts were to be displayed without cases, climate control, necessary for preservation, had to be installed, after standard museum requirements for environmental control had been ignored during construction.

The act of collection itself—quite apart from the results—was a vibrant form of memory work. The design team acted as archaeolo-gists of the Holocaust, digging into the attics of homes, weighing the impact of the physical remnants of a camp, in order to make the Holocaust "real" through physical contact. The signing of agree-ments and the physical exchange of artifacts themselves became acts of Holocaust commemoration. For example, speaking at a ceremony at the Port of Baltimore marking the arrival of the railcar, Polish

Chargé d'Affaires Ryszard Krystosik offered an interpretation of the Polish experience in the war less complex than Polish Jews would render. "The entire country heroically fought for its freedom and for human dignity," he said, "from the first to the last day of this war." Eight days later, on July 14, 1989, the clash of Polish national memory and Jewish memory would intensify when American Rabbi Avraham Weiss scaled the walls of the Carmelite convent at Auschwitz to protest its presence at the site.

The widely publicized council trip to Poland in 1989, during which the delegation received the bricks from the Warsaw Ghetto wall and numerous relics from Auschwitz, was structured as a pilgrimage, complete with wreath-layings, lighting of candles, the recitation of the kaddish, as the group—joined in Auschwitz by a Senate Foreign Relations Committee delegation—visited not only Warsaw and Auschwitz, but Majdanek and Treblinka. In March and June 1990, the German Democratic Republic (GDR) used an exchange of artifacts to symbolize a reconstruction of Holocaust memory. In March 1990, the museum brought from the GDR hundreds of artifacts, including the Hollerith machine and parts of a V-2 rocket, produced by slave labor. The gift, said Dr. Gerhard Herder, the GDR's ambassador to the United States, "underlines that my government is serious in stating that 'the entire German people has a responsibility for the past.' " And in June 1990, two months after the GDR parliament's official apology for the Holocaust, Prime Minister Lothar de Maiziere presented the original keystone of Berlin's Oranienbergerstrasse Synagogue, once the largest in the world, to then Council Chairman Harvey Meyerhoff.

After fulfilling his two-year commitment to the museum, Martin Smith returned to his family in England in September 1990. Fortified with an approved story line and supported by Shaike Weinberg, the design team had radically altered the character of the still-developing permanent exhibition. Even during the ambitious searches throughout Western and Eastern Europe, however, there were some survivors and others on the content committee uneasy with the potential presence of certain artifacts in the permanent exhibition. Decisions about these were part of a whole series of sensitive negotiations among various people representing different interests, all of whom had a role and a stake in the development of the permanent exhibition: survivors, representatives of non-Jewish groups, museum staff, the "lay leadership" of the council, and various advisers, usually Holocaust historians. These negotiations, often spirited clashes over the boundaries of Holocaust memory, eventually resulted in a widely publicized exhibition that became the object of fulsome praise and occasional criticism. It is in these negotiations, in the act of the construction of the permanent exhibition, that the boundaries of Holocaust memory were tested, adjusted, and defined.

CHAPTER FOUR

THE PERMANENT EXHIBITION draws visitors into the Holocaust through a narrative that builds in intensity. From the moment they are herded into the intentionally ugly, dark-gray metal elevators in the Hall of Witness which transport them to the beginning of the exhibition on the fourth floor, they are bunched together. In the elevator, they watch an overhead monitor with black-and-white film of Americans' first encounter with Buchenwald, Mauthausen, and Ohrdruf, while the voice of a GI recalls the horror of what he saw: "The patrol leader called in by radio and said that we have come across something that we are not sure what it is. It's a big prison of some kind, and there are people running all over. Sick, dying, starved people. And you take to an American, uh, such a sight as that, you . . . you can't imagine it. You, you just . . . things like that don't happen."

The narrative builds throughout the fourth floor, where the exhibition is a "primer" on the rise and content of the murderous world of National Socialism; it intensifies on the third floor, where visitors see the world of ghettos, deportations, and death camps; and breaks on the second floor, with thematic exhibits on resistance and rescue, children and killers, liberation and emigration. The narrative resumes in a second-floor amphitheater where *Testimony*, a film in which survivors share their stories, ends the exhibition. (Interestingly, project director Cindy Miller recalls that she and Appelbaum thought about creating an exhibition with *no* narrative voice. Quotes from perpetrators, historians, witnesses, and survivors, along with photomurals, would carry the story. "We thought of this as another method of storytelling," Miller said. "It would have been much more open-ended for visitors, engaging them directly.")

As in many history museums, the permanent exhibition appears as a seamless tale, presenting its story through an anonymous voice that conceals those who shaped the exhibition. Visitors will, by and large, not think about the exhibition as a "narrated interpretation of one particular view of the past," but will be satisfied that major interpretive dilemmas have been resolved in the exhibition.

Interior Space:
The Mood of Memory

THE DESIGN TEAM had to shape the exhibition within the confines of the space that Freed provided, for building construction preceded the design of the permanent exhibition, and Appelbaum and others often felt constrained by these limitations. Believing that "a museum functions from the inside out," Appelbaum understood that part of the design team's challenge was to make Freed's set of complex spaces work, to create a "whole environment that supported the interpretive story." They decided to present, in Appelbaum's words, "a play in three acts": "Nazi Assault—1933–1939," "Final Solution—1940–1945," and "Last Chapter."

Fourth- and third-floor bridges that connect large exhibition spaces with the tower exhibits were designed to be transitional. From them, visitors view the Hall of Witness through glass covered with names of destroyed communities and people. Architectural critic Adrian Dannatt wrote that the bridges provide "a double sigh, of relief from the pressures of history on either side and of sadness at the tale that continues before and after. It is also only from these bridges that the full crookedness and distorted propor-

Elevators to the permanent exhibition *(© Timothy Hursley)*

tions of the main hall below can be understood . . . a distorted, rup-
tured structure, just as the classical foundations of fascist society
seen from the overview of history appear as barbarism, insanity,
chaos." The towers were to be places of special intensity, power
points in the exhibition.

The design team believed that the interior mood had to be "vis_cer-
al" enough so that visitors would gain no respite from the narrative.
"The permanent exhibition," Appelbaum remarked, "has a vocabulary much like Freed's building. We built it in glass and steel and
stone. There is no wood or Plexiglas. We wanted to emphasize that
the story was a permanent one." Appelbaum thought that one reason
former exhibition designers had failed to satisfy the council was their
belief that some kind of singular design would make this museum
memorable. "We tried to bleach out the idea that a designer's style
was important. We used basic abstract concepts of style—contrast,
proportion, scale—within a modular matrix."

The feel and rhythm of space and the setting of mood were important. Appelbaum identified different qualities of space that helped to
mediate the narrative: constrictive space on the third floor, for exam-

ple, where, as visitors enter the world of the death camps, the space becomes tight and mean, with a feeling of heavy darkness. Indeed, walls were not painted, pipes were left exposed, and, except for fire exits and hidden elevators on the fourth and third floors for people who, for one reason or another, had to leave, there is no escape. Slanted glass was used in exhibit cases to draw visitors in.

Appropriate rhythms of space were important, because the exhibition was intended to take visitors on a journey. "We knew early on," said Appelbaum, "that one of the extraordinary parts of the event was that Europe was in flux and the victims were in flux because the perpetrators were moving rapidly throughout the countries. We realized that if we followed those people under all that pressure as they moved from their normal lives into ghettos, out of ghettos onto trains, from trains to camps, within the pathways of the camps, until finally to the end . . . if visitors could take that same journey, they would understand the story because they will have experienced the story."

Visitors, then, are twice removed from Washington, D.C. Freed wanted his building to take visitors out of the city as they negotiated oppressive space and were lifted from the Mall through his architecture of suggestion. For the journey through the world of the Holocaust planned by the design team, this was not enough. Visitors had to be removed from American ground on elevators, and introduced to Holocaust space that would both house the experience and suggest with what kind of spirit they should approach it. The mood of exhibit space offered not only aesthetic but moral direction. Visitors were to take this journey with a heart and soul "heavy and dark," like the space itself.

Personalizing the Story:
Faces and Artifacts

FROM THE OCCASIONAL SUGGESTIONS and stillborn plans of the 1980s through the content committee's unanimous approval of Berenbaum's story line in 1988, there was concern that the millions of individual deaths that made up the Holocaust would be lost in a story of mass death and overwhelmed by a fascination with the technique of destruction. The design team was determined to personalize the Holocaust, since it wanted visitors to eschew forever the role of bystander, and this, it was felt, could be accomplished effectively through a painful link with the faces of Holocaust victims.

Both Radu Ioanid and Arnold Kramer played significant roles in the selection and production of photographs for the exhibition. Ioanid came to the United States in 1987 from Romania, where he had written his doctoral thesis on Romanian fascism; he was hired by the museum as a part-time archivist in oral history in 1990, and then began to work with photographs. Eventually, he became director of photo research. Arnold Kramer was hired by the museum in 1986 and became a full-time photographer for the museum.

There was acute sensitivity regarding the historical accuracy of photographs to be used in the exhibition, particularly since one of the oft-cited justifications for the museum's existence was to refute the claims of Holocaust deniers. Smith, Appelbaum, and Miller believed strongly that the museum should not do any photo retouching at all. Even though the photographs acquired by the museum were copies of copies, and scratches, dust, and dirt had been introduced in making generations of copies, they argued that, if people knew the photograph had been retouched, they would wonder if the image itself had been altered. Kramer successfully argued that, by leaving these accretions, the museum was calling attention to the photograph, not the image. "It was an unconvincing badge of honor," Kramer said, "to show 'dirty' photographs." In one case, the museum *did* reconstruct an image, one of a winter scene at

Polish teacher Marian Jurek, a few moments before his execution in 1939
*(Main Commission for the Investigation of Nazi War Crimes, Warsaw, courtesy
of the United States Holocaust Memorial Museum)*

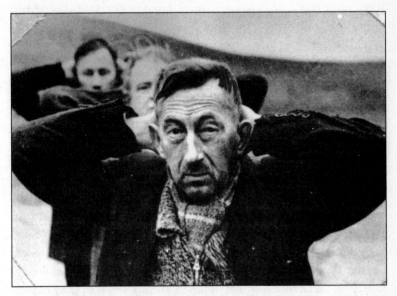

Polish primary-school teachers, moments before they were executed. The first in line is Władysław Bieliński. *(Main Commission for the Investigation of Nazi War Crimes, Warsaw, courtesy of the United States Holocaust Memorial Museum)*

Auschwitz, which appears as a large photomural in the museum. Having received three five-by-seven-inch photographs held together with Scotch tape, the museum digitized the image, in order to reveal the landscape of Birkenau.

Faces of Holocaust victims in the exhibition are shattering in their power. From the perspective of the killers, visitors encounter the stoic countenance of a Polish Catholic priest facing execution. Polish schoolteachers, moments before their execution, look at visitors in agony, sullen anger, and despair. Photographs taken by Germans of emaciated ghetto dwellers from Warsaw, Łódż, and hundreds of other ghettos are in marked contrast to those taken by a resident of Kovno's ghetto, Hirsh Kadushin. He was able to convey a gentle and loving glimpse of doomed people. His pictures focus on individual faces, unlike those taken by murderers, which focus on the suffering of emaciated bodies. There are powerful images of people desperately seeking to flee Europe before the war, and the sorrow, fear, and resignation in the faces of those being deported from countries throughout Europe. And after visitors walk through the railcar on the third floor, to their right are extraordinarily painful photographs, taken by a member of the SS in May 1944, of Jews deported from Hungary standing on the ramp at Auschwitz, most of them destined for immediate murder in the gas chambers. Two brothers, dressed alike in matching coats and caps, fear etched on their faces, gaze at the camera, into the eyes of the visitors. One old woman cradling an infant knew what awaited. Having heard that young women with children were immediately killed, she convinced her daughter to give *her* the baby, and the daughter, unknowing of the fate awaiting her mother and child, gained respite from death. This story, told by the young mother's sister in the *Testimony* film, which concludes the exhibition, imbues the face with a story. The faces of many victims, not all Jews by any means, assault, challenge, accuse, and profoundly sadden visitors throughout the exhibition.

These photographs bring out the "truth" of Susan Sontag's oft-cited reflection about photographs of Bergen-Belsen and Dachau: "One's first encounter with the photographic inventory of ultimate

Hungarian Jewish boys on the ramp at Auschwitz, shortly before they were murdered in the gas chambers *(Yad Vashem, Jerusalem, courtesy of the United States Holocaust Memorial Museum)*

horrors is a kind of revelation, the prototypically modern revelation: a negative epiphany. . . . Indeed, it seems plausible to me to divide my life into two parts, before I saw those photographs . . . and after. . . . Some limit had been reached, and not only that of horror: I felt irrevocably grieved, wounded, but a part of my feelings started to tighten; something went dead; something is still crying."

One of the distinctive and highly publicized ways in which the exhibition sought to personalize the Holocaust was through its presentation of Yaffa Eliach's collection of photographs of the Jews of her childhood shtetl, Ejszyszki. Jews had lived in this Lithuanian town since the early years of the eleventh century. By early in the twentieth century, it had become an agricultural center for nearby Polish villages, and was home to many rabbis and scholars. Only twenty-nine Jews, including four-year-old Yaffa Sonenson (Eliach), her two brothers, and Zipporah and Moshe Sonenson—her mother and father—survived the murder of the area's four thousand Jews by the *Einsatzgruppen* (German mobile killing squads) and Lithuanian collaborators on September 25 and 26, 1941. During three years of desperate and successful attempts to avoid being captured, Eliach's immediate family survived, with the exception of a baby brother, who was smothered to death in a hiding place by Jews fearing that a cry would result in their capture.

Returning to Ejszyszki in October 1944, after the Russians liberated the area, Eliach's family found that their house had been demolished, because "my mother hid her wedding band and earrings when the Germans were collecting all the gold and the furs and the radios and the linen." A Christian family had moved into her grandmother's house and used her grandmother's clothes, "her furniture, her utensils, everything. They didn't like the idea that they had to move out, and our house became the center for the twenty-nine surviving Jews."

On October 20, 1944, another baby brother—who had been born to Eliach's mother while they were in hiding—was murdered along with his mother as they hid from Polish partisans who wanted to finish the work of killing Jews. When the partisans discovered their hid-

Selection of Hungarian Jews for extermination, on the ramp at Auschwitz. At the left is Rosa Goldenzeil, shortly before she was murdered in the gas chambers with her grandson Dani Jakubovitch. She had learned that young women with children were immediately gassed, and convinced her unknowing daughter to give her the baby, thereby saving her daughter's life. Visitors hear this story in the museum's *Testimony* film. *(Yad Vashem, Jerusalem, courtesy of the United States Holocaust Memorial Museum)*

ing place, Eliach recalled, "there was my mother with the baby in her arms. She stood up, walked out . . . and I was just in back of her. And she said, 'Have mercy on my baby. Please kill me first.' She didn't ask for her life. She knew exactly what it was all about. At that moment he shot my baby brother . . . and he shot my mother. . . . She fell back on me, my brother, and my father. And they sprayed with the . . . machine gun, but she protected us with her body, and the bullets went into her body. They shot very low, but her body got all the bullets . . . and I was covered with blood, and they left." Eliach's father was arrested a few days later by the Russians and sent to Siberia; after his release, years later, he emigrated to Israel. Eliach assumed the identity of an uncle's murdered daughter, escaping with him through Europe to Israel—where she was reunited with her surviving brother—and in 1954 moved to the United States.

Eliach had been a member of the commission, and "it was during our trip in 1979," she said, "that I decided to document the history of the shtetl. It was clear to me that I had to bring the town back to life. I wanted to rescue this one town from oblivion. I decided to write its history, to remember the people through this act. I was determined that these Jews would not be remembered only as victims."

After the commission's trip, Eliach took a sabbatical from Brooklyn College, and unsuccessfully applied for grants that would support the project. She and her husband, David, took out loans on their life insurance, she used honoraria from lectures (her book *Hasidic Tales of the Holocaust* had attracted widespread attention), and in 1987 she received a Guggenheim Fellowship. She began locating émigrés from Ejszyszki in Israel, Europe, South America, and the United States. "The search for . . . documents," she wrote, "took me to archaeological excavations in Israel. One . . . where the Wilkanski family buried its Ejszyszki records in order to hide their deportation by the Turks in 1915. The other . . . where in 1946 Peretz Alufi-Kaleko buried photos and documents of his association with the right-wing Zionist movement, Betar."

After more than a decade of work, Eliach gradually acquired documents, artifacts, and more than six thousand photographs from which to write her history of the shtetl. In 1987, Eliach and her husband went to Ejszyszki. What she found confirmed her fears that Jews "died a double death," not just being "murdered physically," but having their memory "obliterated in the post-Holocaust era." Archives often omitted the words "Jew" and "Jewish," and in the town itself, "all traces of Jewish life were systematically eradicated. . . . Jewish cemeteries . . . were demolished. Tombstones were ground up and the streets paved with their gravel." The main synagogue became a sports complex, and "on the mass graves, where 4,000 Jews from Ejszyszki and its environs are buried, stands a drab, gray monument with a sign that reads, 'victims of Fascism, 1941–1944.' None of the younger people knew that these victims were Jews. Today there is not a single Jew among Ejszyszki's 12,000 residents."

Such memories came alive for Yaffa Eliach on this trip. She met the woman who had saved her life by hiding her when the killing began. She went to the hospital where her mother had been taken after being murdered. She stood on the mass graves, where, she recalled, "I felt the shtetl beneath my feet, teeming with life. I was sinking into this place," and, she said, "only the image of my grandchildren helped me hold on to the present." (As Yaffa Eliach told this extraordinary story, her husband David nodded, adding that he could *see* her "slipping away" as she stood on the grave, and how shaken he had been by the event.)

Yaffa Eliach's maternal grandparents, Yitzhak Uri Katz and his wife, Alte Katz, had been the town's photographers. Katz, trained as a pharmacist, had graduated from City College of New York, and had brought photographic equipment from the United States to the town, where, after their marriage, Eliach's grandparents opened a photographic studio on the third floor above their bakery and pharmacy. Eliach remembers watching her grandmother take photographs of the townspeople, and both she and her brother managed to smuggle some of her grandmother's photographs out of the shtetl after their mother's murder. "Since I had assumed the identity of my uncle's murdered daughter, I couldn't carry photographs showing me with a different set of parents. Without the knowledge of my uncle, I hid them in my shoe as we made our way across borders. My brother tried to enter Palestine on a ship illegally, and the British intercepted it. He was forced to jump overboard, was captured and deported to Cyprus, but had photographs strapped to his body. We were reunited in Palestine, but I did not ask him for the photographs until 1979."

Eliach characterized the photographs as "survivor photos": some were "sent to relatives overseas or taken along by emigrants; others were snatched by looters as souvenirs; a number were deposited for safekeeping with friendly neighbors; many were buried in the ground or stashed in unusual hiding places—like those of my grandmother . . . hidden in the litter of her Siberian cat during the entire war. . . . the photos [have] the weightier task of restoring identity and individuality to the otherwise anonymous victims of the Nazis," redeeming them, she said, from the "conflagration that left behind mere ashes, smoke, and pits filled with bodies."

After her extraordinary visit to Ejszyszki, Eliach was determined to find a proper memorial location for the photographs. She met officially with the Museum of the Diaspora in Tel Aviv—which told her, "Come back in 1997, we're booked until then"—and spoke with individuals at the Simon Wiesenthal Center's Museum of Tolerance in Los Angeles, at the Museum of Jewish Heritage—A Living Memorial to the Holocaust, in New York, and at Yad Vashem.

Martin Smith knew of Eliach from Raye Farr's interview with her for Smith's television series *The Struggles for Poland*, and asked Cindy Miller to meet with her. They spoke in Eliach's Brooklyn home on March 1, 1989. "I sat there for eight hours on Yaffa's couch looking at all her material," Miller said, "and walked away completely stunned. What one saw was the entire vibrancy of a small shtetl." Miller recalled the emotional power of the photographs, the way they evoked everyday life. They had the intimacy of family photographs, with "scalloped edges . . . cut in the shape of hearts to become part of cards, birthday cards and greeting cards . . . stained edges ... cut edges ... edges that had been colored and pasted down. We wanted to preserve that character."

That same day, Miller wrote Appelbaum, Smith, Berenbaum, and Weinberg, reporting on Eliach's collection. She was especially interested in having the exhibition portray those murdered in ways apart from Nazi definitions—prisoner, inmate, victim—terms, she argued, "which in our democratic society connote some measure of guilt, whereas in the case of Nazi Germany ... [they] applied to innocent people." A large exhibit on "life before" the Holocaust had gradually eroded because, Miller said, "it was impossible to capture the richness and complexity of life through a small grouping of artifacts. It just never worked to our satisfaction." Eliach's collection, she wrote, provided a dramatic solution. It illustrated the evolving, complex life of a Jewish shtetl, "more than the usual, somewhat fixed and easily-evoked nostalgia associated with the loss of beautiful, old-world traditions." It would also personalize the Holocaust, connecting museum visitors to "real faces of real people." Miller became, Eliach recalled, "the strongest advocate for the photographs."

There was no immediate response from the museum's staff, and Miller reissued the memo on November 10, 1989. Eventually, Miller took Martin Smith to see the collection in New York, and he became enthusiastic when Miller offered another argument for its use: it provided a dramatic memorial to these victims of the *Einsatzgruppen*. Appelbaum recalled, "There was a very inadequate response ... in our museum to the activities of the *Einsatzgruppen*. ... We couldn't quite capture how to handle what happened in the shtetls of Europe as the Germans advanced into the Soviet Union."

Smith and Appelbaum had already decided that they needed a way to "punctuate" the story on each floor of the exhibition, and asked Freed to cut away some cement flooring in space that was shaped like a tower from the outside but, because of solid flooring, was not a towerlike space on the inside. Originally, they planned to put prisoner "mug shots" from Auschwitz in the tower as a way to personalize the story.

There were various ideas for framing the photographs in the tower space: Smith and Appelbaum considered a tower open at the top, thereby allowing the elements to weather the space. They thought of it as a chimney—with all the ominous implications chimneys had in this narrative—lined with brick, and they even wondered whether having pre-blackened brick, perhaps charred through a controlled fire, would be appropriate. The mug shots, however, would have been out of sequence, for visitors were not "in" Auschwitz yet. Furthermore, Appelbaum recalled, "it was a very inadequate solution, because the people were already victims. They were in striped pajamas at that point." Eliach's photographs offered a glimpse of people before they were classified as "victims."

For several reasons, then, Eliach's collection fit well into the museum's narrative. She hired a lawyer to negotiate the terms of use with the museum. "Photographs are not treated with the same dignity as other written documents," Eliach said, "and I feared that photos might be altered. I wanted to protect the collection and make sure that I was involved in every stage of the process: particularly choosing the photographs and placing them in the tower." (For example, she did not want photographs of families that had feuded to be placed next to each other.) For her, the collection was an organic whole, a living memory of the town, and it could not be broken up any more than could a human body. She recalled that Arnold Kramer had initially selected too many portraits of individuals, leaving out others, she thought, that had to be displayed because they expressed a sense of "the town, the buildings, photographs that communicated a sense of place."

She was unwavering in her commitment. Ninety percent of those whose pictures appear in the tower were murdered; the rest had left the shtetl prior to the mass murder. In their first discussions, Shaike Weinberg and Michael Berenbaum told Eliach that they wanted in the tower only photographs of those who were murdered. "I

OPPOSITE: Details of Yaffa Eliach's tower exhibition
(© Jeff Goldberg/Esto)

was stunned," Eliach said. "I remember feeling, 'Here I am rescuing my town from a double death, and they want to excise part of it.' They wanted to make a kind of arbitrary selection. I used that term with them: 'selection.' Eventually, everyone came to agree on the importance of showing the life of the town."

This disagreement revealed the tension between Eliach's commitment to commemorative integrity—the collection being the photographic embodiment of the life of the village—and the museum's interest in the collection as part of a Holocaust narrative that dramatized the activities of Nazi mobile killing squads in the third-floor narrative of the destruction process.

Although Eliach would have refused permission to use the collection had the museum insisted on displaying only those murdered, the staff needed the photographs. Berenbaum said, "I desperately wanted them. I was afraid that, had we not been able to use them, the alternative would have been some kind of artwork that would have been a disaster."

Arnold Kramer also became an advocate for Eliach's photographs, and she sent them to him by personal courier a hundred at a time. Eventually, Kramer copied sixteen hundred; 1,032 appeared in the tower. Originally, the photographs were to have been mounted on enamel, but Eliach thought the appearance too "cold"; she wanted them to have the "warmth of a family album." The cost of porcelain mounting was too expensive, over $1,000 each. Enlarged reproductions were finally mounted on aluminum and laminated in plastic, and will in time, remarked Kramer, undergo some fading. Appelbaum, Eliach, Farr, Kramer, and Miller met in New York to plan the final layout of the photographs. All agreed that original color tones should be maintained in photographs of three different sizes mounted on a fifty-four-foot-high frame ascending from the third floor through the fifth floor, narrowing slightly at each level. Eliach and Miller picked photographs that would represent as many families as possible, looking for images that showed town events, buildings, streets, youth movements, and that revealed the process of secularization in this shtetl, from bearded elderly Jews to the clean-shaven young. In some cases, donors placed restrictions that made it impossible to display photographs in the museum. For instance, "One family gave me magnificent photos, but would not allow them to be displayed outside Israel."

The tower is a powerful space because life is present there, in marked contrast to the overwhelming presence of death in the rest of the museum. The photographs profoundly affected many of the museum's staff. Raye Farr thought them important precisely because they convey images of people fully alive, not yet victims of the Holocaust. Yet, because almost all of them were destined to become victims, Kramer found them "excruciating." They are, he said, "the hardest pictures in the exhibit, for you bring a knowledge of the future to these pictures that these people didn't have. You see them in their innocence, and you know their fate." For Appelbaum, the very "ordinariness" of the photographs makes them extraordinary in the context of the museum's narrative. "Weddings, picnics . . . family portraits, it's grandma this, it's grandchild that; so rich, so ordinary, it's the thing that you and I would open in our photograph album to cherish, but in fact it's something which was all wiped out in a space of hours by . . . these killings."

Visitors greet these ascending faces in two quite different moments in the museum's narrative. By the time they encounter the townspeople of Ejszyszki on the fourth floor, war has begun; Germans have engaged in large-scale murder of the handicapped—"the first victims of systematic murder by the Nazis," the exhibit text reads—and the murder of Polish intelligentsia. Visitors cross to the tower spaces on Freed's glass bridge with the etched names of "Lost Communities." They encounter the photographs of Eastern European Jews taken by Roman Vishniac between 1935 and 1939, displayed in a tower room that resembles a mini–art gallery, a space completely disjointed from the rest of the exhibition space. Visitors then meet "The Ejszyszki Shtetl Collection." The exhibit text does not reveal the fate of these people, but says, among other things, that "the Jewish community had a rich religious culture and an energetic secular life." Miller recalled her efforts to keep the tower "about people being alive."

Suggestions were made that there should be ominous touches, foreshadowing their eventual murder—shadows running through the tower, for example. "I argued that there should be no mention in the fourth-floor text nor hints in the overall design about their fate. It was not part of their lives yet."

Visitors meet these faces again on the third floor, after moving through the most intense part of the exhibition, the world of ghettoization, deportation, and extermination. As viewers cross another of Freed's bridges—this one etched with first names of Jewish victims of the Holocaust—tower spaces display shoes, pictures of women's hair, castings of the Mauthausen crematorium, a Majdanek table that had been used for removing valuables from bodies, and a truck frame from Majdanek on which bodies were burned. After this, visitors encounter "The End of a Shtetl." In the same dispassionate text found throughout the exhibition—for Weinberg understood that the power of photographs and artifacts would only be diminished by passionate text—the events were described. "The 'Final Solution' began in Eishishok [the Yiddish name of the shtetl] soon after German troops arrived there on June 23, 1941. A Jewish Council was formed. The Jews' valuables were collected and confiscated. Jewish men and women were abused and humiliated. On September 21, the eve of the Jewish New Year, an SS mobile killing squad entered the town, accompanied by Lithuanian volunteers. Four thousand Jews from Eishishok and its environs were herded into three synagogues and imprisoned there. Three days later, on September 24, the Jews were taken from the synagogues to a horse market on the outskirts of town. The next day, the men were led in groups of 250 to the old Jewish cemetery. There, the SS men ordered them to undress and to stand at the edge of open pits, where they were shot by Lithuanian guards. On September 26, the women and children were shot near the Christian cemetery. . . . Nine hundred years of Jewish life and culture in Eishishok came to an end in two days. Today, no Jews live in Eishishok."

The identity-card project was another attempt to use photographs to convey the personal dimension of the Holocaust. Each visitor was to obtain, upon entrance to the exhibition, a small card with the photo and brief biography of a person corresponding to the visitor's age and sex, and on each floor the story would be updated. (In the first months after opening, the various update stations were plagued with malfunctions, however. Now visitors simply pick up a completed card, categorized only by gender, before entering the elevators.) When Debbie Klingender, of Peter D. Hart Research Associates, interviewed members of focus groups for their reaction to various proposed museum exhibits well before opening, the identity card was a "smash hit." "They very much liked the idea that they could identify with someone like them in the midst of this horrible story." One focus-group member foresaw an unexpected act of defilement emerging out of this popular idea, however. "I can see right outside of the museum 10,000 cards on the ground. . . . They're going to be blowing up and down the street."

The ID cards did not always match visitors with people "just like them." In fact, the project served, without much fanfare, subtly to extend the boundaries of memory to connect visitors with some oft-overlooked victim groups. Dr. Klaus Müller, a historian from the University of Amsterdam, was in charge of preparing identity cards of homosexual victims. For Müller, the work of reconstructing the history of gay victims was directly related to present social concerns, for, he said, shame had hindered the work of memory among gay survivors. Still not recognized as Holocaust victims in many European countries, gay and lesbian groups were not allowed to erect a plaque in Dachau, and, with the exception of Sachsenhausen, Neuengamme, and only a few other places, "resistance to memorialization represents a second form of exclusion, an effacement of memory at the places where gay men and women died."

For Müller, the museum was a beginning. Indeed, in the early 1980s, urged on by the Gay and Lesbian Alliance, which had criticized the commission for remaining "absolutely silent concerning the thousands of human beings exterminated in Hitler's death camps because of their sexual orientation," the council had contacted gay activists in Europe, and eventually conducted searches for artifactual evidence and photographs. Müller himself contributed photographs of gay life in Germany before the war, arrest photographs from Düsseldorf, and mug shots of gays in Auschwitz. He hopes to plan a special exhibit on gay victims for the museum, and believes that representation in the permanent exhibition will motivate gays to "take responsibility for this part of [their history]. In the memory of the Gay and Lesbian community, the Holocaust has been a symbol of the most extreme persecution you can imagine, but the actual historical knowledge . . . is very little."

Müller also warned against the use of false analogy, the tendency in the gay community to equate AIDS with the Holocaust, and to inflate the numbers of gay Holocaust victims. "Who do we remember," he asked. "Up to 1 million dead gays and lesbians as claimed by some gay groups and researchers? Gay historians estimate that between 10,000 and 15,000 gay men were forced into the camps, and lesbians were persecuted to a far lesser degree. Although big numbers create big emotions, here they only document a disturbing attitude in our community. Is there something within us we need to satisfy by inventing an even harsher history than history itself has been for us?" Regarding AIDS, he underscored what he perceived as the "crucial differences between the inaction and hostility of American society and politics toward people with AIDS and the intentional systematic Nazi killing machine. From a gay European perspective, I find it startling that anyone would be interested in comparing the two. By doing so it diminishes the power of each event."

On April 23, 1993, just after the museum's opening, on the eve of the "March on Washington" by those sympathetic to gay liberation from across the nation, the museum became a site of remembrance for these forgotten victims. Both Müller and Michael Berenbaum spoke to a large gathering in front of the museum. "Until now," said Müller, "it is very difficult to reconstruct the individual stories of the men with the pink triangle. The museum tells some of these stories and breaks thus with an unholy tradition of silence." As a part of this break, Müller wrote eight cards for gay victims and one for a lesbian victim to include in the identity-card project. Stretching the boundaries of memory to incorporate this group of Holocaust victims will also stretch, for some visitors, the limits of their tolerance.

Photographs only illuminated part of the museum's Holocaust narrative. The function of small artifacts throughout the museum was to make each segment come alive. There are approximately one thousand artifacts in the exhibition. Some are examples of materials that prepared the way for the Holocaust: anti-Semitic journals, posters encouraging boycotts of Jewish businesses, instruments used in "racial science," but also advertisements for Zionist lectures documenting Jewish responses to societal exclusion. There are artifacts dramatizing American indifference: a passenger ticket and list and telegrams from passengers on the ill-fated SS *St. Louis,* for instance. There are examples of books burned and fragments of Torahs desecrated during Kristallnacht, the "Night of Broken Glass," in 1938; a carved wooden model of the Łódź ghetto made by survivor Leon Jacobson; a doctor's smock from a clinic where disabled children were murdered; and examples of the mass of materials confiscated from those murdered in Auschwitz: prayer shawls and prayer books, umbrellas, leg braces and artificial limbs, brushes, mirrors, toothbrushes, razors, scissors, kitchen utensils, cutlery, and bowls. There are artifacts dramatizing different kinds of resistance: musical instruments, a Bible belonging to a Jehovah's Witness and one used by Pastor André Trocmé of Le Chambon, protective passes probably issued by Raoul Wallenberg, identity cards from those killed in Lidice, resistance leaflets and small arms, and children's artifacts—a wooden toy, a drawing of a deportation train, a doll. There are posters from DP camps, and a facsimile of the Israeli Declaration of Independence.

Despite the presence of such artifacts, some members of the design team thought that individual human stories had been submerged in favor of the grand narrative of the Holocaust. Permanent-exhibition coordinator Ann Farrington believed that the design team was "ruthless" about using "hard material," rather than incorporating small artifacts to tell "poignant stories." Charlotte Hebebrand recalled constant discussions about this, and regretted that many "incredibly touching" small artifacts "never made their way into the exhibition."

The issue arose at a design meeting on June 20, 1991, with the question of how (or whether) to display small items made by inmates in the camps. Shaike Weinberg was not enthusiastic, for, he said, "90 percent of the inmates wouldn't dream of making these." Others wondered if such items—a woman's belt, for example—illustrated "spiritual resistance." Did these artifacts offer a way to show the "counterpoint to the world of death," a way to emphasize that "people's spirit held on in spite of this"? Raye Farr thought them important to use, because, "deprived of their name, their clothes, their hair, people still made things, and those things offer us glimpses of their humanity." Charlotte Hebebrand believed such items would personalize exhibition space devoted entirely to the destruction of human beings. Likewise, Joan Ringelheim, research director for the permanent exhibition (and now director of the department of oral history), argued that it was important to humanize the area to the extent that the "concentration camp universe" was not portrayed as so unique that visitors could not relate to it at all. Museum historian David Luebke disagreed, arguing that such items conveyed inappropriate sentimentality. (Three small artifacts do appear in the exhibition shortly after visitors exit from the Auschwitz barracks—a brooch, a cigarette box, and a tiny pair of shoes—although Raye Farr believes them not displayed prominently enough.)

This discussion was about more than just the inclusion or exclusion of artifactual material. Through its decision, the design team took a stance with regard to the sensitive issue of expressions of "resistance" other than armed revolts in the ghettos or camps. Many of the survivors involved with the shaping of the exhibition insisted that less recognizable but significant forms of resistance were an important part of this story, and that their inclusion was necessary

Exhibition designer Ralph Appelbaum points out a detail in a drawing during a weekly design meeting. *From left to right:* Ann Farrington, permanent exhibition coordinator; Radu Ioanid, photo research director; Shaike Weinberg, museum director; and Raye Farr, director of the permanent exhibition. *(Arnold Kramer, United States Holocaust Memorial Museum)*

to counteract the accusation that victims went like "sheep to the slaughter."

Cindy Miller agreed. She argued that one could understand the behavior of victims by demonstrating the way the Germans used deception and force. Most often, she argued, people had not known what awaited them. "If people brought brushes, potato peelers and tea strainers with them to Auschwitz, what better evidence that they didn't know where they were going. I wanted to show photographs with barbed wire and armed Germans guarding the victims, confronting them at every stage of their degradation, to show that resistance would have meant fairly certain death, while going along with the progress of the terrible events paradoxically held out some chance of survival."

The design team had to negotiate these sensitive waters carefully.

Should the moving story of the Warsaw Ghetto uprising, or revolts in the death camps themselves, or armed resistance by Jewish and non-Jewish groups occupy a central role in the narrative, as they do in Israeli Holocaust museums? And should "resistance" mean much more than physical resistance? Yaffa Eliach felt strongly that spiritual resistance deserved recognition in the museum. She offered an example: "Prisoners in the camps," she said, "would tie seven knots in their dresses in order to know when the Sabbath came." Martin Smith, on the other hand, was unhappy with much emphasis on resistance of *any* kind, fearing that this could easily lead to an "epic" Holocaust narrative in which heroic resistance gained "equal time" with the narrative of destruction. "There was more resistance than many people know about, so maybe it's right to highlight it in some way. But I think you could go away and feel that there were lots of people fighting. . . . It's not so."

The exhibition did not use the term "spiritual resistance." Indeed, in the audio theater on the third floor, where survivors describe daily life in Auschwitz—certainly one of the places where such resistance might have been mentioned—the introduction informs visitors that they will hear survivors tell stories of "terror, brutality, and illness; of filth, exhaustion, and starvation. They speak of separation from family, of despair and harsh physical labor." Acts of kindness are not characterized as resistance, but momentary aberrations that provided psychic nourishment: "Many remember moments of love and hope that sustained them in the midst of so much death and destruction."

Enduring Issues:
Shaping the Boundaries of Memory

THE DESIRE TO COMMEMORATE occasionally clashed with the desire to present an accurate and moving historical narrative. Moreover, the very location of the museum—adjacent to the Mall—meant to some staff that the permanent exhibition had to "behave itself": it had to be a "good neighbor" to the other exhibitions on the Mall by maintaining a certain level of civility in the narrative's text and choices of artifacts, just as Freed's building had been designed as a good neighbor to adjacent public buildings. Finally, during the frenetic work of the design team in the several years before the opening, there was genuine fear that the museum might be too horrible, and that no one would come. This fear was reinforced by the reaction of the focus groups, many of whom had a "deeply ingrained cultural image of the Holocaust" as simply "piles of bodies." People would need to be convinced that the museum would be more than a horror story before they could be persuaded to visit. Each of these impulses—commemorative sensibility and educational imperative, appropriate institutional civility, and public reassurance—became part of the interpretive mix in exhibition planning.

THE BOUNDARIES OF HORROR

The design team had to decide what images the visitor should first encounter, once he or she has been transported into the world of the Holocaust exhibition through elevators, and has emerged into the heavy, dark space of the fourth floor. The beginning of the exhibit continues the elevator monitor's story of the GIs' encounter with the camps through graphic photographs: a skeletal inmate of Buchenwald looks reproachfully at the camera of a U.S. Army photographer; a large video screen shows color film of the dead at Dachau, taken by Lieutenant George Stevens; and a photograph captures the anger and shock of General Dwight D. Eisenhower, hands on hips, as he viewed the horrific landscape of Ohrdruf with members of his staff. These were considered appropriate, but there was disagreement over what image should be chosen for the large photomural that would dominate the entry area. Appelbaum and Miller suggested the landscape of a camp after liberation, with shocked American troops and emaciated survivors "hinting" at the horror. Kramer and Ioanid argued strongly for a color photograph that showed American soldiers viewing a wagon heaped with corpses at

Buchenwald, with onlookers standing beyond the camp fence, the tops of their heads just visible as they peered in. This photo had, said Kramer, a "moral gravity" that others did not. It revealed the grim faces of the liberators, and the guilty presence of bystanders.

There was widespread opposition to the use of this photograph, however. Ralph Appelbaum told Raye Farr that the reaction of the design team in New York was "uniformly negative." Cindy Miller offered a systematic, articulate critique of an "explicit image of mass death," in which the "human flesh of the exposed victims screams out of the picture." Visitors who had been assured that the most shocking material would be shielded would feel betrayed. She believed that, although focusing on American liberators was a "unique and highly appropriate way to begin," this image was more "about dead bodies than liberators, who in this photograph are rather a faceless group of soldiers." She argued that, if such images were kept on the third floor, fourth-floor exhibits could do their job of "contextualizing" the horror. "By showing bodies right after the elevator," the exhibit would cause visitors to experience a "horror show from beginning to end . . . undermining the narrative structure and drama of our presentation."

Shaike Weinberg opposed its use because of his resistance to the display of genitalia in the exhibition. Others noted that the photograph was not taken at the time of liberation, but several days later. Raye Farr initially supported Kramer and Ioanid, then changed her mind when a number of people told her, "I couldn't take it," and when her daughter persuaded her that it might be tolerable at the end but not at the beginning of the exhibit. She recalled thinking that the design team "had to make the exhibit accessible even to those who cannot deal with images we've had to learn how to deal with, day in and day out." Chosen instead of either the graphic horror of the color photograph or a camp landscape after liberation was a black-and-white photo of American troops looking numbly at charred human remains on a pyre, remains that were certainly visually less human—therefore perhaps less threatening—than the flesh-colored corpses and faces at Buchenwald.

Arnold Kramer and Radu Ioanid argued for this photograph to serve as the opening photomural. *(National Archives, courtesy of the United States Holocaust Memorial Museum)*

The "amount" of horror to exhibit, and the related concern over the display of genitalia, were a matter of grave concern to Weinberg. The museum, he believed, had to use "judgment and good taste" in its presentation of murder. "We have to be sparing with images of naked corpses, to have a sense of measure." Consequently, one large photograph—of nude Russian POWs—is cropped at the waist. Another photograph of Russian POWs, which *does* display genitalia, was originally designed to be three-quarters of life size; it was reduced and placed in the midst of other photos in the exhibit segment "Slave Labor."

These issues had percolated throughout the conceptual planning for the museum since the commission days, and in the late 1980s those planning the exhibition had to resolve them. There was discussion about nudity at various content-committee meetings. The committee wrote a "philosophical statement" about the issue, arguing that the museum had to find the appropriate balance between representations of life and death, that some nudity would be appropriate given proper context and interpretation, but that such images should be of appropriate scale and visitors should be "prepared." Some survivors on the committee were uncomfortable with *any* display of nudity, whereas others saw it as a crucial part of the process of dehumanization of victims that had to be included in the narrative. There are graphic, violent photographs of nude victims, many of them women, in video-monitor exhibits focusing on the actions of German mobile killing squads and their collaborators. And, from video monitors within the Auschwitz barracks, photographs document Nazi medical experiments. All of these monitors are hidden behind "privacy walls," designed to limit exposure: visitors walk up to the walls and peer over to the monitors. This resolved the lingering issue of how the exhibit should accommodate children, and also resolved uncertainty regarding the presentation of horror. As Raye Farr remarked, "For Shaike, it was not a question of whether to put these photographs behind privacy walls or in full view. It was privacy walls or nothing."

Not everyone agreed with Weinberg. Martin Smith thought that

Visitors join American troops in confronting this scene in the opening photomural. *(National Archives, courtesy of the United States Holocaust Memorial Museum)*

the decision on the opening photomural was a "real mistake,"and that the color photomural would have set a "slightly tougher agenda." Arnold Kramer believed the failure to use the Buchenwald photograph and the decision to use privacy walls expressed an "excessive desire to avoid being offensive." He thought that people who were inclined to leave because of photographic imagery would just leave, and he strongly disagreed with the oft-stated idea that the exhibition was being designed to tell the story of the Holocaust to middle America, "the Iowa farm family." In Kramer's view, "We're building this to tell the story without softening it, and we can't expect this story to impinge on people's moral faculties if we don't give them the responsibility to grapple with the worst of it." For him, the exhibition was "first and foremost about cultural sensitivities of the nineties, and secondarily about the Holocaust. It is about people reflecting on the past, caught in the midst of various political and social pressures."

The design team faced a difficult decision regarding the presentation of horror. Why put so much effort into constructing an exhibition that was so horrible that people would not visit? They worried about word-of-mouth evaluation after opening, and feared that the first visitors would tell family and friends, "Don't go, it's too horrible." On the other hand, they faced the articulate criticisms that, by hiding material behind privacy walls, they were, in effect, softening the story. This was a dilemma for which there seemed no adequate solution. The museum's mission was to teach people about the Holocaust and bring about civic transformation; yet, since the public had to *desire* to visit, the museum felt the need to find a balance between the tolerable and the intolerable. Martin Smith worried that any attempt to soften the story would mean the museum was in danger of not fulfilling its mission—namely, "to scald people." Acceptance of the story, Smith argued, "means that people must take it on in some profound way." Weinberg, however, held firm to his conviction that the cropping of photographs and the use of privacy walls for some materials struck a necessary and appropriate balance without altering the essence of the narrative.

THE BOUNDARIES OF REPRESENTATION:
THE PERPETRATORS

The commemorative impulse also complicated the exhibition's portrayal of the perpetrators of the Holocaust. Earlier museum plans and an occasional council member—Raul Hilberg in particular—had noted the importance of detailing the machinery of death, of showing how victims were degraded and murdered and how their very bodies were mined for valuable resources (gold from teeth, for example). Hilberg consistently emphasized the need for perpetrators to "speak" in the exhibition, so that visitors could penetrate the murderous logic of their world. However, given the boundaries of the commemorative voice at work, this idea threatened to contaminate what for many was commemorative space. As in so many Holocaust memorials, the common denominator, wrote council historian Sybil Milton, "is a universal willingness to commemorate suffering experienced rather than suffering caused." There was also the gnawing fear that an effective portrayal of the Nazis' world and their industry of murder would be worse than appalling to visitors—it might be perversely fascinating as well. "We didn't want to create an environment where people were being reverent in front of the wrong things," said Appelbaum. "So we avoided putting out a lot of Nazi memorabilia. The songs and the banners and the objects are alluring. So we avoided that and instead we created what we hope to be reverential moments with elements of rescue and righteousness, of people really doing what we would all hope to do in a similar situation."

Concern that the exhibit could, in effect, unintentionally glamorize the Nazis, focus too much on Adolf Hitler, or fail to capture the enormity of Nazi crimes, made the naming and design of exhibit segments problematic. The late Alvin Rosenfeld, who had worked at the museum both as director of external affairs and as senior consultant to the Days of Remembrance program, criticized a segment tentatively titled "Hitler's Ascent to Power." (As a foreign correspondent for the *New York Post*, the *New York Herald Tribune*, NBC News, and the *Washington Post*, he had covered Israel's war for independence, the trial of Adolf Eichmann, and the Six-Day War.) "To stress the rise of HITLER . . . is to fall into a revisionist trap . . . that he alone was evil, that he and a tiny group of buddies were responsible for the horror, and the German people were innocent." He also objected to an exhibit entitled "Anti-Semitism." The museum, he believed, should more properly focus on Nazi racism and prejudice. "Indeed, I would call the exhibit *not* anti-Semitism but racism. . . . This is an American museum, not a Jewish museum." Likewise, Martin Smith reacted contemptuously to a suggestion that the third-floor exhibition be entitled "Encounter with Evil." "I think the title . . . is banal and distasteful. 'An Encounter with Evil' sounds like a come-on for 'Friday the 13th' or the Haunted House at the fairground."

The exhibition's design bespeaks the design team's conscious intent to mute the allure of Nazi symbols. In the fourth-floor exhibits "Nazi Society" and "Police State," the visual impact of a large Nazi flag is shielded from visitors by scaffolding filled with photographs. "This design," remarked Cindy Miller, "was an act of severe mediation." The team worried as well about ennobling Hitler's remarks that appeared on museum walls. Moving quotes from Elie Wiesel's *Night*, Yiddish poet Moses Shulstein's poem about victims' shoes, and Russian poet Yevgeny Yevtushenko's "Babi Yar" appear in raised letters. "We didn't want to treat Hitler's words the same way," said Miller, "but we couldn't be too self-conscious, we couldn't tell visitors how to think about this." They decided to silk-screen Hitler's words onto the wall. "Unlike the raised cut letters, these words could be painted over or washed away," Miller observed. "This was the most temporary treatment of words in the exhibition, a way of letting design suggest a moral distinction between Hitler's words and those of survivors or witnesses."

The commemorative desire to keep museum space free from the presence of murderers, and the fear of public fascination with the Nazis, had an unintentional and potentially insidious consequence. Raye Farr recalled that, when she arrived at the museum in the fall of 1990, she was surprised at the near-invisibility of perpetrators, even though the museum had collected artifacts and photographs

The "Nazi Society" and "Police State" exhibits were designed to reduce the impact of the large Nazi flag displayed behind the screen of photographs. *(© Jeff Goldberg/Esto)*

with which to tell their story. "The fourth floor was Germans doing things to people, with anti-Semitism the only anchor, and the third floor was people having things done to them. We almost fell into the trap of showing Jews and others as victims of an invisible evil." Likewise, Yitzchak Mais, director of the Yad Vashem Historical Museum in Jerusalem, while walking through a model of the permanent exhibition with Michael Berenbaum in August 1991, was bothered that the Nazis appeared as a "superhuman force that just took over," as if, he said, "there was this metaphysical evil that mysteriously killed the Jews."

In July 1990, however, Ringelheim wondered if an exhibit entitled "Killers" did justice to the many who participated in the killing process without actually committing murder. "I think it might be more effective to simply call it something like: 'who is responsible?' Such a title seems to me to suggest a wider scope for the audience to

The face of National Socialism is graphically expressed in this photograph, which appears early in the exhibition. *(Courtesy of the Bundesarchiv)*

consider." Though the purpose of the exhibit was to help visitors identify with the victims, Ringelheim believed they should also reflect on what it meant to be a bystander. At the same time that the design team discussed expanding the circle of who counted as killers, they also weighed the implications of where to locate such an exhibit. They worried about an early-1991 proposal to place photographs of elite Nazis high on a wall on the second floor, directly across from an exhibit on child victims. "Showing the faces high up, as portraits, might seem to memorialize these mass murderers." They discussed alternatives: "showing the faces closer to the ground . . . or in action (behind their desks, with victims and cohorts, etc.) rather than as portraits; and showing the perpetrators elsewhere in the exhibit, for example, on the third floor where and when the decisions to advance the Holocaust were being made."

In November 1991, museum historian David Luebke raised the issue of how best to represent a wide variety of perpetrators within the limited wall space available. Should the design team decide to give wall space to bystanders—for, "knowingly or unknowingly, virtually all Germans were 'bystanders' to genocidal racial persecution," he argued—there would be inadequate wall space for "individuals whose crimes were deliberate and heinous in their result. This . . . would trivialize not only the people who devised, planned, and executed the 'Final Solution,' but also the genocide itself. Can we afford to portray bystanders at the cost of excluding the commandant of Chelmno? I think not." Luebke argued that, given spatial limitations, the exhibit segment should focus on persons "directly involved in genocidal policy, in planning its execution, and in managing its operation . . . decision-makers, facilitators, executioners."

Ringelheim responded that she wanted a wider definition of guilt. "The function of this segment is . . . an attempt to get museum visitors to be thoughtful about a system as well as about individuals who made it possible to designate certain people as less than human, and to decide that certain lives were not worthy to live. . . . I think we need to at least hint at bystanders, collaborators, and a morally culpable set of perpetrators . . . train engineers, judges, order police, accountants, presidents and others of industrial firms who 'hired' slave labor, lawyers, doctors. Because [this segment] follows liberation [it] becomes a commentary on whether the process of death is what matters; or, in addition to that process and the lives it cost, it is also about the question of what and who makes it possible to construct a society in which death is its definition."

Farr's insistence on increasing the perpetrators' presence in the exhibition was apparent. "Now," she said, as the exhibition took final form, "photographs will show perpetrators often enjoying their work, from those in the mobile killing squads, to soldiers smiling as they cut beards off elderly Jews. We will not just have head shots in gallery portraits." Indeed, when the exhibition opened to the public, perpetrators were very much in evidence throughout, in text, photographs, and artifacts. On the fourth floor, for example, as one moves from the powerful images of the American encounter with the camps down a long corridor toward exhibits documenting the rise of National Socialism, one photograph seems to dominate the space: an SS man and a policeman walk with a muzzled dog—ears perked, fierce eyes open—a fitting image for the official killing that would soon be unleashed. In exhibits on "Nazi Society" and "Police State," numerous photographs of Nazi rallies, youth organizations, and business, church, political, and judicial subservience to Hitler dramatize the role of complicit bystanders. Finally, in the exhibit "Murder of the Handicapped," there is a chilling photograph of a doctor standing comfortably in a clinic room with the body of a child killed in the Nazis' euthanasia program.

On the third floor, devoted to documenting the Final Solution, "civilized" photographs of the participants at the Wannsee Conference of January 20, 1942—a pivotal meeting of high-ranking Nazis to discuss the fate of the Jews—are an effective contrast to the barbarism shown behind the privacy walls and the artifacts of extermination in the tower rooms. Text—in, for example, the "Railroads of Death" and "Slave Labor" segments—indicts those whom visitors might not at first glance consider complicit in murder. And on the second floor, the design team resolved the problem in the "Killers" segment by placing photographs of murderers on a wall directly above monitors showing film of various war-crimes trials. These photographs show murderers "at work"—indeed, enjoying their work, as their broad smiles indicate. Groups of naked victims huddle together facing a soldier hunched over a machine gun, and in one particularly powerful image murderers stand amid bodies like hunters, proudly posing with their prey. These photographs are effectively and consciously juxtaposed to the exhibit on children victims on an opposite wall. Weinberg also responded to Ringelheim's concerns by widening the scope of perpetrators and by indicating bystanders in the text.

The perpetrators are also represented by a contemporary "artifact," the white plaster model of gas chamber and crematorium in Birkenau, built by Mieczysław Stobierski, which confronts visitors in the museum's Auschwitz barracks. Wounded while fighting with the Polish Army during the German invasion in 1939, he escaped captivity and became active in the underground, falsifying documents for others. After the war, Stobierski became acquainted with the Poles responsible for creating the museum at Auschwitz, and he was asked to make a small model of a crematorium. He was also asked to listen to the interrogation of an SS guard who had been in charge of the crematorium, and later spoke of beginning his work while "the smell was still there, and bones, whole and crushed into powder for fertilizer, were still on the ground." In working on the crematorium model, he decided to add human figures, then to make a bigger model, and, finally, to show the whole extermination process, complete with individual figures being gassed. He finished this larger model for the Auschwitz museum in 1948—it is still there—and years later was approached by the Holocaust museum to build another, which he finished in December 1992, on the museum site. Stobierski was somewhat unhappy that the model was placed in the Auschwitz barracks, which perhaps would be more evocative space if not cluttered with monitors depicting medical experiments, prisoners' bowls, a casting of a door from the gas chamber at Majdanek, stones from Mauthausen, and, easily overlooked and certainly

The activities of perpetrators are shown in various ways. Here, in Czechoslovakia, a Jew awaiting deportation is subject to humiliation through the cutting of his beard. *(Yad Vashem, Jerusalem, courtesy of the United States Holocaust Memorial Museum)*

OPPOSITE, ABOVE: Austrian soldiers stomp a man to death in Yugoslavia. *(Muzej Revolucije Narodnosti Jugoslavije, Belgrade, courtesy of the United States Holocaust Memorial Museum)*

OPPOSITE, BELOW: Germans pose with their kill—Jews executed near Gielniów, Poland, in 1943. *(Main Commission for the Investigation of Nazi War Crimes, Warsaw, courtesy of the United States Holocaust Memorial Museum)*

The Stobierski model portrayed horrific images—here, the death struggle in the gas chamber. *(Arnold Kramer, United States Holocaust Memorial Museum)*

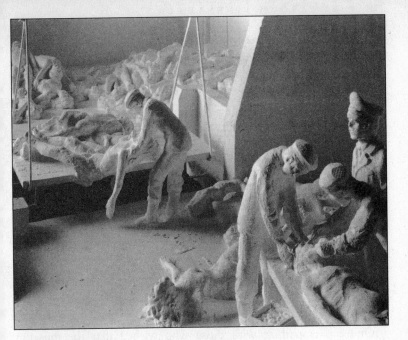

ABOVE: The unloading of bodies and removal of valuables—here, the gold from teeth *(Arnold Kramer, United States Holocaust Memorial Museum)*

LEFT: And, finally, cremation *(Arnold Kramer, United States Holocaust Memorial Museum)*

diminished in impact because of their location, cans of Zyklon-B.

The individual faces in Stobierski's model are among the hardest in the exhibit to look at, for he has sculpted, in exquisite detail, terror-stricken people in their desperate and futile attempt to reach up toward the last air in the gas chamber. En masse, the image is a seething wave, with crushed and broken bodies on the floor. When I stood in the gas chamber at Majdanek, and on the ruins of the crematoria of Auschwitz, and even to some extent at the mass graves at Chełmno and Bełżec, I felt myself an intruder. My feelings were similar as I studied Stobierski's faces, gazing at people not just at a moment of great intimacy—the moment of their death—but at a moment of death imposed, death that was not meant to be, the moment of their murder. I have often observed visitors in the museum's Auschwitz barracks; though many pass slowly by the Stobierski model, not many look carefully at these unforgettable sculptured faces.

One can empathize with those who wished that the museum would not be defiled by the presence of killers, that it would focus attention on the victims of the Holocaust. Yet, without their presence, the human face of evil in the Holocaust was missing. These faces bring alive the material landscape of the Holocaust imported by the museum. And the design team understood well the volatile issues involved: from deciding on who, in fact, were the most important groups of perpetrators to include, to picking appropriate locations for their photographs. The faces of the perpetrators offer visitors the opportunity to reflect on the moral choices made by ordinary people who were not victims.

THE BOUNDARIES OF REPRESENTATION:
AN ARTIFACT OUT OF PLACE

As a result of the agreement between the museum and the State Museum at Oświęcim (Auschwitz), suitcases, umbrellas, can openers, small mirrors, toothbrushes, clothes brushes, prisoners' jackets and trousers, shoes, parts of bunkbeds, bowls, tables, twenty

Zyklon-B cans, four artificial limbs, and nine kilograms of human hair were brought to the museum in Washington. There was no significant objection to the planned display of these objects, with one exception—human hair. The arguments and decision regarding the use of hair in the permanent exhibition dramatically underscore the different voices at work in the creation of the exhibition.

The museum's research brief on human hair notes that, as part of Aktion Reinhardt, the property of those murdered was transported from Poland to various Reich agencies in Germany. The appropriation of goods moved inexorably from the confiscation of land, homes, and personal property, to the confiscation of remaining goods when people arrived at the camps, to the collection of hair, clothes, and, after murder, gold crowns from teeth. "On August 16, 1942, SS Brigadeführer Glücks, chief of the Inspectorate of the Concentration Camps, sent an order regarding 'utilization of cut hair' to the commandants of 13 concentration camps. . . . All human hair cut . . . [is to be] appropriately utilized." Hair was to be used, Glücks went on, "for the manufacture of industrial felt and to be spun into yarn. Out of combed and cut hair of women, hair-yarn socks for U-boat crews are to be made, as well as hair-felt stockings for employees of the Reich railways." Hair was sold for 50 pfennigs per kilo to a number of factories. The SS set fire to various barracks filled with goods a few days before the Soviet Army liberated Auschwitz, yet Russian troops still found approximately seven thousand kilos of human hair.

Smith and Appelbaum were moved by the power of the display of hair in the Auschwitz Museum, and decided it was important to have a similar display in their permanent exhibition. "Now, to the Germans it was simply an industrial product," Smith said. "It was human hair which would be useful in furniture manufacture. There were masses and masses of it. To me it was the one really personal thing. This isn't wood. This isn't metal. This is part and parcel of people. It's hair, and what is hair for most of us? It's our mothers, it's our lovers . . . a spot we nestle into." An exhibit of hair would personalize the story, and dramatically demonstrate that the extermination process, in Appelbaum's words, "didn't conclude with just the death of the victims, but . . . had to include their processing and the auctioning off of the products of their bodies. . . . If we didn't tell that, we're not really telling the whole story."

For several years, members of the museum staff and some survivors on the content committee offered strenuous and vocal objections to the planned display of hair. On February 23, 1989, museum consultant Alice Greenwald, and Susan Morgenstein, former curator and subsequently director of temporary exhibits, wrote, "While we recognize and share with you the concern for a means to convey both dramatically and soberly the enormity of the human tragedy in the death camps, we cannot endorse the use of a wall of human hair, or ashes and bones. These fragments of human life have an innate sanctity, if you will; they are relics of once vital individuals, which do not belong in a museum setting but rather in a memorial setting. You run the very real risk of creating a cabinet of horrible curiosities by choosing to use them . . . and encourag[ing] . . . a more ghoulish than emotionally sympathetic response or painful memorial response."

Greenwald and Morgenstein argued against the use of hair: because it is by its very nature sacred (its "innate sanctity"), the idea of public display of something so intimate, particularly when connected to so great a horror, would register as an act of defilement. The hair would be contaminated—at least in a museum setting— and the museum, by displaying the hair, would be contaminated through the callous disregard of the hair's inherent sacredness. It was evident that the location of a Holocaust museum was crucial in the determination of whether hair from Holocaust victims registered as appropriate artifact or pollutant. "If this museum were situated at Auschwitz or Treblinka or Mauthausen; if it were the very site of the atrocities and the place of death of the victims, then the evidence of their degradation, manifest in the remaining hair, bones and ashes, would have validity. Here, in Washington, DC, that validity does not carry over. Human remains are not a commodity to be shipped, transported, catalogued, and crafted for dramatic display; we have an obligation—morally—to respect these materials, whose most meaningful placement would be one of ritual burial ... which the individuals themselves had been denied. ... The horror, abuse and true inhumanity of the Nazi perpetrators must be conveyed, but not at the continuing expense of the victims or in an emotionally exploitative format for the museum visitor."

The objection was not that hair would be on public display, but that it would be on public display away from its "home" in the camps. It was human "matter" out of place, registering differently from railcars or shoes. Others made the same argument. Well before plans for a display of hair arose, council historian Sybil Milton said, "It must be assumed that objects such as hair, bones, and ashes will not be considered as potential accessions. ... They do not belong in an American setting, where no concentration camps stood and which was not the primary arena for the events now known as the Holocaust." Yaffa Eliach believed that neither the hair nor the shoes "should have crossed the Atlantic." The museum should display, she said, "what survivors and liberators brought back, for this material is a statement about what happened, but we should not contaminate the country with the murderers' loot."

Alvin Rosenfeld added to the litany of objection. "At any standard, the display of human hair and/or ashes and bone is offensive to the memory of the dead." Such displays would, he believed, "offend, repel and sicken many visitors physically, emotionally and spiritually. Many visitors, myself among them—and I am totally non-religious—will consider such displays sacrilegious, a desecration." The fact that Michael Berenbaum had been assured that there would be no rabbinical objection—"There are no human cells in hair and there is no religious objection," he would later report to the content committee—did not assuage Rosenfeld's fears. "There are other groups of Rabbis who will inevitably disagree—and protest and picket and write letters to newspapers."

In addition to objecting on the basis of taste—expressed in the religious language of desecration—Rosenfeld argued that "what is acceptable in the abnormal atmosphere of a death camp—the site of the murders—is not acceptable in the antiseptic atmosphere of the

Nation's Capital. It must not be forgotten that we are a National Museum on the National Mall and we must behave accordingly." So, in addition to objections that victims' hair was out of place in a Washington museum and accusations of contamination came, again, the warning that the museum must behave itself. As in the design team's discussions on the presentation of horror, there was concern about transgressing boundaries in a way that would violate visitor sensibilities and the unspoken but deeply felt code of institutional civility operative in the nation's capital.

None of these arguments, however, proved persuasive in content-committee discussions about the hair, for even some survivors thought its display an important part of the exhibition. On February 13, 1990, the committee discussed whether a privacy wall for the hair might seal off the exhibit from the "casual visitor." Raul Hilberg argued that it was important to display the hair, to illustrate the "ultimate rationality of the destruction process." Berenbaum agreed, saying that, though he understood what a sensitive issue this was for some survivors, and though it was a story that the museum told with "fear and trembling," the display was crucial to the telling of the "dehumanization of the victim who was drained of all mineral life and treated as a by-product of the process of manufacturing and then recycled into the Nazi war economy." Dr. Helen Fagin, a survivor, objected and argued, "We can teach without showing the hair." On the other hand, survivor Sam Bloch declared that he had no objection to its use, and Joan Ringelheim argued that the display of hair would be one of the only places in the exhibit that would focus on what was done to women. After lengthy discussion, the committee voted nine to four in favor of displaying the hair.

Despite the vote, some survivors, particularly Fagin and Dr. Hadassah Rosensaft, pressed for reconsideration. During the content committee's meeting on October 9, 1991, when there was still a question whether a "layer of hair" would accompany a photograph of shorn women in the camps and a photograph of bundles of hair ready for shipment, Helen Fagin made an emotionally convincing argument, declaring that any display of hair would show "insensitivity and a violation of feminine identity," and that, for all she knew, the hair displayed could be from members of her family. Fagin had shifted the attack from debatable arguments regarding taste and appropriate location to the unassailable statement that a display of hair would damage survivors' feelings. Consequently, out of respect for such feelings, announced content-committee chairman Ben Meed, the museum would keep the hair but not display it.

In a design meeting on December 9, 1991, Shaike Weinberg held out a slim hope that perhaps a "single strand of hair" might be used. Concerned that without the hair the third-floor tower rooms would not build to the "crescendo" desired, Weinberg assigned Kramer to go to Auschwitz and photograph the display of hair, in the hope that some of the impact could be communicated. (Weinberg later added that he wanted the exhibit to communicate the effect of a "sea of hair.") Within a few weeks, at a design meeting on January 8, 1992, all hope for any display of actual hair disappeared, yet the design team decided that the segment should be done in such a way that "eventually hair [could] be in the exhibit."

No longer working at the museum when the decision was made, Martin Smith was nevertheless disappointed about it. "I absolutely believe that [the hair] should be in the museum and on display. . . . But it was felt to be too distressing and too wrong. And I think it just says that in the end there are people so concerned about not upsetting people that they actually are willing to hold back on telling the truth of the Holocaust, because I think what the hair does is to actually bring you to a different layer of truth. But it's not going to be there, and this is part and parcel of the whole problem of a museum about this subject, being in Washington, D.C., and being on the Mall. In the end, you mustn't upset too much. And I don't think one can ever upset people too much about this."

Discussions regarding the hair issue were emotional and occasionally bitter. Shaike Weinberg decided that it was more important to have the continuing support of the survivors than to go on fighting about the issue. The decision not to display human hair illustrates the clash between the different voices which shaped the museum, the commemorative and the educational. In this particular case, the commemorative voice, the privileged voice of the survivor, won out. For, as Raul Hilberg once remarked, one of the problematic "rules" of Holocaust speech is that any survivor, no matter how inarticulate, is superior to the greatest Holocaust historian who did not share in the experience.

In the exhibit, in front of Kramer's color photograph of women's hair is an open area, representing the boundaries of commemorative space owed to the survivors. Someday, perhaps, the hair will fill this space. Until then, it remains in storage outside of Washington, in limbo, neither in place at Auschwitz nor in Washington, D.C.

THE BOUNDARIES OF INTERPRETATION: CONTESTED ISSUES AND THE VOICE OF THE EXHIBITION

Martin Smith once cautioned Raye Farr to be "wary against all attempts to turn the exhibit into an encyclopedia"; indeed, a permanent exhibition is *not* an encyclopedia, cannot be all things to all people. Members of the design team have had, and knowledgeable visitors will each have, their own criticisms regarding what could have been taken out, what could have been put in, and what could have received more or less emphasis. Weinberg desired a straightforward narrative at the expense of ambiguity, and this, by definition, precluded sustained focus on controversial issues: the role of the Jewish councils, the kapos in the camps, and even the perhaps too-neat lexicon of perpetrators, victims, bystanders.

There are, on occasion, surprising omissions, most significantly the lack of any attention to the thousands of perpetrators who made their way to the United States after the war, often actively aided by American intelligence officials who saw some of these murderers as valuable resources in the Cold War. Since one of the major aims of the exhibition is to tell the story of American involvement with and response to the Holocaust, this is a surprising omission. The story of the murderers who came to the United States illustrates the treachery of memory, as enemies become friends because of a common enemy, and the murderers' past is best forgotten lest the burden of memory interfere with strategic realities. All this, of course, at the same time that tens of thousands of survivors were also making America their home.

What better opportunity to help visitors appreciate the ease with which nations conveniently, strategically forget, and what better way to help visitors appreciate the bitterly ironic symbol of America as refuge. "We didn't forget about this," Berenbaum recalled, "but there was no visually compelling way to tell the story in the exhibition." Telling the story of American policymakers' strategic forgetfulness in the permanent exhibition would, of course, creatively subvert one of the bedrock assumptions of the institution: that memory itself is instructive and redemptive.

There are also several instances in which the exhibition's voice emphasizes or de-emphasizes significant issues. And here one exhibit stands as a "case study" of the way in which an exhibition can appear omniscient and present as "fact" what is in reality a matter of heated, often bitter controversy.

As visitors make their way through the wrenching exhibits on the death camps on the third floor, and before they walk on Freed's bridge to the tower rooms with shoes, the display on hair, and large artifacts from the camps, they come to a photomural of a U.S. Air Force intelligence photograph of Auschwitz-Birkenau, taken on May 31, 1944. The text informs visitors, "Two freight trains with Hungarian Jews arrived in Birkenau that day; the large-scale gassing of these Jews was beginning. The four Birkenau crematoria are visible at the top of the photograph." Next to the photomural is an artifactual indictment of American indifference, the August 14, 1944, letter from Assistant Secretary of War John J. McCloy in which he "rejected a request by the World Jewish Congress to bomb the Auschwitz concentration camp." Explaining to visitors that the U.S. Air Force "could have bombed Auschwitz as early as May 1944," since bombers had "struck Buna, a synthetic-rubber works relying on slave labor, located less than five miles east of Auschwitz-Birkenau," the text notes that the death camp "remained untouched." And, it concluded, "although bombing Auschwitz would have killed many prisoners, it would also have halted the operation of the gas chambers and, ultimately, saved the lives of many more." Here use of the more definite "would" instead of "might" keeps visitors from appreciating an ongoing controversy, and makes an interpretive stance a statement of fact.

This exhibit is one of the pieces of evidence in the permanent exhibition that the indifference of the Western Allies contributed to the staggering numbers murdered in the Holocaust. One of the early "civic-responsibility" arguments made to justify the existence of the museum was that Americans had, after all, been complicit bystanders. *That* lesson was perhaps the most important to learn, so that coming generations would not again be willing to stand by in the face of overwhelming evil. In addition, for survivors and government officials, the museum represented a penitential response, an official, albeit belated, recognition of the nation's role as complicit bystander, a way of including the shame of the nation within the boundaries of memory, coexisting with more comforting memories of Americans as liberators.

Even before reaching this exhibit, visitors are able to watch five-minute video presentations on the fourth floor concerning American responses to various events in prewar Europe. In "Persecution Begins," amid the growing violence and increasing exclusion of Jews from German society, visitors are informed that, even though Americans were relatively well informed about these activities, "information did not provoke action or change policy." In "Bookburnings," they learn that, despite *Time*'s characterization of the act as a "bibliocaust" and *Newsweek*'s actual use of the term "Holocaust," the "flames did not yet reveal the true menace of what was breaking loose in Germany." In "1936 Olympics," visitors are told that the games were a "huge propaganda success" for the Nazis, partly because American tourists came home with "misleading reports" that all was well with the Jews of Germany. A video presentation on Kristallnacht declares that there may have been strong concern about the violence but "disapproval and the will to act were not linked in the American mind." And in "Search for Refuge," visitors learn that most Americans considered the plight of Europe's Jews either a "Jewish problem or European problem, to which the United States had no obligation to respond."

The refusal to bomb Auschwitz is not the only example of American inaction or indifference to the fate of millions in the exhibition. It also documents restrictive immigration policies, the story of the SS *St. Louis*—turned away from American shores in 1939, with the result that many on board were eventually murdered in the camps. Yet it is in the dramatic story of the refusal to bomb Auschwitz, and the declaration that such bombing *would* have halted the work of the gas chambers and *would* have saved many lives, that the anonymous and authoritative voice of the exhibit appears. Here narrative clarity in support of a major interpretive theme—the significance of being a complicit bystander—obscures a complex issue; a narrative more open to ambiguity and complexity might let visitors in on the contested nature of the interpretation of this "nonevent," lending, it could be argued, a richness and texture to visitors' understanding, even at the risk of a more muddled narrative.

The exhibition accepts the arguments of historian David Wyman—who was a member of the content committee—regarding the reasons for the failure to bomb Auschwitz, and the probable outcome of such bombing. "To the American military," Wyman declared, "Europe's Jews represented an extraneous problem and an unwarranted burden," and, he concluded, the "Air Force *could have* eliminated the Auschwitz killing installations" (emphasis added). Wyman's article "Why Auschwitz Was Never Bombed" appeared in the May 1978 issue of *Commentary*, and was eventually published as a revised chapter in his acclaimed book *The Abandonment of the Jews: America and the Holocaust, 1941–1945*. The "Wyman thesis" was often echoed in commemorative rhetoric at events sponsored by the council, particularly in Days of Remembrance ceremonies, and the Department of Defense's guide for such observances even excerpted several lengthy statements from Wyman's book on the issue.

This interpretation fits so lucidly into the museum's narrative of American indifference, and so well into the moral drama of the role of the bystander, that its status as interpretive argument is lost in the seemingly seamless web of factual narrative. And yet Wyman's thesis, powerfully illustrated in the exhibit, is only one interpretive possibility among others. It ignores, some would argue, the context in which the Holocaust was being carried out—a world at war—as well as taking too lightly the operational difficulties, and the slight chances for success of an attack.

In his review of *The Abandonment of the Jews*, for example, historian Michael Marrus argued that Wyman underestimated "the commitment and the ability of the Nazis to destroy Jews no matter what the Allies did. . . . Much as it may be disparaged now, the argument that real rescue could only come with an Allied victory was compelling and persuasive"—an argument shared by historian John Morton Blum in *V Was for Victory: Politics and American Culture During World War II*. Blum presented a more sympathetic picture of Roosevelt than many Holocaust historians: a president "harassed, preoccupied with overwhelming matters of state, caught in the web of a mammoth war in which no head of government could wholly escape confusion and uncertainty."

Thus, some historians argue, missing from Wyman's analysis and the museum's exhibit is sensitivity to the wider context of the war. What war atrocities, after all, most consumed Americans? Certainly not the image of Jews going to their deaths in the gas chamber, but that of Americans tortured and killed on the Bataan Death March, or accounts of American prisoners of war being beheaded by Japanese soldiers. Even though news of the mass murder of people at the hands of the Nazis reached readers of major newspapers, such reports did not carry the same evocative power as did accounts of the torture and murder of American soldiers at the hands of the Japanese. Japan, not Germany, had attacked the United States, and it was the Japanese, not the Germans, who were classified as subhuman. The power of these violent classifications had been nurtured by "Yellow Peril" literature of the early twentieth century, including fictionalized—albeit prophetic—accounts of the destruction of Japanese cities by American air power. Paul Fussell, one of the most astute analysts of the impact of war on English and American culture in the twentieth century, and a combat veteran of the European theater, declared: "It was difficult, if not impossible, for most Americans to see what the menace and perfidy and cruelty of the Japanese had to do with the ill-treatment of the Jews in Poland. . . . For most Americans, the war was about revenge against the Japanese, and the reasons the European part had to be finished first was so that maximum attention could be devoted to the real business, the absolute torment and destruction of the Japanese. The slogan was conspicuously 'Remember Pearl Harbor.' No one ever shouted or sang 'Remember Poland.' "

A bitterly debated critique of Wyman's arguments was made by historian James H. Kitchens III, archivist of the United States Air Force Historical Research Center at Maxwell Air Force Base, during a 1993 conference, "The Bombing of Auschwitz: Should the Allies Have Attempted It?," at the Smithsonian Institution's National Air and Space Museum. Kitchens argued: "An objective look at targeting possibilities, available intelligence, operational constraints, and the realistic allocation of military resources . . . shows that the effective use of air power against Auschwitz is a chimera having little to do with War Department policies, indifference, military ineptitude, or negative ethnic attitudes."

Kitchens did not consider the photomural of Auschwitz-Birkenau the "smoking gun" that "proved" American intelligence knew but did not care. Working with thousands of photographs, he said, photo-intelligence staff were told specifically what to look for—likely items were smoke (indicating a power plant), rail lines, large numbers of aircraft, and suspicious shapes, which may have indicated new types of aircraft—in likely targets for the strategic bombing offensive. They were not *looking* for evidence of a facility built for mass death. The photomural, so important in the museum's exhibit, was, he claimed, "wholly incidental to the interpreters' work. None of them was tasked to look for concentration camps; their prints and viewing equipment were primitive; none of them had the experience of interpretation guides to make the images talk intelligibly; few, if any, of them had access to other types of intelligence or to Fifteenth AF's [Air Force's] overall air campaign." Escapee reports were not available to them, and, even had they been, Kitchens believed, they were of little use to military planners, since they described more the events at the death camp than the physical layout so crucial for military targeting.

Arguing as well that the camp presented "insurmountable obstacles for precision bombing," and that the prospect of effectively cutting the rail lines was no greater in this instance than in other futile efforts in the European theater, Kitchens concluded, "Any Allied option to frustrate the Holocaust from the air was illusory, a fact so unmistakably obvious to contemporary commanders that it was taken for granted and warranted little policy discussion. Inaction may have been colored by ethnic attitudes, but it was ultimately dictated by the immutable exigencies of intelligence, operational considerations, weapons system performance, and available resources."

Kitchens was attacked in the pages of the *Washington Jewish Week*. Hershel Shanks, editor of *Moment* magazine, noted that he had refused to publish an article submitted by Kitchens because it was "so flawed that it would be irresponsible to print it." And Kai Bird, author of *The Chairman, John J. McCloy: The Making of the American Establishment*, argued, "Even an ineffective raid—or series of raids—would have saved more lives than were lost by inaction." (He estimated that a hundred thousand lives could have been saved.)

Though there were, as Wyman demonstrated, voices raised in the American Jewish community that supported bombing, there were also voices, both in the United States and in Israel, opposed to the bombing, because it would have killed many prisoners. There were also voices of opposition outside the Jewish community, such as former Supreme Court Justice Lewis F. Powell, who during the war was a staff intelligence officer with the Army Air Force, and later an ULTRA officer. When questioned about this controversy in 1985, Powell said, "I am perfectly confident that General [Carl] Spaatz would have resisted any proposal that *we* [emphasis Powell's] kill the Jewish inmates in order temporarily to put an Auschwitz out of operation. It is not easy to think that a rational person would have made such a recommendation." Nor, historian Christopher Browning argued, was it likely that a miraculously successful raid would have stopped the killing, although mass extermination—through shooting and the burning of bodies—would have required more effort.

Browning is also critical of the Wyman thesis. "McCloy and others did not see it as we do now. There *was* no decision made; rather, the matter, since it would not contribute directly to the war effort, was not even seriously considered." However, he is not at all uncomfortable with the museum's theme of "complicit bystander." It might, he said, "make us realize that someday someone else will come along and inquire of us, 'What did you do about analogous events in your time?' " There *was* fatal indifference, Browning said, but the failure to bomb Auschwitz is not the appropriate symbol of this. The failure, he said, was more profound—a "systemic" failure—of "imagination, of a sense of urgency, of historical perspective, of empathy."

The failure to bomb Auschwitz has become a crucial symbol of American indifference, certainly more emotion-laden than the restrictive immigration policies of the 1930s and 1940s. It is also easier, noted former museum historian David Luebke, to "cope with helplessness after the fact, if you can convince yourself that mendacity, not circumstance, had produced it."

None of these critical voices will likely make much impact on survivors who, in retrospect at least, believe that even the death of many prisoners would have been worth a raid on Auschwitz. Wiesel, who mentioned this issue often in commemorative statements, spoke of it at length during the transfer of the land for the museum building from the government to the council at the Capitol, April 13, 1983. In addition to words of thanks, he said: "There will be questions, too, that we will have to include in our memory and program. . . . I have to teach my children and students and tell them that we should have faith. . . . What can I answer them when they ask me 'Why wasn't one military plan altered to liberate the camps one day earlier? Why didn't the Allied forces bomb the railways going to Auschwitz?' Mr. Vice President, Mr. Speaker, friends and members of Congress, ask us and we will tell you: in those days, ten thousand people died daily. If they had bombed the railways, at least ten thousand people would have lived one day longer." Nor will the work of historians likely convince Hyman Bookbinder, who, upon receiving an honorary doctorate of humane letters from Hebrew Union College, asked in his remarks whether "things" might have been different had the Jewish community demanded of Roosevelt that "he make available one single war plane to bomb the railroad tracks to Auschwitz. . . . Is it wrong for me to wonder whether some or all of the 80 members of my parents' families in Poland . . . might thus have survived?"

Given this sentiment—an article of faith for many—and the fact that the Wyman thesis allowed the museum's narrative to proceed smoothly, any attempt to introduce ambiguity and a level of historical complexity into this particular exhibit would certainly have faced strong reaction from those for whom Wyman's interpretation of the "nonevent" has become the crucial evidence in the story of American indifference. Commemorative decorum consists, in part at least, of respecting voices of "tradition," and in the museum, Wyman's voice had been elevated from interpretive stance to historical truth. Though the design team was aware of various historians' positions regarding this issue, any alteration would undoubtedly have registered as a heretical alteration of the Holocaust narrative.

The exhibit's interpretive voice spoke loudly with regard to the bombing of Auschwitz, but it spoke softly about the complex and emotional issue of the actions (or nonactions) of Protestants and Catholics in European nations during the Nazi years. Those commission or council members familiar with the story—Robert McAfee Brown, Harry Cargas, Theodore Hesburgh, Franklin Littell, and John Pawlikowski—agreed wholeheartedly with a nuanced understanding of Christian complicity, and believed that the story needed to be told in the museum. Such presuppositions were not necessarily shared by most members of Christian institutions. Several of them, particularly Franklin Littell, believed that one way of helping Christians confront the story was to involve representatives of Christian churches and organizations in the work of supporting the museum.

Littell recalled that, when he first began arguing for a church-relations committee in 1985, he encountered "barely concealed hostility to [any] Christian participation whatsoever." Littell spoke sadly about the inevitable "turf" battles over Holocaust memory that he had encountered. "I worked for twenty years to overcome Christian indifference," he said; "now, in the last fifteen, I have had to struggle with sectarian Judaism." From his theological perspective, the council failed to remember that "the first wickedness of the Nazis was their idolatry." Littell was insistent that the council recruit the organized churches into the work of building the museum. "I speak as a Methodist clergyman," he told the council. "My people want off the hook, and they want to be told that this is a Jewish enterprise." Littell did not want to let them "off the hook." His insistence occasionally grated on some council members, and he recalled working out plans with Miles Lerman to inform churches, editors of church journals, ecumenical leaders, and professors at schools of theology of the work of the council, and a stillborn plan to ask Sunday-school children to contribute pennies toward the construction of the building. In 1989, Littell became the first chairman of the church-relations committee.

Longtime council member John Pawlikowski, who followed Littell as chairman of the committee, joined in consistently arguing that the story of Christian complicity and Christian resistance and rescue must be told in the museum, albeit delicately. Considering suggestions for museum themes in 1981, for example, Pawlikowski thought it crucial that discussion of Christian anti-Semitism take place in a way that would not anger "Christians coming in, who have not had any preparation . . . because you wind up . . . losing your audience."

The issue was not resolved five years later, when Pawlikowski again reminded council members that "you don't want to immediately . . . turn people against the museum and have groups declare it as anti-American or anti-Christian, but I think we'll have to deal with that."

Visitors confront the role of religion in several places in the exhibit. A twelve-minute film, *Antisemitism*, informs visitors that "some gospel accounts" blame the Jews for the crucifixion of Jesus, and that it was not until the Second Vatican Council that church leaders "officially repudiated the ancient charge that the Jews had murdered Christ." The film traces religious persecution of Jews through the Middle Ages and the Reformation, and shows how anti-Semitism gradually became a "thriving secular, political, and social antisemitism."

In the exhibit segment "Murder of the Handicapped," visitors learn that the "secrecy surrounding this program of medical killing broke down in 1941, when a handful of church leaders, local magistrates, and ordinary German citizens protested." There are several references to religion in "Nazi Society." A photograph of Reich Bishop Ludwig Müller in clerical garb, hand raised in the Nazi salute, dramatizes text that informs visitors that his task was to "unite all Protestant churches into a single, Nazi-controlled organization." "Even the Christian churches," exhibit text declares, "fell under Nazi influence, and many Protestant and Roman Catholic officials openly supported the regime. Only the dissident Protestant Confessing Church declared that unquestioning obedience to the state was not compatible with Christian faith."

There are several references to survivors' struggle with their faith—in a well-known quote from Elie Wiesel's *Night* appearing in raised letters in a third-floor tower room, and in comments on the absence and presence of God in the concluding film, *Testimony*. The exhibit also informs visitors about Christian rescue in stories about the villagers of Le Chambon, and the Catholic Poles who founded the underground resistance group Zegota.

Neither Martin Smith nor Pawlikowski was satisfied that the story of Christian complicity had been told forcefully enough. Smith recalled being told that "the museum had to be careful not to make people feel too guilty," and that the question of Christian complicity and the questions of faith and doubt raised by the Holocaust were "not on the floor" for more than cursory discussion. Smith still feels strongly about this. The failure to confront the issue head-on was, for him, a "moral failing." He also objected to prominent display of Christian rescue, for it was "much more likely," he said, "that you would be saved by a communist or a socialist than a Christian."

Perhaps the exhibit's caution on specific examples of Christian complicity also has to do with the pressure of institutional civility on the Mall. The popular understanding of the role of religion in American life is that it is a force for good, that it humanizes, empowers people to heal grievous personal and societal wounds. Though the *Antisemitism* film clearly locates hatred of Jews in Christian scripture, that story is historically removed from the present. There is no sustained attention to New Testament scholars in German universities, or certain Catholic bishops, or the German Christian movement, which actively engaged in the religious legitimation of National Socialism. What might be the reaction if the exhibit stated even more plainly than it does not only that organized religion often supported National Socialism, but that this is one of the normal functions of religion? In other words, just as religion can humanize and widen the circle of those registering as human in the universe of moral obligation, it can dehumanize, which leads to the constriction of that universe of moral obligation. Insisting on this removes another illusion about the Holocaust—that horrible things are done only "in the name of" religion, for the "really" religious do not do such things, and perpetrators only hide behind the cloak of religion. In an alternative reading, religious functions in both humane and murderous ways in human societies.

The exhibit implicitly raises this issue for the thoughtful visitor, but does not, and perhaps could not, confront it more directly, given the limitations of exhibit space. More important, any more direct critique of the function of religion would have called into question the widespread cultural acceptance of the beneficial role of religion, and, no doubt, caused inevitable resentment about Jews in "their" museum blaming Christians for the Holocaust.

THE BOUNDARIES OF INCLUSION:
ARMENIANS AND GYPSIES

In *After Tragedy and Triumph*, Michael Berenbaum articulated his sense of the historically correct interpretation of the relationship between Jews and other Holocaust victims. "There is no conflict," he wrote, "between describing the uniqueness of the Jewish experience and the *inclusion* of other victims of Nazism. In fact, the examination of all victims is not only politically desirable but pedagogically mandatory if we are to demonstrate the claim of uniqueness."

Berenbaum's claim for uniqueness is based on the understanding that the Nazis' goal of state-sponsored, bureaucratically planned genocide was "unprecedented." Also, he argued, the process—"from definition to expropriation to concentration to deportation to extermination"—broke "new ground, shattering previous boundaries— moral, political, psychological, and religious." Thirdly, the death of six million Jews—over a million of them children—left "an entire world destroyed, a culture uprooted, and mankind left with new thresholds of inhumanity." Berenbaum's argument is mainly directed against those who deny the validity of comparison, who view the Holocaust as "wholly other." Berenbaum believed, however, as did Wiesel, that, unlike any other group of victims, Jews were murdered not because of what they did, but because of who they were. As we have seen, this argument for uniqueness, embedded in the commission's *Report*, provided the framework for the presentation of victim groups in the exhibition, but has never been accepted by all involved. Consequently, the representation of various groups of Holocaust victims in the exhibition satisfies the pluralistic imperative of a national museum to the Holocaust in the nation's capital, and serves as a way to portray Jewish uniqueness *through* comparison with various others.

Armenians and Gypsies struggled throughout the 1980s for what they considered just representation in the exhibit. The Armenian community was willing to accept almost any representation deemed acceptable to the council, for this, in their view, would serve as an important response to Turkish claims that the extermination of the Armenians beginning in 1915 was not genocidal in intent or effect. They asked the council to stretch the boundaries of the Holocaust, arguing that a group dedicated to the preservation of truth in the face of historical denial and the cultivation of redeeming memory *had* to lend a sympathetic ear to their claim.

Argument that recognition and representation of the Armenian genocide was part of the commission's responsibility surfaced in their first meeting in February 1979, when Raul Hilberg declared that "it would not be a fulfillment of the overall task" to ignore Armenians or other victims; in a subsequent meeting, Kitty Dukakis, reporting on the work of the subcommittee on education and curricula, noted: "We discussed the Armenian experience and the sense . . . was to support a curriculum that included the other dramatic examples of genocide in the 20th century, including the Armenians." Leo Sarkasian of the Armenian National Committee pleaded that, if the commission could not recognize that "somewhere, somehow, the Armenian genocide, at least as a backdrop, has a role in [your] work . . . then we are indeed in trouble. . . . Who will listen if not you?"

The potential inclusion of the Armenians troubled Yaffa Eliach. She was willing to include the millions of non-Jewish victims of the Nazis, but not events that took place in 1915. She worried about the slippery slope of inclusion of non-Holocaust-related genocides. "Once you include the Armenians as part of the Holocaust, I don't see why other African tribes which are being annihilated at this very moment should not be included."

Inclusion of memory of the Armenian genocide in the first Days of Remembrance ceremony, held in the Capitol Rotunda on April 24, 1979, involved the commission in a struggle with the Turkish government, which has adamantly refused to acknowledge that any genocide took place. April 24 was, coincidentally, the annual occasion for commemorative ceremonies in the Armenian community, including one scheduled just outside the Capitol. "The Commission," Berenbaum recalled, "faced the choice of including the Armenians within the Holocaust ceremony and thus running the risk of 'universalising' the Holocaust, or of having the Armenians stand outside, opposite the ceremony, while Jewish dead were recalled."

The Turkish government began its persistent campaign to keep any reference to Armenians from entering the boundaries of Holocaust memory—either in commemorative events or in the museum's permanent exhibition—by warning the Carter administration that there would be repercussions should the president mention the Armenians in his remarks. Though the president spoke openly about the Armenian genocide in a White House reception for Armenian Americans on May 16, 1978—"There was a concerted effort made to eliminate all the Armenian people, probably one of the greatest tragedies that ever befell any group," he said—at the 1979 Days of Remembrance ceremony, he did *not* mention the Armenians by name, but referred to them only indirectly: "We recall today the persecution, the suffering and the destruction which has befallen so many other people in this century, in many nations, peoples whose representatives have joined us for this observance."

Rabbi Irving Greenberg, the commission's director, supported a proposal that an Armenian minister, Reverend Vartan Hartunian, deliver a prayer for the dead at the end of the ceremony, and that an Armenian American, Alex Manoogian, light a seventh candle to memorialize victims of genocide around the world. "To the commission staff," Greenberg wrote, "the seventh candle was an appropriately distinguished analogy, particularly since the end result was a seven-branched fully lit menorah. . . . However, the inclusion and associations were sharply criticized by a number of figures important in Holocaust commemoration in the State of Israel."

When the council was formed in 1980, the Armenians were represented by Set Momjian, a first-generation Armenian American whose parents had been orphaned in the genocide. Momjian served as an adviser to President Carter, a representative to the United Nations, and a White House representative to the United Nations Human Rights Commission. In his introductory statement to other council members during their first meeting, on May 28, 1980, Momjian expressed his hope that "all peoples who have been the victims of genocide can look forward to a completed museum and an educational program that will tell the complete story of man's inhumanity to man." On behalf of the Armenian community in America, he announced a pledge of one million dollars.

Throughout the council's anguished attempts both to hold to the uniqueness of the Holocaust and to represent various victim groups, commitment to telling the story of the Armenian genocide waxed and waned. Momjian was troubled by this failure to attend consistently to the story when he spoke at a council meeting on August 4, 1983. "Three years ago, the Museum Committee came to this Council with the unanimous decision that the Armenians would be included in a significant way. . . . The following June this Council voted unanimously again that the Armenians would be included. . . . A month ago . . . the Museum Committee met and there was a consensus of opinion that not only the Armenians but others would be included. It is three years now since that Museum Committee came in with that decision, and I find now that there's a discussion whether there was [an] Armenian genocide or not."

The status of the story of the Armenian genocide was unsettled for many reasons. First, whereas other victim groups had to make the case that they belonged in the museum because their deaths had counted as Holocaust deaths, the Armenians faced double jeopardy. Some on the council were willing to consider that perhaps Turkish claims were at least partly accurate, and that the deaths were *not* the result of genocide. And even for those willing to accept that genocide did indeed take place, there was occasional resistance to including Armenian victims as part of this particular story. Hyman Bookbinder, for example, was willing at least to listen to arguments that what had happened should not register as genocide. In 1983, in response to a letter from Richard L. Chambers, a professor in the department of Near Eastern languages and civilizations at the University of Chicago—who thought any mention of the Armenians in the museum would be a "grave injustice to the Turkish people"— Bookbinder responded that he was looking for some kind of "solution." This attempt at compromise, which worked well in the world of Washington politics so familiar to Bookbinder, was ill-suited to the debate. Bookbinder, no doubt, would recognize immediately the ludicrous strategy of trying to find an appropriate "compromise" with Holocaust deniers. And, echoing Eliach's concerns expressed years earlier, Miles Lerman spoke for the concerns of many when he worried about extending Holocaust memory too far backward. "If you are introducing the Armenian tragedy to the Holocaust, why not the tragedy . . . of the Cambodians? Why not the tragedy of the American Indians?"

Turkish representatives also placed incessant pressure on certain members of the council and Congress to exclude the Armenians. Monroe Freedman, the council's first acting executive director, recalled, "As much as anyone wanted to be represented in the museum, that's how much the Turkish government wanted the Armenians out. There was pressure on us, and pressure on the White House staff working with us, to create the council." Hyman Bookbinder recalled receiving an invitation to a luncheon from the Turkish ambassador to the United States shortly after the council was formed, during which he was told that the well-being of Jews in Turkey might be threatened were Armenians included in a federal Holocaust museum. In 1983, Kitty Dukakis told other council members, "The Turks have been at it with my husband, with myself each time I've been in Washington to speak about the Armenians and will be with every person sitting around this table. Do not be duped by the kind of revisionist history that they will perpetrate on you." In 1986, a joint letter to Wiesel from Momjian and California's governor, George Deukmejian—also a council member—said that the denial of the Armenian genocide was "orchestrated and funded by a nation-state," and the Armenian community looked to the council to "affirm its prior commitments."

The council's "prior commitments" were evident in early exhibition plans. A museum theme, "Death does not have limited targets," adopted on April 30, 1981, included the Armenian genocide as "prelude to the Final Solution." In 1984, Kevork Bardakjian, who had completed a report on the genocide for the council, wrote the museum's interim director of education, David Altshuler, "As I understand it, the Armenian story would be told, exhibited and documented in one half of the interactive learning space. . . . The actual exhibit area allotted to the Armenians would selectively exhibit and document the Armenian Genocide."

Armenians also had reason to be hopeful when Michael Berenbaum returned to the museum, for he proved unwavering in his commitment. Berenbaum's understanding of the various ways that the museum could refer to the genocide was evident in a briefing for Armenian scholars that he and Sybil Milton presented on August 18, 1989. He informed them that Armenians would be included: in a film, *Nazi Rise to Power and Genocidal Precedents*; through display of Hitler's oft-quoted remark "Who today remembers the destruction of the Armenians?"; through reference to the fact that Henry Morgenthau, Jr., secretary of the Treasury in the Roosevelt administration, was moved to confront the president regarding American indifference to the Holocaust largely because of his memories that his father had been American ambassador to Turkey during the genocide; through reference to the inspiration that Jewish resistance fighters from Białystok drew from Austrian writer Franz Werfel's novel about Armenian resistance, *The Forty Days of Musa Dagh*; through photographs of the genocide from the collection of German Red Cross worker Armin Wegner; and also through the museum's commitment to collecting oral histories and archival material and to planning educational programs.

Berenbaum was joined in his quest for a substantial Armenian presence by Martin Smith, who told Shaike Weinberg in July 1990, "At a minimum, the Hitler quotation should be prominently displayed and addressed. Failure to do so would be craven pandering to the mandarins of the Israeli Foreign Ministry, for whom Turkish-

Israeli relations are more important than dealing with the subject of genocide." Facing stiff resistance from some members of the content committee—including survivors—Berenbaum was forced to scale back his plans, informing the museum's executive committee in August 1990 that at least reference to Armenians in the film and Hitler's quote should be in the exhibition. The committee stated, however, that "the only mention of the Armenian genocide would be the quote from Hitler, and that the Content Committee should decide if and how the 'Rise of Hitler' film . . . should include a reference to the Armenian genocide or in fact any reference to precedents. . . . Mr. Abramson asked that the minutes reflect that it is the 'sense' of the Committee that a comparison should not be made in the film or any other place in the Museum to any other mass murder, because the Holocaust is unique."

Berenbaum, who strongly dissented from the committee's decision, continued to press the losing battle for inclusion of the Armenians in the film, the title of which no longer included "genocidal precedents." At a content-committee meeting on February 13, 1991, a prominent survivor and council representative lost control and screamed at Berenbaum, "ordering" him not to mention Armenians in his presence again. In this case, a survivor used his privileged voice as a weapon, and only Franklin Littell and Raul Hilberg spoke in Berenbaum's behalf. At the cost of significant political support within the institution—several people mentioned that Berenbaum lost any chance to eventually become museum director because of this issue—he succeeded in salvaging the Hitler quote for inclusion in the permanent exhibition, for even that had been in jeopardy.

Israeli Holocaust scholar and museum adviser Yehuda Bauer kept his silence during the shouting. Later, however, Bauer, a staunch defender of the uniqueness argument, wrote Ben Meed, chairman of the committee, "For the last two years I have been on the receiving end of direct pressure by the Turkish representative in Jerusalem, by the Turkish embassy in London, by my own Foreign Office representatives, and by the Jewish community in Istanbul (on one occasion, by a member of the Jewish community in Washington as well). . . . The Jewish community in Istanbul, under pressure from their government, provide a very sad example of the kind of behavior we all know from Jewish communities who have to bend their backs and heads before Authority." Though reminding Meed that the museum's insistence on the centrality of the Jewish experience was a "condition of my joining it," Bauer cautioned him that the "denial of other people's genocides would expose us to a tremendous wave of criticism, and would be morally absolutely contemptible." In response, Meed wrote that he hoped for a "resolution," but reminded Bauer that his first responsibility was to Jewish victims.

The museum's memory had constricted since the early 1980s, when a museum/memorial committee unanimously approved the inclusion of the Armenian genocide in a "significant" manner. To this day, Berenbaum is troubled by the failure to include a more substantive Armenian presence in the permanent exhibition. The "only reason for the exclusion of precedents for mass murder," he wrote, "has been the politicization of the Armenian question in part by well paid and seemingly effective lobbyists." He worried about the potential consequences of such exclusionary policies, which he judged "a historical mistake which undermines the integrity of this . . . exhibition, and a pedagogical mistake which diminishes our ability to reach out and to include groups who naturally can see in the Holocaust a sensitive metaphor to their own experience. These groups include Native Americans and Blacks and their exclusion because of the Armenian question is idiocy. It is also short sighted for our visitors and our critics will ask again and again as they have in the past what about Native Americans? What about American slavery? What about the Armenians? The Cambodians? Furthermore, it undermines our professional standing among those who have studied the Holocaust and genocide and it evinces the politicization of our mission."

Both Set Momjian and Dr. Rouben Adalian, director of academic affairs of the Armenian Assembly of America, tried to put the inclusion of the Hitler quote in a positive light. Momjian took some solace that the quote was in the "largest type" of any engraved on an exhibit wall, and Adalian said, "We owe Michael Berenbaum a great deal, that the quote is so unambiguously presented." It was, Adalian thought, a significant inclusion, "an affirmation of the genocide, and its place in Hitler's memory."

As memory constricted in the exhibit, it expanded in other parts of the institution. Other museum staff, particularly those developing educational programs, consciously extended the boundaries of memory to include the Armenians. Educational workshops always included the Armenians in discussions of genocidal precedents; the library and research archive collected related materials; in March 1994, the museum sponsored a discussion of Donald E. Miller and Lorna Touryan Miller's *Survivors: An Oral History of the Armenian Genocide*; and there has been discussion of a temporary exhibit focusing on the Armenian genocide.

The unstated resistance to inclusion of the Armenian genocide rests in part on some survivors' ambivalence regarding any formal linkage between that genocidal event and the Holocaust. As the concept of genocide—used in the late 1940s to describe the murder of the Jews—became popular, other instances of genocide could be recognized, could in fact become "real" through recognition and location in a historical narrative. In this case, the narrative would place the Armenian genocide as a precursor and perhaps even a model for the Holocaust.

For those committed to a radical understanding of the uniqueness of the Holocaust—that *any* act of comparison dilutes the integrity of memory of the Holocaust—locating the Armenian genocide in a historical narrative that led to the Holocaust was threatening. It was, argued Professor Gregory Goekjian, "a dangerous and antecedent supplement that threatens to displace [the] Holocaust in priority. . . . To preserve its singularity, the Holocaust must deny full genocidal stature to the Armenian genocide through a process of differentiation in magnitude, cause, and effect." The 1981 museum plan characterizes the Armenian genocide as a "prelude" to the Holocaust. The language is revealing. It is not to be presented as a model of genocide in the twentieth century, or the first in a series of genocides, but a prelude—that is, an introductory performance setting the stage for the "real" genocide to come. However, just as the Armenian genocide could *threaten* the Holocaust's uniqueness, it could as well *support* it, through an interpretive strategy of situating it in the comparative hierarchy of genocide and Holocaust. This Berenbaum tried to accomplish. In making the case that the *Nazi Rise to Power* film include a segment on genocidal precedents, he argued that this would "place the Holocaust in the context of previous mass murders as a unique, hitherto unprecedented event." Berenbaum argued that, "unlike the Turkish clash with the Armenians during which Armenians living in Constantinople and other cities were safe—and only those living in the East were at risk, all Jews in Europe were targeted. The 1942 Wannsee Conference listed 11 million Jews as potential victims including those in Britain and Spain. Later lists included American Jewry. The goal was the elimination of all Jews—a fundamental realignment of the human species."

Just as memory of the Armenian genocide in an institution devoted to the redeeming and transformative power of memory was contested, so too was its memory in governmental bodies already congratulating themselves for being willing to support the Holocaust museum and therefore cultivating memory of genocide as important for reflection on public policy. Whether Armenian deaths registered as genocidal or unfortunate wartime casualties in American governmental memory depended on the political cost involved. Armenian Americans were enraged in 1982, when, in the context of discussing Armenian terrorism, the State Department, citing the "ambiguous" nature of events in 1915, would not endorse "allegations that the Turkish Government committed a genocide against the Armenian people."

In his April 22, 1981, proclamation recognizing the Days of Remembrance ceremony, President Reagan linked the Armenian *and* Cambodian genocides to the Holocaust; but, speaking to editors and broadcasters at a White House luncheon on October 1983, the president refused to recognize the genocide, stating that the government's stance was opposition to any form of terrorism and, whatever happened, the integrity of memory no longer counted, since, he said, "I can't help but believe that there's virtually no one alive today who was living in the era of that terrible trouble."

In 1985 and 1987, the United States House of Representatives defeated a resolution that would have recognized April 24 as a day to commemorate victims of genocide, particularly those of the Armenian genocide; the United States Senate failed to pass a similar resolution in 1990. This last resolution was introduced by Senator Robert Dole, who during World War II had been treated by an Armenian physician, himself a survivor of the genocide.

Discussions about the earlier resolutions reveal how fragile is the commitment to historical memory when confronted with what are perceived as security interests of the state. The geopolitical importance of Turkey as a NATO ally, and the fear of angering such an ally, was judged as more important than official recognition of the Armenian genocide. On March 29, 1985, for example, President Reagan told a Turkish journalist that he opposed the congressional resolution because it would "reward" terrorism, and "could harm relations with an important ally." Representative William L. Dickinson (R.-Alabama) argued, "What we are doing here today is counterproductive. It adds nothing. . . . So if it would do some good, if it would be helpful to us, if it would strengthen our NATO alliances, fine let us do it. If it is counterproductive, let us forget it and go on to something else." Even former Congressman and Holocaust Memorial council member Stephen Solarz voted against the resolution, arguing that the Holocaust was a "universally accepted historical reality" but what had happened to the Armenians remained unsettled, merely a "hotly disputed view of events."

According to this logic, of course, should Holocaust deniers make further inroads into the mainstream, and someday convince enough congressmen that there was a real question as to whether or not the Holocaust took place, it, like the Armenian genocide, would not deserve the prestige of an official memory.

In 1989, with passage of Dole's resolution a distinct possibility, various interests, all of whom would, no doubt, piously affirm the importance of memorializing the Holocaust, organized an unprecedented campaign against an Armenian day of remembrance. The head of the Jewish community in Turkey joined with Jewish lobbyists in the United States and Israeli diplomats in a successful effort to block the resolution. President Bush, who during his 1988 campaign had stated that the United States should recognize the Armenian genocide, brought back Morton Abramowitz, United States ambassador to Turkey, to lobby against the resolution. Israel worried that Turkey would reduce its embassy's status, and, reported the *Jerusalem Post*, hoped for the "pay-off" of an upgrade of Turkey's Tel Aviv legation to a "full fledged embassy." Israeli diplomats were also aware that Turkey had served as an escape route for Jews from Iran. The United States, of course, had NATO issues most in mind.

This organized resistance caused a firestorm of protest in the Israeli and American press, causing the Israeli Foreign Office to claim, somewhat lamely, that some Washington embassy staff had gone "too far" in making "inquiries" into the status of the resolution. The more profound question regarding the integrity of memory was not overlooked. Such an act of intentional forgetfulness led the *Washington Jewish Week* to declare itself "appalled and ashamed," and it asked, "If Jews join in an effort to whitewash what happened to the Armenians, how can they expect other groups, seeking their own diplomatic gains, to treat the Nazi Holocaust any differently?"

In addition to the organized lobbying effort against the resolution, Israeli officials continued to put intense pressure on council members who spent time in Israel to keep the Armenians out of the museum. Ingeniously, Turks used the uniqueness argument as a persuasive tactic. Defending Turkey against the charges of genocide in *Washington Jewish Week*, Daryal Batibay, minister-counselor of the Embassy of Turkey, called attention to the "unique horror" of the Holocaust, as opposed to Armenian "suffering" in wartime. Playing as well on fear of terrorism, Batibay cautioned that Turkish people would consider it a "shocking affront" if Americans, by way of the museum, "raised the terrorists' banner."

If state interest and the principle of expediency govern what nations choose to remember, any officially enshrined memory can be revised or forgotten. In the past decade, official memory was receptive to the Holocaust and not to the memory of Armenian genocide, thereby weakening one of the stated virtues of remembering the Holocaust. This lends an even more compelling tone to the Armenian challenge to the commission; if there was not room for the Armenians in the permanent exhibition, where would there be room?

Gypsies, on the other hand, were ignored by the council until the mid-1980s, when individual Gypsies argued that they too were murdered simply because of who they were. Consequently, not only did they belong *in* the story, but by rights, they argued, they should be among the storytellers, those who would shape the exhibition's Holocaust narrative. They asked the council to extend the boundaries of memory beyond representation in a story shaped by others and to recognize their "right" to appropriate location at the center, alongside Jews, for both, according to the Gypsy argument—one shared by many historians—were primary and unique victims of the Holocaust.

Like the Armenians, Gypsies—or, more accurately, Rom—perceived that representation in the permanent exhibition was an act of remembering what had been unjustly forgotten: for them, the genocide of Romani victims in the Holocaust, or, in their terminology, the Porrajmos, the "great devouring." The failure of the commission and the council to recognize Romani suffering in the Holocaust had not become an issue until 1984, when Rom from six states met at the Simon Wiesenthal Center in Los Angeles to announce the formation of the United States Romani Holocaust Committee, whose purpose was to gain representation on the council and to make sure that "Nazi genocide against the Rom is fully documented in the planned Holocaust Memorial Museum."

Grattan Puxon, co-author of *The Destiny of Europe's Gypsies*, asked Elie Wiesel to attend the meeting, arguing, "Even Armenians have been invited to participate [in the council], although they were not targets of racial persecution." Wiesel's mission, Puxon argued, was to "preside over a national project to preserve the memory of *all* victims of the Holocaust." Wiesel's "bias" toward Jewish victims "is understandable," said Puxon, "and it is unjust." James Marks II, a member of the International Romani Union—an umbrella organization accorded Non-Governmental Organization status by the United Nations in 1979—implored Wiesel, "Your people and my people died together in Auschwitz concentration camp. We, together are the victims of the Nazi genocide. Why then are Jewish and Gypsy representatives not sitting together on the U.S. Holocaust Memorial Council? Why has not one Gypsy been invited to any of the functions, conferences and remembrance day celebrations? We feel strongly that we are being left out and discriminated against." Leita Kaldi, a member of Romania of Massachusetts, Inc., urged Wiesel, "Your presence at the meeting would be an inspiration to the Romani leaders, and would assure them that they have not been forgotten by fellow victims who shared the same sufferings during the Holocaust."

Wiesel, unable to attend, informed Puxon, "The plight of the Gypsies has been part of our memory. It will remain part of our memory. . . . I had nothing to do with [the council's] composition. All the appointments came from the White House. However, I will see to it that members of your community are invited to our functions."

In an attempt to resolve the issue, the council's executive director, Rabbi Seymour Siegel (formerly professor of ethics at the Jewish Theological Seminary), Micah Naftalin, Anna Cohn, and David Altshuler met with a group of Rom in the Department of Labor's auditorium on July 20, 1984. Siegel and Naftalin tried to assuage their fears, promising that they would hereafter be "fully included," and claiming that, "as a government agency, we don't speak for any community, including the Jewish community." Romani spokesmen, however, continued to press the staff for seats on the council. John Tene, who had organized Romani of Massachusetts, Inc., asked if there was "any way you see fit that we can have the seats that belong to Gypsies." Marks offered the opinion that Romani representatives should be involved in the planning of the museum: "It would not be

. . . right if you do not have Gypsy people working on the Gypsy section." Grattan Puxon declared that he believed the council had intentionally ignored Romani victims, because the council understood the Holocaust to be a Jewish story. "We . . . will continue to say, give the Rom ten seats. Because that would be respect for the dead, and acceptance for the living."

Naftalin again said that the council had no responsibility for appointments, and agreed that an "oversight" had been made. "You have an obvious and persuasive case," he said. Barry Fisher, a Jewish lawyer from Los Angeles, serving as counsel to the Romani Holocaust Council, pressed Siegel and Naftalin to correct this "reckless disregard" of Romani experience by at least creating "auxiliary status" for Romani representatives, in order that they could review plans, discuss decisions with staff members, and be allowed access to books and records "so that they can begin . . . to augment the decision-making." Fisher continued to press this issue, writing President Reagan on July 12, 1984, "In view of the tragic suffering of the Rom during the Holocaust, comparable only to that of the Jews, fairness requires allocation of at least ten voting positions on the Council." And on January 30, 1985, Fisher and his colleague Rabbi William Kramer urged Naftalin to create "associate status for 3 or 4 members of the Gypsy community leadership" on the council, as well as representation on the Days of Remembrance planning committee.

Former Director of Museum Development Anna Cohn characterized the July 1984 meeting as a "profound event, one in which the bureaucratic voice of museum planning met people with a real voice and stake in the story." After the staff explained their actions and their plans, Cohn said that Rom told "compelling stories, with the elders speaking first." Significant goodwill was generated in the meeting. "We really listened," Cohn said, "and were moved by what they had to say."

If seeds of trust were planted in this meeting, they were trampled the next day, when Siegel was quoted in the *Washington Post*, characterizing as "cockamamie" the Rom request that perhaps some council members would leave to make room for Romani representation, or that Romani representatives could be added. "The council," said Siegel, "is too unwieldy as it is." Adding fuel to the fire, Siegel said that, though he would not object to Romani representation, he wondered if in fact Rom even "existed" as a people. "There should be some recognition or acknowledgment of the Gypsy people . . . if there is such a thing," said Siegel. "I guess there is. There was a suffering element under the Nazis."

In 1985, the Holocaust Memorial Council responded to these claims for restoration of the Romani story in two ways. First, it commissioned University of Vermont and Concordia University Professor Gabrielle Tyrnauer to write a report on the Romani experience in the Holocaust. Second, in May 1985, it created the post of special adviser on Holocaust-related Gypsy matters to the council, filled by University of Texas, Austin, English and Linguistics Professor Ian Hancock. Tyrnauer's report, "The Fate of the Gypsies During the Holocaust," claimed that between one-quarter million and one-half million Rom died in the Holocaust, and that "Gypsies and Jews were marked for total annihilation by the same Nazi death machine. They must be represented on the Council in proportion to their suffering. No other ethnic group beside[s] the Jewish people, have as great a claim. . . . To remember them together is both an act of justice and a correction of a distorted chapter of history."

Hancock had little influence on council matters as special adviser, a position characterized by Micah Naftalin as "honorary." He never met with Wiesel, and had particularly prickly relationships with numerous council members and staff. Hancock, the United States representative of the International Romani Union to the United Nations and to UNICEF, framed the neglect of Romani experience as a part of the continuing oppression of Rom throughout the world, victimized by German law before the Holocaust, murdered in the Holocaust, forgotten after the Holocaust. Hancock's writings made the claim that the Romani and Jewish experiences in the Holocaust were the same, that the claim of the uniqueness of the Jewish experience was historically untenable, that enduring stereotypes of Rom hindered widespread knowledge and acceptance of their suffering, and that restoration of this story in the museum was one way to bring to public consciousness the continued violence inflicted upon Rom throughout Europe and the United States in contemporary times.

Not all Romani spokespersons were pleased about this appointment. James Marks II, writing as a "senator" in the "Gypsy Nation" to Wiesel on August 21, 1985, cautioned, "Don't appoint one Gypsy, especially Mr. Ivan [sic] Hancock, and just forget about the rest of us. . . . Just because he is educated should not be his qualifications."

With eleven council terms expiring in January 1986, Romani spokesmen and council staff believed that there would be a Romani representative appointed by the White House. Surprisingly, one was not. In June 1986, Hancock and John Megel of Alexandria, Virginia, who, in the early 1980s, had been one of the first to press the council for representation, met with the council. In a subsequent letter to the council's executive director, Hancock observed, "Three times at that meeting, the phrase 'getting into the act' was heard in relation to other Holocaust victims' attempt to obtain fair representation. This implies that the act is Jewish and the rest of us are trespassers." Hancock and others believed that crass political motives of the Reagan administration were responsible for the continued exclusion of Romani representatives from the council. "We have been told this by a White House spokesman; if we were wealthier and more generous, we would have a better chance. . . . We feel strongly . . . that whether or not an appointee is a Republican should not have the slightest bearing upon his or her selection."

Despite the failure of the Rom to gain representation, the council was making a modest attempt to rectify the invisibility of Romani suffering. On September 16, 1986, a special Days of Remembrance ceremony "in memory of the Gypsy victims of Nazi genocide" was held in the Russell Senate Office Building. Elie Wiesel—who had consistently said that he had pressed the White House to appoint a Romani council member—confessed in his address that he felt "guilty" that the council had not done enough to "listen to your voice of anguish," and promised "that we shall do whatever we can from now on to listen better." At the end of the ceremony, several Romani participants poured water on soil brought from camps where Rom were murdered. Even this ceremony, however, was marred for some Romani guests. In a letter to Wiesel, Hancock complained that only five council members attended, that he—Wiesel— had left early, and that Romani participants were not allowed to sing because "it would disturb office workers in nearby rooms." Elsewhere, he noted that he didn't like the idea of a separate ceremony: "Our ashes were mingled in the ovens, why should that be remembered separately today?"

In 1987, William Duna, who taught music at St. Thomas (Minnesota) University, became the first Romani representative on the council. He immediately charged the council with "overt racism," characterized it as a body that had "willfully downplayed" Romani suffering, and referred to himself as the "token Gypsy." He also accused the council—incorrectly—of suppressing Tyrnauer's report, since they had "refused" to publish it. "These were fundamental planning documents," Cohn said; "they were never intended for publication." Like Hancock, Duna compiled a litany of complaint against the council, including failure to represent Rom adequately in the Days of Remembrance ceremonies—Duna was a member of the Days of Remembrance committee—and failure to consult Rom in the planning of the 1987 "Other Victims" conference.

In 1991, however, the council's commemorative memory expanded measurably, when, for example, the council flew a Romanian Romani survivor to the Days of Remembrance ceremony. He played a selection of Rom music from the camps on the violin; his wife, also a Rom survivor, joined hands with a Jewish survivor to light a memorial candle. In 1992, the council helped sponsor an exhibition of Austrian Romani artist and Birkenau survivor Karl Stojka's *A Childhood in Birkenau* at the Austrian Embassy. During the exhibit's opening, council historian Sybil Milton, whose research had led the council to Stojka, translated his moving comments, and Duna, an accomplished musician in his own right, played the piano. Stojka also participated in the memorial candle-lighting at the Days of Remembrance ceremony in the Capitol Rotunda.

The relationship between the council and Romani communities was difficult for many reasons. In contrast to scholarship on the Jewish experience in the Holocaust, Hancock observed, "Only a handful of Romani scholars exists, and research on the Romani Holocaust is in its infancy." Failure to recognize the Romani Holocaust in the formative years of the project planted seeds of distrust that grew as the White House failed to rectify an obviously unjust situation until 1987. By that time, at least for some Romani spokespersons, deep suspicion ruled their interaction with the council, fueled by clear evidence that some council members viewed Rom participation in the museum the way a family deals with unwelcome, embarrassing relatives.

Nevertheless, although Holocaust memory was often bitterly contested in matters of council representation, commemorative events, and personal relationships, the museum's staff was energetically working to include the story of the Romani Holocaust in the museum. In her letter to Duna on October 4, 1990, Sara Bloomfield—who played a major role in ensuring Romani representation in the museum's educational work—carefully detailed the museum's activities. There were, she said, "scholars, curators, archivists and researchers conducting extensive searches in several European countries in an effort to secure, with the help of Roma and Sinti survivors, photographs and artifacts as well as archival materials pertaining to their fate." She informed him that the museum was in contact with numerous individuals and institutions: "For example, from the Documentation Archive of the Austrian Resistance Movement, we have recently received a set of documents pertaining to the 1941 deportation of Austrian Sinti from the Upper Danube region to the Lodz Ghetto from which they were deported to Chelmno and gassed." She told Duna that researchers microfilming documents in the Soviet Union and Eastern Europe "have implicit instructions from the

Museum to search for material on the Nazi persecution of the Roma and Sinti." And, she concluded, the museum was interested in adding to its collection of Romani survivors' oral histories, and asked for Duna's help.

Unlike the case of the Armenians, reference to Romani victims appears in various places in the permanent exhibition, in artifacts, photographs, and text. For example, visitors learn that Rom were classified as a racial threat to the Aryan race, that they were subjected to official discrimination well before 1933, and that, as laws against Rom grew more severe, a Nazi racial theorist argued, "In the long term, the German people will be freed from this public nuisance only when [Romani] fertility is completely eliminated." Visitors view a Romani wagon from Czechoslovakia, a photograph of Romani victims deported from a Vienna suburb, and a violin, clothing, and jewelry that belonged to Rom murdered by the Nazis.

Mention is also made of Romani inhabitants of the Łódź and and Warsaw ghettos, and the fact that Rom were murdered at Babi Yar. Text and photographs note that Jews and Rom were subject to the same process of deportation to killing centers in Poland, and that the fate of two hundred thousand Rom "closely paralleled that of the Jews."

Reference to the Romani experience throughout the exhibition still did not resolve the problem of representation for those—like council historian Sybil Milton or former museum historian David Luebke—who believed that Romani victims shared exactly the same fate as the Jews. For them, the exhibit still defined Rom as "other" than Jews, somewhat removed from the center, their presence defined through their difference from Jewish experience. Milton has argued for an inclusive definition of the Holocaust that comprehends Jews, Gypsies, and the handicapped as racial victims of the Nazis, sharing the same fate. She strongly disagrees, for example, with Israeli historian Yehuda Bauer's contention—adopted by the museum—that some groups of sedentary Gypsies avoided persecution. Not surprisingly, Milton believes that the exhibition could have integrated the Romani experience much more fully. For example, Milton argued,

"There could be discussion of the harassment of Gypsies in the early years, the monitor showing restrictive laws against the Jews could have included those against the Gypsies, and they should *not* be lumped together with Jehovah's Witnesses and homosexuals. Some of the Rom whom I have taken through the exhibition think the wagon promotes the stereotypical view of all Rom and Sinti peoples as migratory." Furthermore, she said, the stated number of Romani victims—two hundred thousand—"is much too low. The most accurate estimates are about half a million."

Despite the remaining serious differences of opinion, even Ian Hancock expressed cautious optimism, noting that there has "been a steadily growing acknowledgment of the Romani tragedy. . . . From having no representation at all on the Council, we now have one member; from having no Gypsy-related entries in the data-bank [in the museum's learning center] we now have some." He still hopes, however, that eventually Romani victims will be "fully recognised as the only population, besides the Jews, which was slated for . . . eventual eradication from the face of the earth."

The Center and the Periphery
of Holocaust Memory

THE EXHIBIT USED Berenbaum's strategy of comparison to make the case for the uniqueness of the Jewish experience, although the Romani experience was presented as similar in almost every respect. As always happens in trying to make sense out of historical materials, resolution depends on the criteria used and is a matter of perspective and definition. Historian Christopher Browning said, for example, "If the criterion is the place of various groups in Hitler's worldview, then Gypsies and everyone else are at the periphery. Hitler was, after all, a phobic anti-Semite, not a phobic anti-Gypsiite. If, however, the question is the effect of the Nazis' machinery of destruction, it is certainly legitimate for Gypsies to claim 'we should be with you' at the center of the story."

"Cultures," wrote Henry Jenkins and Mary Fuller, "endlessly repeat the narratives of their founding as a way of justifying their occupation of space." Groups can also repeat the narratives of their destruction as a way of achieving status in a story deemed "officially" significant, and, in this case, a way of laying claim to occupation of exhibition space in a national museum. From the formation of the commission and council, the insistence by so many was, first, "We belong in this story." Then various positioning strategies evolved with regard to the uniqueness of the Jewish experience in the Holocaust.

Some Jews zealously guarded the story as *only* about Jews, and grudgingly allowed others to "rent" space in the story because of the pluralistic imperative of a national museum. Others found Wiesel's aphoristic solution, "All Jews were victims but not all victims were Jews," unsatisfactory. They wanted to reduce the space between Jews and "others." Jaroslav Drabek claimed that Czechs were killed for who they were, not for what they did, and John Pawlikowski made the same argument for Poles.

Some non-Jewish council members—Pawlikowski, for example—were willing to acknowledge the "unique dimensions" of the Jewish experience and at the same time argue that "others" also died because of who they were, not what they did, and should be more than "interruptions" in the narrative of Jewish suffering. Armenians argued that their experience foreshadowed what was to come, and pressed for inclusion but not for centrality; Romani spokespersons argued that, whereas "others" rightly occupied a less prominent "rung" on the hierarchy of victimization, *they* belonged at the center, with the Jews, and they were being unjustly deprived of their "right" to tell the story in "their" way. Each group argued that they belonged within the boundaries of the Holocaust, and then their representatives made a case for their "space," their position—*always defined, however, in relation to the Jewish center.*

The permanent exhibition does not—cannot—resolve the complex tensions that seek to shape ethnic identity and status through the prestige of victimization and location in a Holocaust-museum exhibit. And whereas the permanent exhibition has chosen a particular formulation, solidifying the boundaries in a particular way, other memory systems in the museum—temporary exhibitions, archives, educational programs, for example—allow for an interpretive flexibility, a continuing probing of acceptable and appropriate representation at the periphery and the center of Holocaust memory.

Endings: The Lure of Redemption

THE LATE TERRENCE DES PRES, professor of English at Colgate University and author of *The Survivor: Anatomy of Life in the Death Camps,* wrote of the Holocaust, "The predicament of aftermath defines us, and not merely as individuals but as creatures of an age that has never been able to assimilate the implications of the event we call the Holocaust." One of the most difficult interpretive challenges for the museum's design team was to construct a proper ending to the exhibition. Should visitors be sent away with a greater appreciation of Des Pres's "predicament of aftermath"? Or was there some way to offer a more intellectually and emotionally satisfying ending to the story, an ending that would make use of the comforting language of "lessons" to be learned, and the comforting rhetoric of insulation that declared that, despite the horrors visitors had viewed, the spirit was ultimately triumphant? Just as James Freed was forced to reduce the size of and set back the Hall of Remembrance, and alter his plans for its bricked-up windows, so that the building would not contaminate the Mall with a message of despair, so too the design team faced pressure to soften the impact of the powerful story told in their exhibition.

Part of the problem lay in the structure of narrative itself. Hayden White argued that narrative imposes a structure of meaning upon events. It demands resolution, demands that "real events be assessed as to their significance as elements of a moral drama." From the earliest plans for a permanent exhibition, the issue of appropriate ending was contested. Many—particularly survivors—believed that, like Israeli Holocaust museums, this museum should emphasize resistance and rescue and the creation of the State of Israel. Death would precede rebirth. Consequently, the Holocaust could be "resolved" as a horrible prelude to its redemption through the birth of Israel. "It is," wrote James E. Young, "almost as if violent events—perceived as aberrations or ruptures in the cultural continuum—demand their retelling, their narration, back into traditions and structures they would otherwise defy. For upon entering narrative, violent events necessarily reenter the continuum, are totalized by it, and thus seem to lose their 'violent' quality." Others, including Elie Wiesel, objected to what amounted to a triumphal, redemptive ending, arguing that the ending could reflect both the continuation of life and the sober realization that the "predicament of aftermath" would remain.

In the two years before the museum's opening, pressure on the staff to create a "happy ending" increased. Lay leaders, particularly Albert Abramson, believed that the ending needed to convey hope in order to satisfy the American public. There was a short-lived plan to have Israeli and American flags placed at the end of the exhibit. In the spring of 1989, the content committee discussed the wisdom of having visitors sign a presidential statement about genocide and be offered a copy when they left. There was also discussion of the installation of television sets with film of contemporary genocidal events.

German-government officials attempted to moderate portrayal of Germany in the museum. In 1986, Wiesel had established the U.S.-German Committee on Learning and Remembrance with Peter Petersen, a member of the West German Bundestag. Aside from Wiesel, there was little enthusiasm for this among council members, and his resignation ended the connection. In February 1988, however, Miles Lerman met informally with Petersen and reported that Petersen had wondered whether the story of the "new" Germany would be told. In a follow-up letter to Lerman, Petersen wrote, "The

Holocaust is part of your history, it is also part of our history, the darkest part any people can carry. If we Germans face the truth . . . then obviously that truth will have to have formed the basis of the Federal Republic. We would like to have a chance to show how this has been translated into our constitution, our laws, our relationship to Israel, the attempts of restitution. . . . In another way Israel . . . is also a result of the Holocaust, and here we could imagine that the story of the Federal Republic and the story of Israel should have a part in a Holocaust museum, not in an attempt to cover up anything, but as an encouragement for people and nations to learn from this past and become free for the future."

Briefly considered was the idea of including in the exhibition a photograph of the former West German chancellor Willy Brandt kneeling in contrition at the Warsaw Ghetto Monument. Both Weinberg and Berenbaum were in favor of this, but met strong opposition from several survivors on the content committee, who thought it a way of letting the Germans "off the hook." Berenbaum read it differently. "Why not use a powerful photograph of a German leader admitting German guilt through an act of penance?" he asked. "It would be useful against Holocaust deniers." Given emotional opposition, however, the content committee decided not to proceed, and Shaike Weinberg chose not to fight their decision.

Appelbaum and Smith worried about ending with an overemphasis on resistance and rescue, or making it appear that the Holocaust was a necessary precursor to the birth of Israel. Smith wanted an ending that would intentionally *not* bring closure to the narrative. Ending with resistance and rescue would, he said, "come dangerously close to a falsehood." He argued for recorded voices of survivors, an "eternal flame of memory which would be . . . people talking totally at random so that you would be left with something which was forever changing." His idea was not adopted; instead, as visitors conclude their walk through exhibits on the second floor, many stop to watch *Testimony*, a one-hour-and-seventeen-minute film made up of short segments of interviews with survivors. The space in which the film is shown is in stark contrast to the dark space of the rest of the exhibition—softer, with walls of dark-gold Jerusalem stone.

Filmmaker Sandra Wentworth Bradley—who also produced the *Antisemitism* film—received the contract from the museum to make *Testimony*. She was directed to construct it around themes of resistance, rescue, and defiance, themes chosen in part to satisfy lay leaders who insisted on a hopeful ending. "Through the whole project," she said, "I had difficulty understanding the difference between resistance and defiance, and no one at the museum seemed able to articulate it well, either." Bradley interpreted these themes "loosely." Spiritual resistance, mentioned not at all in the exhibition, was the emphasis of many of these stories. "For me, spiritual resistance *was* resistance, just as real as physical resistance," Bradley said.

She developed short biographies of several thousand survivors, did in-depth research on approximately three hundred, and filmed thirty-three, twenty of whom appear in the film. Making the film was painful, for several reasons. "The overwhelming impact on me was my shame at how little I knew," she recalled, "and I was stunned by the similarity of what was done to these people, despite the fact that they reacted in quite different ways." Editing out people whom she had come to know and care about was particularly painful. "I do not consider the film a triumph, or even really complete, because it hurt me so much to have to leave people out. I wanted it to run for three hours."

It is easy to imagine a film on themes of resistance, rescue, and defiance insidiously subverting the brutal Holocaust narrative told in the permanent exhibition, sending people away comforted, believing, in fact, that the human spirit did triumph, that good did triumph over evil. Bradley's film, however, avoids such Holocaust sentimentality. Though not in the random form that Smith preferred, the voices in the episodic film help remind visitors that the individual reality of the Holocaust was much more chaotic than the museum's coherent narrative.

In the midst of moving and horrible accounts of resistance, rescue, near-rescue, theological certainty, and theological doubt, the presence of the Holocaust as a living thing is overpowering. Bradley helped museum visitors focus on survivors' faces by filming them with the background out of focus, and these striking faces reflect the presence of the Holocaust in many ways. It weighs heavily as faces sag during the telling of a story; it is looked upon as a despised life-companion by those who recall seeking to rescue shreds of human dignity in their experiences; and it explodes on the faces of those who sob as unacceptable memories erupt into their present.

One voice in the film seemed to provide a fitting expression of unresolved closure. Survivor Gerda Weissmann Klein, who, with others, was abandoned in a factory in the Czech town of Volary during a death march in the last days of the war, speaks with a quiet dignity of being liberated by a young American soldier, Kurt Klein, who, we later find out, became her husband. At another point in the film, however, this "happy ending" is itself subverted, for she speaks of finding the body of a friend who had died the morning of their liberation. She recalled that they had met three years earlier on a train taking them to a camp, and spoken of their chances to survive until the war ended. For a wager of strawberries and whipped cream, "I said we would be liberated, she said we would not." Bradley, who has grown close to Klein, recalled, "She believed that she had, in fact, lost the wager. I told her before filming, 'But you didn't lose. Don't you see? You were both right.' I don't think Gerda had considered this." After telling the story in the film, in a long moment of powerful silence, Klein looked at the interviewer, and it was clear that she could not then, or perhaps ever, settle the matter. No survivor of the Holocaust could ever be completely liberated.

CONCLUSION

IN HIS SPIRITED EXCHANGE with James Baldwin in 1971, Shlomo Katz not only deplored Baldwin's appropriation of the Holocaust to describe the legal situation of black activist Angela Davis, but bitterly condemned as well the use of the term "genocide" to describe a wide variety of social ills, from poverty to abortion. What was needed in order to restore historical integrity to discussion about the Holocaust, Katz argued, was a clear definition of "that which is, who is who and what is what."

The museum project has been such an exercise in officially sanctioned conceptual ordering and control, establishing boundaries both firm and permeable around a way of remembering the Holocaust. Official memory would authoritatively define the Holocaust, provide evidence for its uniqueness, and determine what events, if any, might be compared to it and remembered alongside it. Definitional clarity would, it was hoped, lead to guidelines for establishing a hierarchy of Holocaust victims, which would, in turn, guide representation of such victims in the museum. Official Holocaust memory would remain primarily an ethnic memory, because the storytellers would remain primarily Jewish, but it would move beyond ethnic memory through what Michael Berenbaum called the "Americanization" of the Holocaust, the attempt both to link Americans to the story and to highlight professed American values through stark presentation of their antitheses in Nazi Germany.

Official memory required proper location, the nation's capital; proper site, adjacent to the Mall; a proper "house" of memory, Freed's building; and a core exhibit to provide "proof" of the event and the dramatic rendition of the narrative. Archives and educational-outreach programs, for example—would spread the web of Holocaust memory throughout the nation. In this way, the memory was located in space, contained in a public institution, embodied in an exhibit, and projected throughout American culture.

Even after the opening of the museum, however, the prestige of a national Holocaust memory did not permanently set its boundaries. In an angry attack, Nation of Islam spokesman Khalid Abdul Muhammad attacked the Holocaust as the pre-eminent example of genocide—thereby threatening the doctrine of uniqueness—by presenting the case for what he believed was the far worse example of genocide against African Americans. On April 18, 1994, after touring the museum, Muhammad, speaking in Eisenhower Plaza, next to the Hall of Remembrance, declared, "We, over the past 6,000 years, the past 400 in particular, have lost over 600 million, which means that the black 'holocaust' is 100 times worse than any recorded." And yet even his attempt to proclaim a "proper" hierarchy of holocausts bore witness to the power of the Holocaust: it was that event from which he drew contrasts, and it was in museum space that he sought recognition.

The permanent exhibition stands as an authoritative public narrative, but not an uncontested one. Romani spokespersons still press for more substantive inclusion. And, on the other hand, some people are angered by the museum's memory. Reverend Dale Crowley, Jr., host of an evangelical radio program in Virginia, who had previously picketed the laying of the museum's cornerstone, accused the museum of a "theological attack on our faith" (Christianity), because the *Antisemitism* film mentions that early Christian teachings contributed to hatred of Jews.

Also angered by the museum's Holocaust narrative was Romania's right-wing party, Greater Romania. The museum in Washington is, according to staff historians Radu Ioanid and David Luebke, the "only museum in the world that mentions the forgotten Holocaust," which murdered at least 250,000 Romanian and Ukrainian Jews and 25,000 Gypsies. The exhibit was significant, they noted, because, alone among European nations, Romania conducted its own "autonomous genocide . . . without following German instructions or models of operation." Greater Romania was part of a campaign to deny the Romanian Holocaust, and it threatened to initiate a suit against the museum at the International Court of Justice in the Hague, "because of what it perceives as slanders against the Romanian people."

Still unsettled as well was the issue of whether the museum was a "Jewish" or an "American" museum. Though certainly settled in one important sense—it was created by a federally sponsored council operating on appropriated funds and built on federally donated lands, and would, after opening, rely extensively on federal appropriations for annual operating costs—the question arose in other important ways. Should the museum, for example, be closed on Yom Kippur? Some council members worried that such closing would be viewed by non-Jews as an inappropriate ethnic statement and bring to the surface lingering resentment of a Jewish presence on the Mall. Other council members argued, successfully, that Congress itself does not work on Yom Kippur, and that both Jews and non-Jews would react with disbelief if the museum did not honor this sacred day, just as it did Christmas.

As the dedication and opening of the museum on April 22, 1993, approached, a battle for the direction of the institution took place behind the scenes between those who feared that the museum would appear "too Jewish," and attract only a Jewish audience, and those who feared that, in the attempt to sell itself to a wide audience, the museum would jettison its focus on the Holocaust and eventually become a museum of contemporary genocide. As a member of the opening committee who worried that the museum was "too Jewish" told me, "It is terribly important what picture of the opening appears on the front page of *The New York Times*. Do we want a picture of survivors crying, or a picture of a young American family walking inside?"

The issue came to a head during spirited discussions among those planning the opening ceremonies regarding the wisdom of having Israeli President Chaim Herzog—who, while serving with the intelligence branch of the British Army, encountered the horrors of the Bergen-Belsen concentration camp—speak at the dedication ceremony. Council Chairman Harvey Meyerhoff and Vice-Chairman William Lowenberg, a survivor of Auschwitz, were opposed, as were others who thought the museum should not link itself too closely with Israel. Compromise proposals were considered: Herzog could be invited to speak at the Tribute to Liberators and Rescuers ceremony April 21, at Arlington National Cemetery; or the Israeli ambassador could give greetings on behalf of Israel at the dedication ceremony (this was quickly dismissed as being diplomatically impossible, for it would mean the president of Israel would sit in the audience while an ambassador spoke). The opening committee decided not to invite Herzog to speak at any event, but White House staff, continuing the tradition of understanding the museum in the manner of previous administrations—that is, as an affirmation of American support for the State of Israel—told Meyerhoff in early April that Herzog *would* speak.

Meyerhoff's opposition, along with a separate and more serious charge that the council, once populated by scholars and theologians like Raul Hilberg, Robert McAfee Brown, Irving Greenberg, Franklin Littell, and the former president of Notre Dame, Father Theodore Hesburgh, was now mainly made up of "wealthy Republican donors," convinced the White House to replace both Meyerhoff and Lowenberg. The president appointed Miles Lerman, who was involved in the project from its inception, as chairman, and selected as vice-chair Dr. Ruth Mandel, professor of political science at Rutgers University and a child survivor of the SS *St. Louis*. A document transmitted to the White House characterized this as a restoration of the "spiritual task of the Council," but the timing of the

LEFT: Council Chairman Harvey Meyerhoff speaking at the opening ceremonies *(Bill Fitzpatrick, United States Holocaust Memorial Museum)*

BELOW: Council Chairman Meyerhoff, President Bill Clinton, and Elie Wiesel light an eternal flame during opening ceremonies. *(AFP photo)*

announcement, three weeks before the opening, was criticized even by some who welcomed the change.

The overwhelming popularity of the museum among non-Jews—polling data in the fall of 1993 revealed that 62 percent of visitors were not Jewish—did not eradicate concern about the museum's appearing too Jewish. The original cover of Michael Berenbaum's *The World Must Know: The History of the Holocaust as Told in the United States Holocaust Memorial Museum,* included a photograph of a frayed yellow Star of David, with the word *"Jude"* in black letters. In subsequent printings of this popular book, a drawing of the museum building and, more recently, a photograph of victims' shoes have covered the Star of David, which symbolized, for some senior staff, too much emphasis on Jewish victimization in an "American" museum.

Mobilizing Holocaust Memory

IT WAS ONE of the cherished assumptions of those who created the museum that Holocaust memory would be able to aid in the recognition and ending of genocidal situations. A critical mass of Holocaust memory, produced in institutions like the museum, could, it was thought, alter for the better the present and future. It was also the hope, as Elie Wiesel put it, that "whoever enters this subject is purified by it. . . . is humanized by it." The uses of Holocaust memory, however, are more complex.

BURDENSOME MEMORY

Throughout the history of this project, the commission and the council had steadfastly resisted the persistent call to create a museum in which various genocides would be represented. The Holocaust, it was argued, presented most starkly the challenge to governments and

President Clinton toured the permanent exhibition shortly before the opening. Here he stands in front of the "Terror in Poland" exhibit.
(White House photograph)

individuals. By visiting the permanent exhibition, policymakers and policy might be changed.

To this end, the museum hosted scores of foreign leaders from over fifty countries, the United Nations, and the European Parliament. It hosted numerous officials from various bureaus in, for example, the State Department, the National Security Agency, and the Foreign Service Institute, as well as members of Congress and the White House staff. Occasionally, these visitors would meet with Michael Berenbaum or other senior staff to talk about their reaction to the exhibition. "They think immediately about their jobs," recalled Ralph Grunewald, the museum's director of external affairs, "and talk about the day-to-day dilemmas they face. It is impossible to tell what direct influence the museum has, but it is clear that we have become a place where policymakers can think about the relationship between the Holocaust and a variety of contemporary issues."

Agreeing that there is a "soft correlation" between Holocaust memory and policy influence, Warren Zimmerman, former ambassador to Yugoslavia (1989–92) and former head of the Bureau for Refugee Programs (1992–94)—who resigned his ambassadorship partly because of his frustration at the failure of the United States to intervene in Bosnia—said, "Memory of the Holocaust has at least reminded policymakers of the importance of human rights. It intrudes on their thinking more, making it harder to ignore these kinds of issues."

By the day of the museum's dedication ceremonies, contemporary events in Bosnia made the museum strikingly relevant. Here was both an opportunity (given the unprecedented attention directed toward the museum) to show that Holocaust memory could make a difference, and a risk, that the failure of Holocaust memory to alter policy would strike at the heart of one of the museum's reasons for being.

In his remarks at the dedication, Elie Wiesel turned to the president and said, "As a Jew, I am saying that we must do something to stop the bloodshed in that country! People fight each other and children die. Why? Something, anything must be done." (As was true of

President Reagan when Wiesel implored him not to go to Bitburg in 1985, President Clinton was not pleased by this unexpected public confrontation.) Wiesel was calling for a selective mobilization of Holocaust memory, but he was aware, given his long engagement with the museum project, that the government had always been nervous about Holocaust memory's moving beyond commemoration and education to a direct impact on public policy.

Recall that the commission's *Report to the President* in 1979 had recommended that a committee on conscience, made up of "distinguished moral leaders," be appointed to monitor instances of genocide; these should "have access" to Congress, the president, and the public, to "influence policy" and "alert the national conscience" in order to help stop genocide. In 1980, the council envisioned a "Platform of Conscience" within the museum upon which members of the committee on conscience would stand and, like town criers, "warn the world through the United States Holocaust Memorial that a holocaust is pending and is possible." Throughout several presidential administrations, the State Department strongly opposed this idea, and by 1984 Wiesel informed council members that, when needed, the "entire Council would act as the Committee on Conscience." No platform was ever erected.

Clearly, Holocaust memory was to be taken seriously when it was convenient to do so, and ignored when other priorities intruded. We have seen evidence of this already. In the midst of rhetorical allegiance to the importance of memory and the need to be sensitive to genocides worldwide, Armenian memory was virtually effaced from the permanent exhibition, and some Israeli and American Jews, supposedly sensitive to the virtues of remembrance, joined forces to prevent the United States Congress from officially remembering the Armenian genocide. They were joined in this effort by American politicians—who were not at all hesitant to declare that, when integrity of historical memory clashed with the need to mollify a NATO partner, Holocaust memory was a burden that should be jettisoned.

Beginning with Roy Gutman's Pulitzer Prize–winning accounts

for *Newsday* of Serbian genocide in August 1992, Americans were assaulted with images that might have been extracted from the liberation of the camps at the end of World War II. On August 17, 1992, *Time*'s cover shocked readers with a photograph of emaciated Muslim prisoners standing behind barbed wire in a Serbian camp. For those convinced that genocide was taking place, policy direction was clear. The United States could not stand by as it had in the 1930s and 1940s. Appearing on *World News Tonight with Peter Jennings* the night before the museum dedication ceremony, Holocaust survivor and member of the council's education committee Helen Fagin declared, "It is our business to get involved. It is our business to prevent the killing. It is our business to interfere with ethnic cleansing and to say to the world, 'A human being's value is the same, no matter what religion, what nationality, what ethnicity, and what race."

Holocaust memory could not, however, provide clear policy direction. It was not the only historical model invoked in order to make sense of Bosnia. The production and mobilization of historical memories—especially those deemed central guides to contemporary life—compete with one another for influence. There was no consensus about the character of the conflict; rather, there were a number of possible analogies. Was the appropriate analogy the Holocaust, which damned indifference and demanded intervention? Was it Vietnam, which cautioned against becoming trapped in a quagmire? Should the events be understood as a civil war, lending support to those who claimed America had no stake in the fighting? Was the fighting an expression of ancient ethnic hatreds, which implied an endless course of blood-letting impervious to outside intervention? Expressing his own confusion three days after the museum opened, Secretary of State Warren Christopher asked, "Am I able to sort out which of these things are possible situations like the Holocaust. . . . Is it Cambodia, or is it Bosnia or is it Haiti?"

Another analogy—quiescent since the end of the Cold War—was resurrected as it became clear that the United States would not intervene. Invoking memory of Neville Chamberlain's policy

ABOVE: Rob Rogers captured the way powerful historical memories led to indecision, not to clarity of policy. *(Rob Rogers, reprinted by permission of UFS, Inc.)*

BELOW: Dana Summers's cartoon reminded readers that memory of the Holocaust can be mobilized in murderous ways. *(© 1994, The Washington Post Writers Group. Reprinted with permission.)*

of appeasement at Munich, Zbigniew Brzezinski, who had been national-security adviser to President Carter, asked readers of *The New York Times* on the day of the museum's dedication if the rhetoric of Holocaust commemoration was a "proclamation of a moral imperative," or a "pompous affirmation of hypocrisy." Arguing that it was easy to be "Churchillian" in retrospect, Brzezinski angrily accused the United States and Great Britain of inexcusable evasion and appeasement of Serbian aggression.

Several Jewish organizations pressed for intervention. They were willing at least to acknowledge a family resemblance between the Holocaust and the genocide in Bosnia. Failure to act would be a failure to heed the lessons of the Holocaust. These groups were also concerned that failure to speak out would leave Jews open to criticism that they cared only about Jewish victims. On December 22, 1992, eighteen Jewish organizations staged a rally outside the museum to protest evidence of atrocities against Bosnian Muslims. In April 1993, four days after the dedication of the museum, the American Jewish Congress published a full-page open letter to President Clinton in *The New York Times*, calling for intervention. It asked, "If the memory of those [Holocaust] victims does not move us to respond to suffering and persecution in our own time, what conceivable purpose does memory serve?" By April 1993, of course, it was clear that the Holocaust analogy had *not* affected policy, and for Brzezinski and others the point was now not that memory of the Holocaust might push the Clinton administration to act but, rather, that a declaration of shame that such memory had *not* worked might be persuasive.

Rather than providing a clear road map for policy decision, however, Holocaust memory was an unwelcome burden for both the Bush and Clinton administrations, even though, in his remarks at a White House reception held in honor of the opening of the museum, President Clinton expressed his hope that the Holocaust would remain "ever a sharp thorn in every national memory." In the fall of 1992, the State Department failed to charge Serbia with genocide because of fear that the United States would be forced by the

Genocide Treaty to intervene, and in the months leading up to the opening of the museum, State Department personnel were reportedly discouraged from drawing close parallels between the Holocaust and events in Bosnia.

Elie Wiesel's plea to President Clinton was not only for Bosnians, but for evidence that Holocaust memory could make a difference. Political will—including the willingness to sacrifice many American lives—strategic considerations, a feel of urgency, all *might* have blended together to create an environment in which the awareness of the cost of governmental indifference and inaction during the Holocaust would lead to intervention in Bosnia. But it did not.

This failure to affect public policy dramatically rests in part on inflated expectations about the clarity and power of Holocaust memory. Such memory does not exist "out there," independently. It is not a sole cause that will be able to bring about the effect of stopping genocide. Just because an event is perceived as transformative, epochal, a watershed, a break in human history—all the sweeping phrases used to separate the Holocaust from the ongoing stream of history—*memory of that event is not necessarily equally transformative,* no matter how much we would like it to be. Furthermore, even had there been a consensus among policymakers that the lessons of the Holocaust (we must never again be indifferent to genocide, for example) should lead to United States intervention in Bosnia, what specific *kind* of intervention? And what of the many genocidal situations in other nations in which the imperative of "never again" demanded a response? Memory of the Holocaust does *not* necessarily lead to a clear case for a specific policy.

TREACHEROUS MEMORY

Official Holocaust memory may also function as a "comfortable horrible" memory, allowing Americans to reassure themselves that they are engaging profound events, all the while ignoring more indigestible events that threaten Americans' sense of themselves more than the Holocaust. This is clear from the presence of the black-and-white POW/MIA flag—honoring those Americans some believe are still held captive in Southeast Asia—prominently displayed during the annual Days of Remembrance ceremony in the Capitol Rotunda. As the result of a congressional resolution passed in January 1989, the flag will be displayed in the Rotunda "until a satisfactory accounting of all America's POW/MIA's has taken place."

There are several ways to read the meaning of this flag. It can signify the commitment of a nation to remember its soldiers, to provide hope to their families that the same government that sent them to war will attempt to resolve their fate. Or it can indicate treacherous memory expressed in the rhetoric of self-pity: an attempt to transform the United States into an innocent and righteous victim of a war supposedly inflicted upon it. Other memories of the war are effaced; uncomfortable readings of history are ignored. The United States can position itself as the wounded party in the war, conveniently ignoring the undigested, and perhaps indigestible, realities of being party to the massive infliction of war upon Southeast Asia. In this reading, the POW/MIA flag stands for memorialized forgetting, and its presence at the Days of Remembrance ceremonies indicated that memory can be mobilized in order to destroy an uncomfortable or incriminating past.

MURDEROUS MEMORY

It is often assumed that memory of the stark horror of the Holocaust engenders *only* the commitment to avoid repetition. However, just as memory of the Holocaust has inspired and will inspire resistance to genocide, expressed in the phrase "Never again," the continued and widespread use of genocide as state policy is no less a use of Holocaust memory. Governments "remember" the Holocaust by making it a model for present action and future prospects. Organized hate groups mobilize Holocaust memory in their political rhetoric, hate literature, Nazi-style uniforms, adoration of Nazi leaders, and racist violence in the streets.

Consequently, the declaration "Never again"—which implies that Holocaust memory can serve to keep genocide from recurring, can prevent the eruption of the past into the present—is more accurately rendered, "Will it ever stop?"

HOPEFUL MEMORY

If official Holocaust memory does not often dramatically affect public policy, and if such memory can, in fact, serve as a convenient way of forgetting more threatening events, or, in the worst case, if it actually provides certain governments with a model of genocide applicable to contemporary problems, does the museum exist only to serve as a way for visitors to pay their respects to the Holocaust? Will it become just another tourist attraction in the nation's capital for visitors to consume, a part of what Erving Goffman calls "the ceremonial agenda of obligatory rites"? Will it function, in the words of Tom Freudenheim, assistant secretary of museums at the Smithsonian Institution, to enable people to "feel engaged without being engaged . . . encouraging us to live with the illusions we seek: namely that thoughtful observation is a substitute for active engagement"?

We continue to hope that the consequences of official Holocaust memory will not end with mere observation or acts of commemorative respect. Perhaps official Holocaust memory will serve individuals and communities as a stark reminder that extreme situations begin modestly, and so too do attempts to stop them. In this regard, recent events in Billings, Montana, are illuminating.

In 1993, this city with forty-eight Jewish families in a population of eighty-one thousand faced an explosion of racist violence. Skinheads disrupted services at the African Methodist Episcopal Church. With members of other hate groups, they mobilized Holocaust memory in their own fashion. Hate literature appeared in mailboxes; swastikas were placed on the door of Beth Aaron Synagogue, along with a photograph of a Jew kneeling at the edge of a mass grave, about to be executed by a member of a German mobile killing squad; and tombstones were vandalized in the synagogue's cemetery. Denial literature also appeared, creating a bizarre situation in which hate groups employed images of an event that their literature declared never took place. In November and December, the homes of two Jewish families—including one owned by the conductor of the Billings Symphony—decorated with Hanukkah menorahs, had windows broken. When a cinder block crashed into her children's room— "The lights were on, so you could see that it was a children's room," said Tammy Schnitzer—she immediately connected it with Nazi terror. "My God, is this Kristallnacht? Is this the night of broken glass? Is there going to be a death after this?"

The jarring intrusion of violence into their domestic life reminded Tammy's husband, Brian Schnitzer, of what black people had lived with for so long in the United States. "I'll bet many a black family slept with their babies under their bed every night. And we never knew it, never paid attention to it. . . . I can't go back to make that different. But I would like to think I'm not going to let it happen again."

Memory of the Holocaust motivated some members of the Christian community in Billings to counter the violence. Margaret MacDonald, executive director of the Montana Association of Churches, said that memory of the Holocaust was "absolutely present" in the response of many in the community to what was understood as an "insidious, virulent ideology." The Holocaust, she said, "offered us an example of where this kind of hatred ultimately leads."

Keith Torney, senior minister at the First Congregational Church in Billings, was angered by a suggestion that Jewish families take the menorahs out of their windows. He said, "The suggestion reminded me of what happened in Germany when people who may have had good intentions did not speak out."

With the notable exception of their more conservative brethren, local churches passed out printed copies of menorahs for their parishioners to hang in their windows. For a time, acts of violence increased. Windows of several homes and churches were broken, vehicles of those displaying the menorah were damaged, and owners were told on the phone, "Go look at your car, Jew-lover." In a December 5, 1993, sermon, Torney had asked his parishioners to join him in displaying a menorah. "I only know that I, and I hope many of you, will take a menorah and place it in your window. It might mean you will receive a brick through that window, it might mean late night telephone calls. . . . I will put a menorah in my window, for what happens to the Jew happens also to me." He was "touched" when he saw menorahs appear in windows throughout the city. "Many people understood the risk of participating," he said, "and many of them were willing to take the risk. I was surprised that some of the older people, particularly those who had no families for support, displayed them, for acts of intimidation were ugly."

The sporadic acts of violence and hate telephone calls spurred the *Billings Gazette* to publish a full-page menorah that could be cut out and displayed. Margaret MacDonald reported, "Small stores of all kinds started handing them out and I feel certain that thousands went into windows and doors at that time." Some businesses, she recalled, also put up signs that announced, "No hate in our community."

As more and more people placed the menorah in their window, Chief of Police Wayne Inman recalled, "it became physically impossible for the hate groups to harass and intimidate thousands and thousands of Billings citizens. . . . We have spoken out with one very loud voice."

The boundaries of Holocaust memory in Billings encompassed those who understood the Holocaust to be an appropriate model for a murderous vision of the American future, as well as those who understood the danger of indifference in the face of such a vision and would not be silent. Memory of the Holocaust, which, as we have seen, can be used as a weapon of exclusion—in, for example, rigid hierarchies of victims—was here used as a force for inclusion, as when, on Martin Luther King Day, many in the community were willing to march to express their support of Billings' black citizens. In dramatic fashion, they were also willing to "become Jewish" as an act of engagement, both with the Holocaust and with the life of their community. They spoke with a "very loud voice," the kind of courageous and compassionate voice that will need to be raised again and again if Holocaust memory is to serve us well.

NOTES

Paragraph numbering begins with the first full paragraph on each page.

INTRODUCTION

P. 3, ¶ 1. See, for example, Michael Kernan, "A National Memorial Bears Witness to the Tragedy of the Holocaust," *Smithsonian*, vol. 24, no. 1 (April 1993), pp. 54–62; Jonathan Rosen, "The Misguided Holocaust Museum," *New York Times*, April 18, 1993; George F. Will, "Telling Their Truth," *Washington Post*, April 22, 1993; Ken Ringle, "The Holocaust Museum: An Album of Agony," *Washington Post*, April 22, 1993; Lance Morrow, "Never Forget," *Time*, April 26, 1993, pp. 56–57; Kenneth L. Woodward, "We Are Witnesses," *Newsweek*, April 26, 1993, pp. 48–51; Leon Wieseltier, "After Memory," *New Republic*, vol. 208, no. 18 (May 3, 1993), pp. 16–26 (Wieseltier had been critical of the museum in an earlier article, "The Milk Can," *New Republic*, vol. 204, no. 16 [April 22, 1991], p. 47); Charles Krauthammer, "Holocaust: Memory and Resolve," *Time*, May 3, 1993, p. 84; Kay Larson, "Where Does It End?," *New York*, May 10, 1993, pp. 66–68; James Bowman, "American Notes," *Times Literary Supplement*, May 21, 1993; Edward Norden, "Yes and No to the Holocaust Museums," *Commentary*, vol. 96, no. 2 (Aug. 1993), pp. 23–32; Suzanne Slesin, "Through a Child's Eyes, History and Tragedy," *New York Times*, June 3, 1993; Philip Gourevitch, "Behold Now Behemoth," *Harper's*, July 1993, pp. 55–62; Stuart E. Eizenstat, "Holocaust Memorial Deserves Capital Place," *Christian Science Monitor*, April 28, 1993; Estelle Gilson, "Americanizing the Holocaust: The Museum in Washington," *Congress Monthly*, vol. 60, no. 6 (Sept.–Oct. 1993), pp. 3–6; Ken Johnson, "Art and Memory," *Art in America*, vol. 81, no. 11 (Nov. 1993), pp. 90–98. For children, see Sarah Jane Brian's "Museum Shows the Danger of Hate," *Scholastic News*, vol. 55, no. 23 (April 30, 1993), pp. 1–2; and for air travelers on United Airlines Chairman and Chief Executive Officer Stephen M. Wolf's "Guilt of the Bystander," *Hemispheres*, Aug. 1993, p. 11.

P. 5, ¶ 1. Raul Hilberg, "Developments in the Historiography of the

Holocaust," in Asher Cohen, Joav Gelber, and Charlotte Wardi, eds., *Comprehending the Holocaust: Historical and Literary Research* (Frankfurt am Main: Verlag Peter Lang, 1988), p. 21. Historian Gerd Korman notes: "In 1949 there was no 'Holocaust' in the English language in the sense that word is used today. Scholars and writers had used 'permanent pogrom' . . . or 'the recent catastrophe' or 'disaster.' " (Gerd Korman, "The Holocaust in American Historical Writing," *Societas*, vol. II, no. 3 [Summer 1972], p. 259.) See also "Names of the Holocaust: Meanings and Consequences," in James E. Young, *Writing and Rewriting the Holocaust: Narrative and the Consequences of Interpretation* (Bloomington: Indiana University Press, 1988), pp. 83–98. Robert H. Abzug, *Inside the Vicious Heart: Americans and the Liberation of Nazi Concentration Camps* (New York: Oxford University Press, 1985), p. 44.

P. 5, ¶ 2. I thank Benjamin Meed for allowing me to read his collected speeches in his office in New York City. Quoted material is from "After Forty Years We Are at Home," 1986.

P. 6, ¶ 1. Greenberg interview, Aug. 8, 1991. Holocaust memorial events did take place in public in New York City, however, even during the war. James E. Young noted that on December 2, 1942, "some five hundred thousand Jews in New York City stopped work for ten minutes, both to mourn those already killed and to call attention to the ongoing massacre." Other mass gatherings took place in New York during the war, and in 1947, Young reported, "tens of thousands of people" went to Riverside Park to attend the dedication of a Holocaust memorial, one that was never built. (James E. Young, *The Texture of Memory: Holocaust Memorials and Meaning* [New Haven: Yale University Press, 1993], pp. 287, 289.)

P. 7, ¶ 2. Henry Friedlander, "The Trials of the Nazi Criminals: Law, Justice, and History," *Dimensions: A Journal of Holocaust Studies*, vol. 2, no. 1 (Winter 1986), p. 5. See Leon A. Jick, "The Holocaust: Its Use and Abuse Within the American Public," *Yad Vashem Studies*, vol. 14 (1981), p. 305. Jick also noted that Paul Benzaquin's 1959 account of the tragic Cocoanut Grove nightclub fire in Boston in 1942 was titled *Fire in Boston's Cocoanut Grove: Holocaust!* (Boston: Branden Press, 1959). The word had not come, by 1959, to signify the extermination of European Jewry during World War II. In 1970, Gerd Korman complained that "America's textbook writing historians still do not understand the demands the death camps place on each of them as scholar and as educator of the young in our public schools and universities." He argued that texts did not deal with the culture of Eastern European Jewry, chronological charts did not offer information on Gentile-Jewish relations, and in maps of Europe "this special silence truly reigns supreme. . . . The maps are silent about Dachau and Buchenwald, Bergen-Belsen and Ravensbruck, Mauthausen and Theresienstadt and other camps where the Germans imprisoned and destroyed Jews." (See Gerd Korman, "Silence in American Textbooks," *Yad Vashem Studies*, vol. 8 [1970], pp. 183, 188–89.) More recently, Glenn Pate offered criticism of elementary-school, high-school, and college textbooks in the United States (Glenn S. Pate, "The United States of America," in Randolph L. Braham, ed., *The Treatment of the Holocaust in Textbooks: The Federal Republic of Germany, Israel, the United States of America* [New York: Columbia University Press, 1987], pp. 232–332).

P. 8, ¶ 1. Deborah E. Lipstadt, "The Holocaust: Symbol and Myth in American Jewish Life," *Forum on the Jewish People, Zionism and Israel*, vol. 40 (1980–81), p. 75. Jick, "Holocaust: Use and Abuse," p. 308. Stephen J. Whitfield, "The Holocaust and the American Jewish Intellectual," *Judaism*, vol. 28, no. 4 (Fall 1979), pp. 394–95. Whitfield also noted that in 1944, only a year after the Warsaw Ghetto uprising, a symposium of Jewish writers assembled by the *Contemporary Jewish Record* "expressed no sense of urgency, no sense of obligation, as writers or as Jews, to incorporate the experience of mass murder in their depictions of human actuality."

In *Commentary*'s 1966 symposium, Rabbi Richard Rubenstein, one of the first to grapple with the religious implications of the Holocaust, accurately predicted the coming emergence of the issue: "I do not think that the full impact of Auschwitz has yet been felt in Jewish theology or Jewish life. Great religious revolutions have their own periods of gestation. . . . No religious community can endure so hideous a wound without vast inner disorders." ("The State of Jewish Belief: A Symposium," *Commentary*, vol. 42, no. 2 [Aug. 1966], p. 134.)

P. 8, ¶ 2. For the history of the interpretation of Anne Frank in American culture, see Judith E. Doneson, "The American History of Anne Frank's Diary," *Holocaust and Genocide Studies*, vol. 2, no. 1 (1987), pp. 149–60; Alvin H. Rosenfeld, "Popularization and Memory: The Case of Anne Frank," in Peter Hayes, ed., *Lessons and Legacies: The Meaning of the Holocaust in a Changing World* (Evanston, Ill.: Northwestern University Press, 1991), pp. 243–78.

In Jeffrey Shandler's analysis, the episodes of the popular television series *This Is Your Life* in the 1950s and early 1960s that focused on Holocaust survivors and liberators (at least five) celebrated survivors' triumph over death, "unhaunted by anger, grief or guilt over the millions of dead" (" 'This Is Your Life': Telling a Holocaust Survivor's Life Story on Early American Television," *Journal of Narrative and Life History*, vol. 4, nos. 1 & 2 [1994], p. 64; I thank Mr. Shandler for a copy of his article).

P. 8, ¶ 3. Greenberg interview.

P. 8, ¶ 4. Dorothy Rabinowitz, *New Lives: Survivors of the Holocaust Living in America* (New York: Alfred A. Knopf, 1976), p. 193.

P. 9, ¶ 1. Abraham Joshua Heschel, *Israel: An Echo of Eternity* (New York: Farrar, Straus & Giroux, 1973), pp. 196–98.

P. 9, ¶ 2. Jacob Neusner, *Stranger at Home: "The Holocaust," Zionism, and American Judaism* (Chicago: University of Chicago Press, 1981), p. 63.

P. 10, ¶ 1. I am indebted to Peter Novick for this insight, during a conversation in the spring of 1991.

P. 10, ¶ 2. Rabinowitz, *New Lives*, p. 194.

P. 10, ¶ 4. Hilberg interview, Aug. 30, 1992; Raul Hilberg, "The Holocaust Today," B. G. Rudolph Lectures in Judaic Studies, Syracuse University, April 1988, p. 7.

P. 11, ¶ 1. See Aryeh Neier, *Defending My Enemy: American Nazis, the Skokie Case, and the Rise of Freedom* (New York: Dutton, 1979); David Hamlin, *The Nazi/Skokie Conflict: A Civil Liberties Battle* (Boston: Beacon Press, 1980).

P. 11, ¶ 2. Allan A. Ryan, Jr., *Quiet Neighbors: Prosecuting Nazi War Criminals in America* (San Diego: Harcourt Brace Jovanovich, 1984), pp. 335, 340.

P. 12, ¶ 1. Lance Morrow, "Television and the Holocaust," *Time*, May 1, 1978, p. 53; exchange between Elie Wiesel and scriptwriter Gerald Green, *New York Times*, April 16, 1978.

P. 12, ¶ 2. Judith Doneson, "American Films on the Holocaust: An Aid to Memory or Trivialization?," in *Remembering for the Future, Theme II: The Impact of the Holocaust on the Contemporary World* (Oxford: Pergamon Press, 1980), p. 1677; see also her chapter "Television and the Effects of Holocaust" in *The Holocaust in American Film* (Philadelphia: Jewish Publication Society, 1987); and her article "History and Television, 1978–1988: A Survey of Dramatization of the Holocaust," *Dimensions: A Journal of Holocaust Studies*, vol. 4, no. 3 (1988). See also the harsh judgments on the film made in the following: Charles Allen, Jr., " 'Holocaust': On Commercializing Genocide," *Martyrdom and Resistance*, vol. 4, no. 4 (May–June 1978), pp. 8, 10; Bernard Martin, "NBC's Holocaust: The Trivialization of the Tragic," *Journal of Reform Judaism*, Summer 1978, pp. 43–46; David R. Blumenthal, " 'Holocaust' and the Holocaust," *Martyrdom and Resistance*, vol. 5, no. 1 (Sept.–Oct. 1978), p. 8; Gitta Sereny, "BBC Condones Distorted History," *New Statesman*, vol. 29 (Aug. 1980); Aviva Cantor, "TV's 'Holocaust': A Sellout to Assimilation," *Lilith*, vol. 5 (1978), pp. 32–37; Lawrence L. Langer, "The Americanization of the Holocaust on Stage and Screen," in Sara Blacher Cohen, ed., *From Hester Street to Hollywood: The Jewish-American Stage and Screen* (Bloomington: Indiana University Press, 1983), pp. 213–30. Keith Bird discusses *Holocaust*'s impact in Germany in "Germany Awakes: The 'Holocaust'—Background and Aftermath," *Shoah*, vol. 1, no. 4 (Summer 1979), pp. 5–9. The Irving Greenberg quotation is from "Letters from Readers," *Commentary*, vol. 71, no. 6 (June 1981), p. 5.

P. 12, ¶ 4. Jacob Neusner, *The Jewish War Against the Jews: Reflections on Golah, Shoah, and Torah* (New York: Ktav Publishing House), 1984, p. 56.

P. 13, ¶ 1. Yaffa Eliach, "President's Commission on the Holocaust: Reflections," n.d., Yaffa Eliach Papers. I thank Yaffa Eliach for sharing this material with me.

P. 14, ¶ 2. John Murray Cuddihy, "The Elephant and the Angels, or The Incivil Irritatingness of Jewish Theodicy," in Robert N. Bellah and Frederick E. Greenspahn, eds., *Uncivil Religion: Interreligious Hostility in America* (New York: Crossroad, 1987), p. 32; John Murray Cuddihy, "The Holocaust: The Latent Issue in the Uniqueness Debate," in Philip F. Gallagher, ed., *Christians, Jews and Other Worlds: Patterns of Conflicts and Accommodation* (Lanham, Md.: University Press of America, 1988), p. 77. I am indebted to Peter Novick for bringing this last article to my attention. James Baldwin's quotation comes from his "My Sister, Angela Davis," *New York Times*, Jan. 7, 1971; see also the response by Shlomo Katz, "An Open Letter to James Baldwin," *Midstream*, vol. 12, no. 4 (April 1971); James Baldwin and Shlomo Katz, "Of Angela Davis and the Jewish Housewife Headed for Dachau," *Midstream*, vol. 6 (June–July 1971), pp. 3–9. Even the *Holocaust* miniseries engendered black resentment. In Letty Cottin Pogrebin's *Deborah, Golda, and Me: Being Female and Jewish in America* (New York: Crown Publishers, 1991), a black friend tells her, "Over and over again I heard blacks complain that the . . . mini-series on television was the Jews' way of stealing the spotlight from *Roots*" (p. 225).

P. 14, ¶ 3. Marc H. Ellis, *Ending Auschwitz: The Future of Jewish and Christian Life* (Louisville: Westminster and John Knox Press, 1994), p. 24. See Robert Alter, "The Masada Complex," *Commentary*, vol. 56, no. 1 (July 1973), p. 20; Robert Alter, "Deformations of the Holocaust," *Commentary*, vol. 71, no. 2 (Feb. 1981), pp. 48–54. For a brief overview of some of the debates, see Paula E. Hyman, "New Debate on the Holocaust," *New York Times Magazine*, Sept. 14, 1979. See also Ellis's *Beyond Innocence and Redemption: Confronting the Holocaust and Israeli Power* (New York: Harper and Row, 1990), and *Towards a Theology of Jewish Liberation: The Uprising and the Future* (Maryknoll, N.Y.: Orbis Books, 1989). See also Paul Breines, *Tough Jews: Political Fantasies and the Moral Dilemma of American Jewry* (New York: Basic Books, 1990). Similar concerns about the role of Holocaust memory in Israel are raised in Tom Segev, *The Seventh Million: The Israelis and the Holocaust* (New York: Hill and Wang, 1993), and Avishai Margalit, "The Kitsch of Israel," *New York Review of Books*, vol. 35, no. 18 (Nov. 24, 1988), pp. 20–24.

P. 15, ¶ 1. Neusner, *Stranger at Home*, p. 85. Greenberg is quoted in "Holocaust Remembrance in Local Communities," *Shoah*, Fall–Winter, 1981–82, p. 17.

P. 15, ¶ 2. For an introduction to these issues, see "The Silence of God: Philosophical and Religious Reflection on the Holocaust," in Richard L. Rubenstein and John K. Roth, *Approaches to Auschwitz: The Holocaust and*

Its Legacy (Atlanta: John Knox Press, 1987), pp. 290–336; John K. Roth and Michael Berenbaum, eds., *Holocaust: Religious and Philosophical Implications* (New York: Paragon House, 1989). One of the first major Holocaust conferences in the United States focused on the religious legacy of the Holocaust. See Eva Fleischner, ed., *Auschwitz: Beginning of a New Era? Reflections on the Holocaust* (New York: Ktav Publishing House, 1977).

CHAPTER ONE

P. 17, ¶ 1. For those who continue to read the story more cynically, Michael Berenbaum, former deputy director of the commission, project director of the museum, and appointed director of the United States Holocaust Research Institute in 1993, wrote, "Jewish tradition has always recognized mixed motives and sought to utilize them in positive ways; the rabbis have continually negotiated between realpolitik and prophetic demands. They taught: 'That which is originally done not for its own sake may come to be done for its own sake.' " (Michael Berenbaum, *After Tragedy and Triumph: Modern Jewish Thought and the American Experience* [Cambridge: Cambridge University Press, 1990], p. 41.)

P. 17, ¶ 2. Siegel interview, Jan. 29, 1992. Goldstein to Siegel, June 21, 1977. I thank Ellen Goldstein for providing me with a copy of this memorandum. The Genocide Treaty, which had the support of many nations, had been introduced for ratification in the United States Senate by President Truman in 1949. It had failed, in large part because of fear that it could be applied to domestic civil-rights violations. It finally passed in 1986, when the Reagan administration reversed its previous opposition. See Haynes Johnson, "The Genocide Treaty: Still Not Ratified 34 Years Later," in *The Obligation to Remember: The American Gathering of Jewish Holocaust Survivors in Washington, D.C., April 14, 1983* (Washington, D.C.: Washington Post, 1983); Hyman Bookbinder, *Off the Wall: Memoirs of a Public Affairs Junkie* (Washington, D.C.: Seven Locks Press, 1991).

P. 18, ¶ 1. Rochelle Saidel, "The Genesis of the U.S. Holocaust Memorial Museum: A Case Study of the Politics of Memorializing the Holocaust," paper delivered at 23rd Annual Scholars Conference on the Holocaust, University of Tulsa, March 7, 1993, p. 5. Excerpts from Siegel's resignation letter are found in "Resignation—He Had No Choice," *Near East Report*, vol. 22, no. 44 (March 15, 1978), p. 44. I thank Mark Siegel for giving me a copy of the full letter.

P. 18, ¶ 2. Goldstein to Eizenstat, March 28, 1978, Goldstein files.

P. 19, ¶ 1. Elzenstat to Wiesel, Feb. 15, 1980, Eizenstat, box 216, Holocaust Memorial Commission (CS, O/A-728); Lipshutz and Eizenstat to Carter, April 25, 1978, Staff Offices Counsel Lipshutz, box 18, Holocaust Memorial Commission, 4/77–12/78 (CF, O/A-437), Carter Library.

P. 19, ¶ 2. "The White House: Remarks of the President and His Excellency Menachem Begin, The Prime Minister of Israel, at White House Reception Honoring Prime Minister Begin and Jewish Leaders, May 1, 1978, 2:10 pm," Press release, author's files.

P. 20, ¶ 1. Goldstein to Eizenstat, May 2, 1978, Goldstein files.

P. 20, ¶ 2. Goldstein to Eizenstat, May 10, 1978, Goldstein files. Krieger would eventually serve as executive director of the council from April 1986 to Feb. 1987.

P. 20, ¶ 3. Goldstein to Eizenstat, May 10, 1978. Goldstein attached an initial list of possible commission members. The categories were: former and current government officials, historians and educators, arts and letters, science, Nuremberg trials and camp survivors, fine arts, writers and commentators, religious leaders, prominent Democrats, business and labor, and "other" recommendations. Of the eighty people named on this list, thirteen would eventually be appointed to the commission—Kitty Dukakis; Justice Arthur Goldberg; Senator Henry Jackson; Representative Stephen Solarz; historians Lucy Dawidowicz and Raul Hilberg; Elie Wiesel; writer Isaac Bashevis Singer; Dr. Hadassah Rosensaft, a survivor; Telford Taylor, who directed the proceedings of the American Military Court trials at Nuremberg; Hyman Bookbinder, Washington representative of the American Jewish Committee; Father Theodore Hesburgh, president of Notre Dame; Rabbi Bernard Raskas of St. Paul, Minnesota—and two would be appointed to the advisory board, Richard Krieger and Steven Ludsin, son of survivors, and founder of the Holocaust Remembrance Foundation, respectively. Interestingly, only Rosensaft and Wiesel were survivors; Senator Jackson, a member of the House of Representatives at the time, was brought by Eisenhower to Buchenwald in the immediate aftermath of the war.

Goldstein clearly felt other plans threatened the president's initiative. On July 17, 1978, she told Lipshutz and Eizenstat, "Senator Anderson is being pressured to pursue his legislation; this could be embarrassing to the President" (Staff Offices Counsel Lipshutz, box 18, Holocaust Memorial Commission, 4/77–12/78 [CF, O/A-437], Carter Library).

P. 21, ¶ 1. Krim's reply recorded by hand in Goldstein to Lipshutz, May 31, 1978; Goldberg's recommendation in Lipshutz to Eizenstat, June 13, 1978; Starr to Goldstein, June 16, 1978; Eizenstat and Lipshutz to Tim Kraft, July 20, 1978, all in Staff Offices Counsel Lipshutz, Carter Library.

P. 21, ¶ 2. Goldstein to Eizenstat, July 26, 1978, Eizenstat, box 216, Holocaust Memorial Commission (O/A-6242) (2), Carter Library; Wiesel interview, March 15, 1993. Wiesel tried to get Carter to agree to an annual joint session of Congress in remembrance of the Holocaust, but settled on an annual memorial ceremony. Carter, of course, did not have the power to authorize congressional ceremonies.

P. 22, ¶ 2. Quoted material in previous two paragraphs from Eizenstat and

Lipshutz to Tim Kraft, n.d., Staff Offices Counsel Lipshutz, box 18, Holocaust Memorial Commission, 4/77–12/78 (CF, O/A-437), Carter Library; Greenberg to Eizenstat, Aug. 16, 1978, Eizenstat, box 216, Holocaust Commission (O/A-6242) (2), Carter Library; Goldstein to Eizenstat, Aug. 25, 1978, Eizenstat, box 216, Holocaust Commission (O/A-6242) (2), Carter Library.

P. 23, ¶ 1. Goldstein to Eizenstat, Oct. 16, 1978, Eizenstat, box 216, Holocaust Commission (O/A-6242) (2) Carter Library; Eizenstat and Lipshutz to Mondale, Oct. 18, 1978; Carter's note in Lipshutz and Eizenstat to the President, Sept. 18, 1978, Staff Offices, Offices of Staff Secretary, box 107, Hand Writing File, 10/25/78, Carter Library.

P. 23, ¶ 2. Text of executive order found in *Report to the President: President's Commission on the Holocaust*, Washington, D.C., Sept. 27, 1979, (hereafter *Report to the President*), p. 20. Although the museum would be built with donated funds, both the commission and the council were funded by appropriated funds. Commission funding came from the Department of Interior. Secretary of the Interior Cecil B. Andrus informed his assistant secretary for fish and wildlife and parks on June 21, 1978, "I am requesting the reprogramming of funds [$125,000] from the National Park Service's operating funds for the support of the Commission" (Federal Gov't—Organizations box, FG 225, 1/20/77–6/30/79, Carter Library). The budget was eventually raised to $175,000.

P. 23, ¶ 3. Greenberg to Eizenstat, Nov. 30, 1978, Federal Gov't—Organizations box FG 221, 1/20/77–6/30/79, Carter Library; Sanders to Eizenstat, Nov. 30, 1978, Special Advisor to the President Moses, box 7, Holocaust Memorial Council, 1/27/78–4/27/79, Carter Library.

P. 24, ¶ 1. Yaffa Eliach, "President's Commission on the Holocaust: Reflections," n.d., p. 3, Yaffa Eliach Papers.

P. 24, ¶ 2. Commissioners' written comments in President's Commission on the Holocaust, United States Holocaust Memorial Council miscellaneous files, box 15, "Commissioners' views—staff summary: February 6, 1979." Berenbaum to Wiesel, Feb. 6, 1979, Wiesel files.

P. 25, ¶ 1. President's Commission on the Holocaust transcript, Feb. 15, 1979, p. 140 (hereafter PCOHT). On Lerman's life, see Carol Horner, "Make Sure We're Not Forgotten," *Philadelphia Inquirer*, March 28, 1993; "Making a Holocaust Memorial a Reality," *New York Times*, May 28, 1993; "Memory of Atrocities Haunts New Holocaust Council Leader," *Jewish Exponent*, June 4, 1993.

P. 25, ¶ 2. PCOHT, Feb. 15, 1979, pp. 7, 126.

P. 26, ¶ 1. Greenberg to Gabriel Cohen, April 13, 1979, President's Commission on the Holocaust miscellaneous files (hereafter PCOH-mf), box 15, "composition of the commission"; Krol to Greenberg, April 2, 1979, Yaffa Eliach Papers.

P. 27, ¶ 1. Blanchard quoted in PCOHT, Feb. 15, 1979, p. 106;

Berenbaum's quote in "Memos from Michael Berenbaum, President's Commission on Holocaust," Feb. 8, 1979, Wiesel files.

P. 27, ¶ 2. Carter quotes from appendixes to *Report to the President*, passim.

P. 28, ¶ 1. Berenbaum interview, June 1, 1992.

P. 29, ¶ 1. Isaac Goodfriend, "Returning to the Unknown," PCOH-mf, box 15, "Trip to Holocaust Memorials"; Hadassah Rosensaft, "My Journey into the Past," *Midstream*, April 1980, p. 26.

P. 29, ¶ 2 and 3. Quoted material from preceding two paragraphs from Benjamin Meed, "The President's Commission on the Holocaust in Poland and the Soviet Union," PCOH-mf, box 15, "Trip to Holocaust Memorials."

P. 30, ¶ 1. First quote is from ibid.; the second, Elie Wiesel, "Pilgrimage to the Country of Night," *New York Times Magazine*, Nov. 4, 1979. Commenting on discussion with Polish officials, Raul Hilberg said that the Polish government neither denies the Holocaust nor obscures the fact that Jews died, but "will remind the world of the Poles who died as Poles, and it will present the two fates in a formula suggesting parity" (Raul Hilberg, "The Holocaust Mission," PCOH-mf, box 15, "Trip to Holocaust Memorials").

Some of the documents shown to commissioners by the Polish minister of justice, Jerzy Bafia, strained even their endurance. Meed recalled the family photograph album of a German officer that included "photographs of his family from his early childhood, through church ceremonials, weddings, etc. The second part . . . contained pictures relating to his military activities . . . executions, shooting of Jews, walking among the corpses of his victims, all carefully and proudly arranged to show the story of his life." (Meed, "President's Commission on Holocaust in Poland and Soviet Union.")

P. 30, ¶ 2. Wiesel, "Pilgrimage to the Country of Night"; Hilberg, "Holocaust Mission."

P. 30, ¶ 3. Goodfriend, "Returning to the Unknown"; Wiesel, "Pilgrimage to the Country of Night"; Hilberg, "Holocaust Mission."

P. 30, ¶ 4. Meed, "President's Commission on Holocaust in Poland and Soviet Union"; Lily Edelman, "In Search of Memory," *ADL Bulletin*, vol. 26 (Oct. 1979), p. 14.

P. 31, ¶ 1. Meed, "President's Commission on Holocaust in Poland and Soviet Union"; Rosensaft, "My Journey."

P. 32, ¶ 1. Wiesel, "Pilgrimage to the Country of Night"; Bookbinder, *Off the Wall*, p. 98.

P. 32, ¶ 2. Meed, "President's Commission on Holocaust in Poland and Soviet Union"; see also Hilberg's recollections of discussions with Soviet officials in "Holocaust Mission." Rustin vigorously objected to a visit scheduled to Lenin's Tomb, refusing to get off the bus.

P. 33, ¶ 1. Roy and Alice Eckardt, "Travail of a Presidential Commission Confronting the Enigma of the Holocaust," *Encounter*, vol. 42, no. 2 (Spring 1981), pp. 110, 113.

P. 33, ¶ 2. Gideon Hausner, "Opening Address to the First World Council of Yad Vashem, August 9, 1979," Wiesel files.

P. 34, ¶ 1. Hyman Bookbinder, "From Auschwitz to Jerusalem," Washington Hebrew Congregation, Sept. 7, 1979, "Trip to Holocaust Sites," PCOH-mf. For insightful comments on the function of tours to Holocaust sites for both American Jews and Israelis, see Jack Kugelmass, "The Rites of the Tribe: American Jewish Tourism in Poland," in Ivan Karp, Christine Mullen Kreamer, and Steven D. Lavine, eds., *Museums and Communities: The Politics of Public Culture* (Washington, D.C.: Smithsonian Institution Press, 1992), pp. 382–427; Tom Segev, *The Seventh Million: The Israelis and the Holocaust* (New York: Hill and Wang, 1993), pp. 487–507.

P. 36, ¶ 1. Richard L. Rubenstein, *The Cunning of History: The Holocaust and the American Future* (New York: Harper and Row, 1975), pp. 6, 36; other quoted material in preceding two paragraphs from *Report to the President*, passim.

P. 38, ¶ 1. Quoted material in the preceding four paragraphs from *Report to the President*, passim.

P. 39, ¶ 1. Mazewski to Greenberg, April 12, 1979. I thank Father John T. Pawlikowski for a copy of this letter.

P. 39, ¶ 2. Slotkowski to Greenberg, March 30, 1979; Berenbaum to Slotkowski, May 23, 1979; both in Pawlikowski files. Father John T. Pawlikowski, professor of social ethics at Catholic Theological Union, who had written widely on Jewish-Christian relations and was a member of Greenberg's Zachor Holocaust project, was an observer at the first commission meeting; like Mazewski, he would become a member of the council.

P. 40, ¶ 1. Bolten to Sanders, Sept. 18, 1979, Special Advisor to the President Moses, Box 1, Holocaust Memorial Council, 4/28/79–9/27/79, Carter Library. Greenberg to Eizenstat, Sept. 21, 1979, Federal Gov't—Organizations box FG 225, 1/20/77–6/30/79, Carter Library.

P. 40, ¶ 2. Letter to President Carter, Sept. 20, 1979, box 15, PCOH-mf.

P. 41, ¶ 1. Information on Eizenstat's Oct. 25, 1979, memorandum to the president taken from letter from Wiesel to Eizenstat, Sept. 29, 1980, in which Wiesel quoted Eizenstat's words. I thank Monroe Freedman for providing a copy of this letter. The first mention of the two estimates of Jewish victims—5.7 million and six million—is found, according to the council's senior historian, Sybil Milton, in the records of the International Military Tribunal at Nuremberg. "The first published figures were based on extrapolations of pre-war and postwar populations as well as on fragmentary information derived from captured German records evaluated and used by the Allied prosecution team at Nuremberg. American prosecutor Justice Robert Jackson used 5.7 million," and the six-million figure, "attributed to Eichmann," was used by the tribunal in 1946. "This 6 million figure," Milton wrote, "is based on an affidavit at Nuremberg, dated 26 November 1945, by SS Major

(Sturmbahnführer) Dr. Wilhelm Höttl. Höttl had previously served as deputy director of the Security Service (SD) branch in Budapest. Höttl stated that Eichmann mentioned the 6 million figure to him in Budapest in late August 1944." I thank Sybil Milton for a copy of her memorandum.

P. 41, ¶ 2. Berenbaum to Sanders, Nov. 16, 1979, Special Advisor to the President Moses, box 7, Holocaust Memorial Council, 11/2/79–9/2/80, Carter Library.

P. 42, ¶ 2. Quoted material in the preceding two paragraphs from Freedman interview, March 15, 1993.

P. 43, ¶ 2. Material in the preceding two paragraphs from Bolten to Eizenstat and Sanders, Nov. 30, 1979, Eizenstat, box 216, Holocaust (CS, O/A-723), Carter Library. Bolten had long been uneasy with what he considered a restrictive definition of the Holocaust. Only several weeks before his meeting with Wiesel, he attached a copy of a *Time* article, "The Nazis' Forgotten Victims" (Nov. 19, 1979), on the experience of Gypsies in the Holocaust and their continued persecution in Germany in a handwritten note to Sanders and asked him, "How does our Holocaust definition look in the light of this article?" (Bolten to Sanders, Nov. 15, 1979, Special Adviser to the President Moses, box 7, Holocaust Memorial Council, 11/2/79–9/2/80, Carter Library).

P. 43, ¶ 3. Wiesel to Eizenstat, May 5, 1980. I thank Monroe Freedman for providing a copy of this letter. See Freedman's various accusations against Berenbaum in "Michael Berenbaum's 'Distortions of the Holocaust,' " *Midstream*, May 1991, pp. 47–48.

P. 44, ¶ 1. Berenbaum interviews, Feb. 8, 1994, April 14, 1994.

P. 44, ¶ 2. Berenbaum interview, April 14, 1994.

P. 45, ¶ 2, 3. Monroe H. Freedman, "Memorandum for the File," April 3, 1980. I thank Monroe Freedman for providing me with a copy of this.

P. 46, ¶ 1. Eizenstat, box 216, Holocaust (CS, O/A-723), Carter Library.

P. 46, ¶ 2. Bolten to Eizenstat and Rubenstein, Feb. 5, 1980, Eizenstat, box 216, Holocaust (CS, O/A-728), Carter Library. The details of a meeting between Freedman, Berenbaum, and a representative of the Ukrainian Anti-Defamation League are found in a memorandum from Sanders and Freedman to Eizenstat, Jan. 24, 1980, Federal Gov't Organizations, boxes FG-231, FG 352, 1/20/77–1/20/81, Carter Library. The same file contains a memorandum from Freedman to Eizenstat on Feb. 1, 1980, which mentions the "intensive search" for ethnic representatives, and lists various groups contacted.

P. 47, ¶ 1. Eizenstat to Wiesel, Feb. 15, 1980; Freedman to Eizenstat, Feb. 19, 1980; both in Eizenstat, box 216, Holocaust (CS, O/A-728), Carter Library.

P. 47, ¶ 2. The handwritten response from Rubenstein to Eizenstat, and memorandum from Eizenstat to Freedman—both undated—are in Eizenstat, box 216, Holocaust (CS, O/A-728), Carter Library.

The White House was under pressure not only from ethnic groups who demanded representation on the council, but from those who opposed such a move. On Feb. 27, 1980, a worried Robert Strauss, chair of the Carter/Mondale Presidential Committee, Inc., informed Eizenstat about a cable from the former commission member Alfred Gottschalk, president of Hebrew Union College: "Current White House thinking on this council will lead to public rejection of plan by representative leaders of organized Jewish community and members of President Carter's original Holocaust Commission." No doubt Strauss, deeply involved in the presidential campaign, understood that a vote of no confidence in the project from a group supportive of Democratic candidates might well translate into fewer votes in November. (Domestic Policy Staff, Eizenstat, box 216, Holocaust [CS, O/A 728], Carter Library.)

P. 47, ¶ 3. See Roberta Strauss Feuerlicht, *The Fate of the Jews: A People Torn Between Israeli Power and Jewish Ethics* (New York: Times Books, 1983); Morris Fine and Milton Himmelfarb, eds., *American Jewish Yearbook* (New York: American Jewish Committee, 1978–80); Edward Tivnan, *The Lobby: Jewish Political Power and American Foreign Policy* (New York: Simon and Schuster, 1987).

P. 48, ¶ 2. Wiesel to Eizenstat, Sept. 29, 1980; Eizenstat to Wiesel, Oct. 22, 1980. The Hungarian referred to was not Tibor Baranski, whom Wiesel supported. I thank Monroe Freedman for providing me with a copy of Wiesel's memorandum and Eizenstat's response.

P. 49, ¶ 1. Monroe Freedman, memorandum "for the file," April 3, 1980.

P. 49, ¶ 2. Freedman's detailed history of the language controversy is in ibid.

P. 50, ¶ 1. Rubenstein to the President, March 21, 1980, Office of Staff Secretary, box 176, President's Hand-Writing file, folder 3/21/80 (2), Carter Library.

Language used to define the Holocaust in "official" correspondence changed according to the interest of the writer and the intended audience. In an undated letter from Carter to Wiesel, asking him to chair the council, the president used Wiesel's "dash" formula. A press release from the White House announcing the membership of the council defined the Holocaust as the extermination of six million Jews and the "murders of millions of other people," and a council press release on May 5, 1980, spoke of a memorial to the six million Jews, and "appropriate regard" to "other victims of genocide in the Twentieth Century."

In other contexts, the attempt was to lessen, rather than widen, conceptual distance between victims. In 1984, for example, the chairman of the National Republican Heritage (Nationalities) Group informed President Reagan that the *commission* [*sic*] should include "representatives of all American ethnic communities whose nationalities suffered persecution and death in holocausts." The White House response revised the council's mandate to read, "the systematic murder of six million Jews, and the murder by the Nazis of millions of others representing a score of nationalities during World War II."

P. 51, ¶ 1. Wiesel to Eizenstat, May 5, 1980. I thank Monroe Freedman for providing me with a copy of this memorandum.

P. 53, ¶ 1. PCOHT, April 24, 1979, p. 126.

P. 53, ¶ 2. Wiesel's words quoted in Bookbinder to Wiesel, April 26, 1979, Staff Offices Counsel Lipschutz, box 18, Holocaust Memorial Commission, 4/77–12/78 (CF, O/A-437), Carter Library.

P. 54, ¶ 1. Yehuda Bauer, *The Holocaust in Historical Perspective* (Seattle: University of Washington Press, 1978), p. 38; Yehuda Bauer, "Whose Holocaust?," *Midstream*, vol. 26, no. 9 (Nov. 1980), p. 46; Henryk Grynberg, "Appropriating the Holocaust," *Commentary*, vol. 74, no. 5 (Nov. 1982), pp. 56–57. See also Uriel Tal, "Holocaust and Genocide," *Yad Vashem Studies*, vol. 13 (1979), pp. 7–52. Likewise, Henry L. Feingold worried that the Holocaust would be "subsumed under a generalized scream of ethnic pain" ("Determining the Uniqueness of the Holocaust: The Factor of Historical Valence," *Shoah*, vol. 2, no. 2 [1981], n.p.).

P. 54, ¶ 2. Irving Greenberg, "The Dialectics of Power: Reflections in the Light of the Holocaust," in Daniel Landes, ed., *Confronting Omnicide: Jewish Reflections on Weapons of Mass Destruction* (Northvale, N.J.: Jason Aronson, 1991), p. 19. Bauer, "Whose Holocaust?," p. 45; Freedman, "The Particular Holocaust," *Moment*, vol. 5, no. 6 (June 1980), p. 61.

CHAPTER TWO

P. 57, ¶ 1. *A National Commitment to Remembrance: Official Ground-breaking* (Washington, D.C.: United States Holocaust Memorial Council, 1986), pp. 9, 17. The idea of a ceremonial burial of earth containing remains of Holocaust victims was discussed in the work of the President's Commission on the Holocaust in 1979. The burial of this symbolically charged earth, it was felt, would provide a ceremonial link between contemporary Americans and Holocaust victims. For survivors, it would be a "symbolic burial of their kin who perished and were never properly buried" ("Summary of Views received to date 3/21/79: Museums and Monuments," box 15, Holocaust Museum—1979, Commission History, PCOH-mf. Even this "quest for remembrance" was not without controversy, however. One survivor denounced the mix of ashes used: "Included were ashes from concentration camps for political prisoners and the Jews . . . but excluded [were] those from strictly Jewish death centers" (Henryk Grynberg, "Don't Universalize the Holocaust Memorial!," *Midstream*, vol. 32, no. 4 (April 1986), p. 7).

P. 57, ¶ 2. Dawidowicz's statement in "opening and closing remarks, Elie Wiesel," box 15, pp. 5–6, PCOH-mf; Eliach's statement in "Subcommittee: museum & monument," box 20, PCOH-mf, p. 5; statement of the president of senior citizens' club in PCOHT, April 24, 1979, pp. 47–48. I thank Elie Wiesel for allowing me to read these transcripts in his office at Boston University.

P. 58, ¶ 2. Quoted material in the preceding two paragraphs from Bookbinder and Bernstein, "Subcommittee: museum & monument," box 20, PCOH-mf; various concerns expressed in "Summary of views received to date (3/21/79)," box 15, Holocaust Museum—1979, Commission History, PCOH-mf; Michael Berenbaum to Elie Wiesel, June 5, 1979, Berenbaum files. As early as April 22, 1979, Berenbaum had advised Wiesel that it was "important that we receive Commission consensus for Washington, D.C., rather than New York so that the debate can be over once and for all" (Michael Berenbaum to Elie Wiesel, April 22, 1979, "Memos from Michael Berenbaum, President's Commission on the Holocaust," Wiesel files).

P. 59, ¶ 3. Dawidowicz's statement in "opening and closing remarks, Elie Wiesel," box 15, pp. 5–6, PCOH-mf; Schatz's statement in PCOHT, Feb. 15, 1979, pp. 72–73.

P. 60, ¶ 1. PCOHT, April 24, 1979, p. 12.

P. 60, ¶ 2. "Summary of views received to date (3/21/79)," PCOH-mf; site-selection folder, p. 6, United States Holocaust Memorial Museum Files (hereafter HMMF).

P. 60, ¶ 3. Talisman interview, Aug. 1, 1991. Previously, Talisman had for thirteen years been administrative assistant to Congressman Charles Vanik of Ohio, and helped draft the Jackson-Vanik amendment, which linked special-trade and most-favored-nation status for the Soviet Union with Soviet Jewish emigration policy.

P. 61, ¶ 1. United States Holocaust Memorial Council transcript (hereafter HMCT), April 30, 1981, pp. 20, 17.

P. 61, ¶ 2. HMCT, Sept. 24, 1981, p. 8.

P. 63, ¶ 1. HMCT, Dec. 2, 1982, pp. 14, 17.

P. 63, ¶ 2. Written responses to fund-raising materials found in "DM Sample Letters—incoming," HMMF. Hirsch quoted in *Atlanta Jewish Times*, May 15, 1992. Letter in *Washington Post*, July 10, 1987.

P. 64, ¶ 1. Letter to President Ronald Reagan, March 6, 1983, HMMF; two quotes from *Time*, July 20, 1987; Peter D. Hart Research Associates, Inc., "Materials from Focus Groups Conducted for the U.S. Holocaust Memorial Museum," HMMF; Avineri's article, originally published in *Jerusalem Post*, was carried on July 17, 1987, in *Jewish Week*, and letters in response are found in the Aug. 7 issue.

P. 65, ¶ 1. Howard Husock, "Red, White, and Jew: Holocaust Museum on the Mall," *Tikkun*, vol. 5, no. 4 (July–Aug. 1990), pp. 34, 92; Hart, "Materials from Focus Groups."

P. 65, ¶ 2. Bloomfield's letter in *Washington Post*, March 24, 1990, was in response to Richard Cohen's *Post* article of March 14, 1990, in which he said that the museum was "extraneous to the broad American experience."

P. 65, ¶ 3. George F. Will, "Holocaust Museum: Antidote for Innocence," *Washington Post*, March 10, 1983.

P. 65, ¶ 4. "Braden Report," April 23–24, 1983, HMMF.

P. 66, ¶ 1. Levine interview, May 3, 1992.

P. 66, ¶ 2. Hart, "Materials from Focus Groups."

P. 67, ¶ 1. Lance Morrow, "The Morals of Remembering," *Time*, May 23, 1983, p. 88; Rustin, *New York Times*, May 18, 1984. The council's fund-raising literature—letters, color brochures—usually included either a map of the Mall and the location of the museum, or a picture of the Mall, usually with the Washington Monument as a point of orientation, and an indicative mark of the museum's location. One large fund-raising booklet, *The Campaign for the United States Holocaust Memorial Museum*, stated that the museum belonged "at the center of American life because as a democratic civilization America is the enemy of racism and its ultimate expression, genocide" (author's files). In a fund-raising videotape, *Campaign to Remember*, narrated by ABC's Ted Koppel, the museum was linked visually with the Lincoln, Jefferson, and Iwo Jima memorials and the Washington Monument. Koppel said that the museum would teach visitors that "racism and hatred didn't disappear," and that the museum was "essential for the future of this country." (Author's files.)

P. 67, ¶ 2. James E. Young discusses the interplay between site and monument in various American projects—including Rapoport's—in *The Texture of Memory: Holocaust Memorials and Meaning* (New Haven: Yale University Press, 1993).

P. 68, ¶ 1. L'Enfant's plan for the Mall is in a letter to George Washington, June 22, 1791. His comment on the "Grand Avenue" is found in almost any discussion of the L'Enfant plan. See, for example, Paul D. Spreiregen, ed., *On the Art of Designing Cities: Selected Essays of Elbert Peets* (Cambridge, Mass.: MIT Press, 1968), p. 88.

P. 68, ¶ 2. Pamela Scott, " 'This Vast Empire': The Iconography of the Mall, 1791–1848," in Richard Longstreth, ed., *The Mall in Washington, 1791–1991* (Hanover, N.H.: University Press of New England, 1991), p. 46; George J. Olszewski, *History of the Mall, Washington, D.C.* (Washington, D.C.: Office of History and Historic Architecture, United States Department of the Interior, National Park Service, 1970), p. 25.

P. 68, ¶ 3. Quoted in Constance M. Green, *The Secret City: A History of Race Relations in the Nation's Capital* (Princeton: Princeton University Press, 1967), p. 28.

P. 68, ¶ 4. The description of Downing's plan is found in Therese O'Malley, " 'A Public Museum of Trees': Mid-Nineteenth Century Plans for the Mall," in Longstreth, ed., *Mall in Washington*, p. 65. Downing quoted in John W. Reps, *Monumental Washington: The Planning and Development of the Capital Center* (Princeton: Princeton University Press, 1967), p. 53.

P. 70, ¶ 1. Quotations in this and the preceding paragraph from Jon A. Peterson, "The Hidden Origins of the McMillan Plan for Washington, D.C., 1900–1902," in Antoinette J. Lee, ed., *Historical Perspectives on Urban Design: Washington, D.C. 1890–1910*, occasional paper no. 1 (Washington, D.C.: Center for Washington Area Studies, George Washington University, 1983), pp. 3, 8. This is, of course, only a brief characterization of the McMillan Plan. See also Frederick Gutheim, *Worthy of the Nation: The History of the Planning for the National Capital* (Washington, D.C.: Smithsonian Institution Press, 1977); Thomas S. Hines, "The Imperial Mall: The City Beautiful Movement and the Washington Plan of 1901–1902," Jon A. Peterson, "The Mall, the McMillan Plan, and the Origins of American City Planning," and David C. Streatfield, "The Olmsteds and the Landscape of the Mall," all in Longstreth, ed., *Mall in Washington*.

P. 70, ¶ 2. Gutheim, *Worthy of the Nation*, p. 135.

P. 71, ¶ 1. Public Law 101–185, Nov. 28, 1989, sec. 3; Claudine Brown, comp., "Final Report of the African American Institutional Study," Smithsonian Institution, 1991, p. 1.

P. 71, ¶ 2. Savage spoke on a Howard University television program, *Evening Exchange*, summer 1992. Mack quoted in Cassandra Burrell, "Supporters of African-American Museum Object to Smithsonian Control," Associated Press, Sept. 15, 1992. Mack believed that the Smithsonian did not fairly represent minorities, and he began to enlist support for a museum of slavery on the Mall, appropriate, he thought, given the history of slave pens on the Mall in antebellum times. He also had plans for an adjoining "think tank" for educational and economic development. Mack believed that the Smithsonian had inappropriately taken the idea and changed it, and he thought, given their record of "142 years of discriminatory behavior," that they were not fit to control the institution (Mack interview, July 20, 1992).

P. 72, ¶ 1. Charles L. Griswold, "The Vietnam Veterans Memorial and the Washington Mall: Philosophical Thoughts on Political Iconography," *Critical Inquiry*, vol. 12, no. 4 (Summer 1986), p. 689.

P. 72, ¶ 2. Hilberg to Rabbi Bernard Raskas, Feb. 20, 1981, Hilberg folder, HMMF. Technical studies of the old building began in Nov. 1982. The council was advised by consultants at the Smithsonian Institution that, in Seymour Siegel's words, "requirements and function should determine the size and shape of the museum buildings, not the reverse" ("Comprehensive Staff Planning Document," Nov. 23, 1982, HMMF). As early as Dec. 1980, however, there were expressions of the need for a new building to replace the annexes. Council member Steven Ludsin, president of the Remembrance of the Holocaust foundation and a child of survivors, told other council members that they "should give serious consideration to the architectural statement of a new building that we could design" (HMCT, Dec. 12, 1980, p. 83). And in April 1981, during an extensive discussion regarding the virtues of the Auditor's Complex and Sumner School, a recommendation was made that a site with an existing structure be selected and a new structure built later on ("memorial/museum committee, April 7, 1981," Wiesel files).

P. 73, ¶ 2. Cohn worked on this project with Mark Talisman and David E. Altshuler, professor of Judaic studies at George Washington University. Altshuler would join Cohn at the Holocaust museum. He went on to become director of the Museum of Jewish Heritage, "A Living Memorial to the Holocaust," in New York City. See David Altshuler, ed., *The Precious Legacy: Judaic Treasures from the Czechoslovak State Collections* (New York: Summit Books, 1983).

P. 73, ¶ 2, and p. 74, ¶ 1. Except for final quote, all quoted material from Cohn interviews, Dec. 9, 1993, and Feb. 16, 1994; Cohn memo, June 9, 1983, "memos, Micah," HMMF. Wiesel had requested that the General Services Administration (GSA) also transfer to the council annex 3, since it was "most suitable for our education and administrative functions and would be an integral part of our unique Memorial/Museum area" (Wiesel to Gerald P. Carmen, June 4, 1982). Carmen refused, because the Department of Agriculture thought the annex an "integral part of its overall Master Plan" (Carmen to Wiesel, July 16, 1982). Wiesel raised the issue again in 1984, and was again unsuccessful (National Capital Planning Commission file, "Museum—Annex 3" [hereafter NCPCF]).

There were scattered objections to the idea of a new building. For example, Dr. I. Harold Sharfman, rabbinic administrator of the Kosher Overseers Association of America, Inc., wrote President Reagan that he was "dismayed" that the old buildings—"in keeping with the somber mood of the holocaust"—would be "cast aside, in favor of a monumental edifice." Sharfman argued that the money would more wisely be used for the rescue of Ethopian Jews and starving African children. (Sharfman to Reagan, Aug. 15, 1983, "White House Correspondence," HMMF.)

When the museum opened in 1993, it occupied approximately 250,000 square feet.

P. 74, ¶ 3. Wiesel memo to council, Nov. 21, 1984, HMMF. See also, for example, "Preliminary Case Report to Advisory Council on Historic Preservation from United States Holocaust Memorial Council, Nov. 27, 1984." This report argues, "It is clear that the museum contemplated by the Congress and developed by the Council in preliminary designs can be constructed on the current site *only if the existing structures are removed*" (file 2016, Statues/Memorials—Holocaust Memorial [1981–87], NCPCF). See also "Holocaust Group to Raze 2 Buildings," *Washington Post*, Dec. 27, 1984.

Naftalin quotes from interview, June 5, 1992. Naftalin was former chief counsel of the U.S. House of Representatives Select Committee on

Governmental Research, and senior official and technology policy analyst at the National Academy of Sciences. Now national director of the Union of Councils for Soviet Jews, he is doing for Soviet Jews, he said, "what we should have been doing in the 1930s for European Jews."

P. 75, ¶ 1. The council was able to delist the buildings largely because of the weak case that had been made for their historic value when GSA nominated them for the National Register of Historic Places in 1978. The Joint Committee on Landmarks of the National Capital recommended in favor of the nomination of the main Auditors Building, but not the annexes, since "the marginal historical significance of these buildings does not outweigh their lack of architectural distinction and the negative impact which their siting has on the Main Auditor's Building" (Lorenzo W. Jacobs, Jr., to Michael F. Mulloy, Historian Preservation Officer, GSA, Feb. 21, 1978, file 2016, Statues/Memorials—Holocaust Memorial [1981–87], NCPCF.) Naftalin's comment in *Washington Post*, Dec. 27, 1984, p. A11.

Don L. Klima, chief, Eastern Division of Project Review of the Advisory Council on Historic Preservation, responded to a citizen's query that their responsibility was to evaluate the council's decision to tear the annexes down, "determine if there were workable alternatives, and decide whether demolition was the only prudent and feasible course of action"; after a tour, Klima said, he saw no other options or a need for public meetings (letter from Klima, Jan. 25, 1985, Wiesel files).

P. 75, ¶ 2. Cohn interview, Feb. 16, 1994; Finegold interview, Aug. 14, 1991. In their Nov. 27, 1984, report to the Advisory Council on Historic Preservation, the council detailed the requirements for their new building. There would have to be a "relatively low scale in keeping with the tightness of the site, the personal nature of the subject matter and the need to create an inviting entry to draw visitors from the Mall." It should be "dynamic, intimate and expressive," and the materials should be masonry and stone, "permanent in nature and suitable for a memorial" (file 2016, "Statues/Memorials—Holocaust Memorial" [1981–87], NCPCF).

P. 75, ¶ 3. Finegold interview, Nov. 5, 1993.

P. 77, ¶ 1. The concept document from Notter Finegold & Alexander is in Wiesel's "museum" file.

P. 77, ¶ 2. Z. R. Enav Architects, Ltd., "Holocaust Memorial Museum, Washington, D.C., Design Concept," Wiesel files; Finegold interview, Nov. 5, 1993.

P. 77, ¶ 4. Benjamin Forgey, in *Washington Post*, May 11, 1985, p. G6; transcript of meeting, July 3, 1985, p. 8, NCPCF. The best introduction to the Commission of Fine Arts is Sue A. Kohler, *The Commission of Fine Arts: A Brief History 1910–1990* (Washington, D.C.: Commission of Fine Arts, 1990).

P. 78, ¶ 1. Comments by Stone and Chase found in Commission of Fine Arts meeting transcript (hereafter CFAT), May 15, 1985, pp. 31, 25.

P. 78, ¶ 2. Brown's letter to Hodel, June 5, 1985, CFAT; see also Benjamin Forgey, in *Washington Post*, May 16, 1985. Letter to editor found in *Washington Post*, June 6, 1985. In his letter to Hodel on July 24, 1985, Brown said, "There was sufficient improvement . . . to warrant conceptual approval of the present scheme" (see CFAT, June 28, 1985).

P. 79, ¶ 1. On Sept. 23, 1985, as a part of meeting the requirements of the sunset clause, the council provided the Department of the Interior "estimates for architectural and construction costs as well as affidavits and supporting documentation certifying that sufficient funds were available in cash and pledges to cover the construction costs." On Oct. 4, 1985, Secretary Hodel "certified that funds were available in an amount sufficient to ensure completion of the museum." (U.S. Congress, House of Representatives, Committee on Appropriations, *United States Holocaust Memorial Council*, 100th Cong., 1st sess., 1988, p. 323.)

P. 79, ¶ 2. "February 13, 1979—Summary of Views Received to Date," and "Summary of Views Received to Date, 3/21/79," box 15, Holocaust Museum—1979, Commission History, PCOH-mf. Among some commissioners, there was clearly a feeling that any representation of non-Jewish victims should be spatially separated from the story of Jewish victims.

P. 81, ¶ 2. The discussion in the preceding five paragraphs is found in "content committee, 9-3-85," "Museum Concept Materials (various) fy '85" box, HMMF. The issue was raised again at a "museum-design" meeting on Dec. 13, 1985. Whereas Sultanik found it inappropriate to honor Daniel Trocmé in the Hall of Remembrance, Representative Sidney R. Yates, a council member, had found it appropriate to speak of him during his remarks at the 1984 Days of Remembrance ceremony held in the Capitol Rotunda. See *Days of Remembrance 1984* (Washington, D.C.: United States Holocaust Memorial Council, 1984), p. 65.

In the permanent-exhibition plan submitted by Stuart Silver in 1986, which will be discussed in the following chapter, the Hall of Remembrance was designated as a place to "symbolize the six million Jews" ("The United States Holocaust Memorial Museum: Design Concept Proposal, January 31, 1986," HMMF).

In the controversy regarding the Hall of Remembrance, I was reminded of Eric Leed's idea of ethnic "arrivals" in culture, characterized by "transforming kinship categories, ethnic and class distinctions into quarters, walls, and rooms" (Eric J. Leed, *The Mind of the Traveler: From Gilgamesh to Global Tourism* [New York: Basic Books, 1991], p. 87).

P. 82, ¶ 1. Brodecki interview, July 23, 1992; Berenbaum interview, Aug. 17, 1991.

P. 82, ¶ 2. Hausenberg in CFAT, May 22, 1987, pp. 65–66; Kolodny in CFAT, June 19, 1987, p. 26.

P. 83, ¶ 1. "Second Installment: Museum Concept by Elie Wiesel," Aug.

1985, Wiesel files; Finegold interview, Aug. 14, 1991; Rosenblatt interview Aug. 8, 1991.

P. 84, ¶ 1. Pei's firm is now named Pei Cobb Freed & Partners. Quoted material in the preceding two paragraphs from Rosenblatt interview, Aug. 8, 1991. For interpretations of Rosenblatt's role in the museum, see Carla Hall, "Celebrating the Will to Remember: Arthur Rosenblatt and the Holocaust Museum," *Washington Post*, April 29, 1987, pp. D1, D14; Larry Cohler, "Holocaust Museum Director Expected to Resign," *Washington Jewish Week*, vol. 24, no. 27 (July 7, 1988), pp. 1–2, 37. I thank Kevin Roche for detailing his part in this story in a June 9, 1993, letter.

P. 84, ¶ 2. Freed interview, March 18, 1993; transcript of Freed interview, WETA-TV, *For the Living* (hereafter *For the Living*), roll 93, tape 6, p. 53.

P. 85, ¶ 1. Freed interview, March 18, 1993; *For the Living*, roll 93, tape 6, p. 61.

P. 86, ¶ 1. Finegold interview, Aug. 14, 1991. After the trip, Finegold remained as associate architect, and is proud of the part he played in the making of the museum. "I knew by the end of the trip that Freed would do it right," he recalled, "and I am glad I stayed on and pushed for a new building rather than resigning earlier" (Finegold interview, Nov. 5, 1993). I have taken Freed's recollections of the significance of his trip from these sources: Freed interview, March 18, 1993; *For the Living*, roll 93, tape 6, p. 65; Jean Lawlor Cohen, "James Ingo Freed," *Museum and Arts Washington*, March–April 1988, p. 41. Interestingly, in 1981, Hilberg had had a similar sense of what elements would make for an appropriate building: "It should be a contemporary statement about the Holocaust. It should not be an old structure converted to house a new museum. The outer shell and the interior view must be a unified whole. Our building should not be erected with smooth lines. Its atmosphere should not be 'serene.' In no conventional sense should it be 'beautiful.' The materials must be rough and they should evoke the primitive, elemental forces that generated the Holocaust." (Hilberg to Rabbi Bernard Raskas, Feb. 20, 1981, Hilberg folder, HMMF.)

P. 86, ¶ 2. Freed also expressed his dislike for a neutral building in Paul Goldberger, "A Memorial Evokes Unspeakable Events with Dignity," *New York Times*, April 20, 1989. On the building as "expressive," see *Washington Post*, Nov. 21, 1986. *For the Living*, pp. 90–92; on his building, Freed interview, March 18, 1993.

P. 88, ¶ 1. Herbert Muschamp, "Shaping a Monument to Memory," *New York Times*, April 11, 1993, p. 32; first Freed quote in "James Ingo Freed: The United States Holocaust Memorial Museum," *Assemblage*, vol. 9 (1989), p. 70; second Freed quote in *For the Living*, roll 93, tape 6, p. 69.

P. 89, ¶ 1. *For the Living*, roll 93, tape 6, pp. 72–73.

P. 89, ¶ 2. California State Representative Thomas Lantos and his wife, Annette, both saved as children by Wallenberg, were largely responsible for this act of renaming, and for keeping alive Wallenberg's memory in the United States. Lantos's first piece of legislation, signed by President Reagan on October 5, 1981, made Wallenberg an honorary citizen of the United States, an honor extended to only one other: Winston Churchill. The Lantoses also were responsible for moving the plaque from a largely ignored grassy area across the street from the museum to a prominent place on the wall of annex 3. (Annette Lantos interview, June 21, 1993.) I also wish to thank Representative Lantos's legislative assistant, Michelle Rae Marinelli, for her assistance. See also Annette Lantos, "My Fight for Raoul Wallenberg," *Moment*, Oct. 1987, pp. 21–25, 58–59. On the significance of renaming city streets, see Maoz Azaryahu, "Renaming the Past: Changes in 'City Text' in Germany and Austria," *History and Memory*, Winter 1990, pp. 33–53.

P. 89, ¶ 3. Albert Abramson championed the idea of presidential statements as a way of emphasizing the importance of Holocaust memory for contemporary American culture.

P. 91, ¶ 1. Benjamin Forgey, "A Miraculous Monument to Catastrophe," *Washington Post*, April 18, 1993, p. G4; Herbert Muschamp, "Shaping a Monument to Memory," *New York Times*, April 11, 1993, sec. 2, p. 1. Freed has stated that he meant the façade on 14th Street to represent the false face that Nazi Germany showed the world, and his intricate entryway introduces "a selection, a segregation of movement, arbitrary if you will, not a life and death situation, but a selection" ("James Ingo Freed," p. 70).

P. 91, ¶ 2. James Ingo Freed, "The United States Holocaust Memorial Museum: What Can It Be?," HMC publicity sheet; Joseph Giovannini, "The Architecture of Death," *Los Angeles Times Magazine*, April 18, 1993, p. 38; Freed interview, March 18, 1993.

P. 94, ¶ 1. Freed interview, March 18, 1993. Freed said of the skylight that it "carries a great deal of information in the way it is built. It is not sleek, it is not pleasant. It is the war structure that we want to see. And when we see it, we will find that it is twisted and deformed as the Holocaust twisted and deformed our perception of justice and our perception of what to expect from a civilized country" (HMCT, Nov. 18, 1987, p. 74).

Architect Michael Sorkin asked, "And what of the names to be chiseled in the granite of the first floor, those of the big donors. . . . What strategies must be imposed to reconcile this commemoration with that of the names painted on the glass bridges . . . the towns obliterated . . . the first names of victims? Those carved names are a reminder that the memorial lives the life of a modern institution, that however powerfully it addresses to the Holocaust, it fits comfortably into familiar cultural routines" (Michael Sorkin, "The Holocaust Museum: Between Beauty and Horror," *Progressive Architecture*, Feb. 1993, p. 74).

P. 94, ¶ 3. Quoted material in preceding two paragraphs from Freed interviews, March 18, 1993, and March 24, 1994.

P. 96, ¶ 1. Berenbaum's letter on inscriptions and various proposals from Berenbaum files.

P. 98, ¶ 1. Berenbaum interview, April 13, 1994. Moved into the Hall of Witness was an inscription Berenbaum wanted in the Hall of Remembrance, from Isaiah 43:10—"You are my witnesses"—although it left out the rest of the sentence, "says the Lord." There were two reasons for this omission: some people were sensitive that the museum might be "too" religious, and the imperative may be viewed by visitors as coming from Holocaust victims and not from God.

P. 99, ¶ 1. Freed's "good neighbor" comments in CFAT, May 22, 1987, pp. 10, 12. The decision that the Hall of Remembrance would face the Washington Mall was made in 1984 by Maurice Finegold. There had been discussion of putting it in the center of the building, and the Kaufman sketch suspended it from the museum building. Though Freed rejected any necessary religious meaning, there may be an interesting memorial relationship from his own childhood. During Kristallnacht, when the streetcar stopped for a moment, his father jumped out and grabbed a hexagonal piece of tile from a synagogue, gave it to Freed, and asked him to keep it. I thank architect Harry Barone for telling me this story.

For his comments on the "spiritual" nature of the building, see *Jewish Exponent* (Philadelphia), May 29, 1987. In his June 2, 1987, letter to Hodel, J. Carter Brown said that the commission was "greatly encouraged by what we saw. Many of our previous concerns appear well on the way to being met, and I believe that with some additional study we will have an acceptable design in the near future," CFAT, May 22, 1987.

P. 99, ¶ 2. CFAT, May 22, 1987, p. 6. At the Fine Arts meeting on June 19, 1987, Frank Speh of the Steuben Society also opposed the building, arguing that "Talmudic/Zionist symbols should not be permitted to overpower the area's monuments symbolizing American leaders and American . . . events" (CFAT, p. 32).

P. 100, ¶ 1. Quoted material in the preceding two paragraphs from *Washington Post*, May 23, 1987; Forgey interview, Aug. 14, 1991; on the annex controversy, see Forgey's article, "Annex 3: Worthy—and Endangered," *Washington Post*, Feb. 20, 1988, pp. B1, B6. The council's request to demolish the annex was formally withdrawn in a letter to the executive director of the Advisory Council on Historic Preservation on April 14, 1991.

P. 100, ¶ 3. I am indebted to Professor Lawrence Langer for giving me a copy of the unpublished speech in which his comments appear.

P. 101, ¶ 1. CFAT, Feb. 18, 1988, pp. 50, 53, 84.

P. 101, ¶ 2. See Forgey's comment in *Washington Post*, May 23, 1988. Wolf and Freed's comments in CFAT, March 17, 1988, pp. 15, 16–17, 25–26.

P. 102, ¶ 1. *For the Living*, roll 93, tape 6, pp. 86, 88. Visitors *can,* through two of the narrow openings in the Hall of Remembrance, see the Washington

Monument and the Jefferson Memorial. This was important for Charles Krauthammer, who wrote that the "juxtaposition is not just redemptive. It is reassuring. The angels of democracy stand on watch on this temple of evil. It is as if only in the heart of the world's most tolerant and most powerful democracy can such terrible testimony be safely contained." (Charles Krauthammer, "Holocaust Museum," *Washington Post*, April 23, 1993.)

P. 103 ¶ 1. Quoted material in CFAT, March 17, 1988, pp. 36–38, 40–41, 67, 55. Freed recalled other attempts to soften his building. Some donors complained about its apparent harshness. One donor asked, "Why can't it be more like the National Gallery?" There were constant pressures, he said, to make the building an easier one to look at and move around in. Freed interview, March 24, 1994.

P. 103, ¶ 2. Cohen, "James Ingo Freed," p. 44.

P. 104, ¶ 1. Berenbaum interview, April 14, 1994.

P. 104, ¶ 2. Stanley and Adam Prill interview, June 24, 1993.

P. 106, ¶ 1. Fact sheet in author's files. Herbert Muschamp, "How Buildings Remember," *New Republic*, Aug. 28, 1989, p. 32.

P. 106, ¶ 2. For a related discussion, see Nelson Goodman, "How Buildings Mean," in Nelson Goodman and Catherine Elgin, *Reconceptions in Philosophy* (Indianapolis: Hackett Publishing Company, 1988); Lawrence J. Vale, *Architecture, Power, and National Identity* (New Haven: Yale University Press, 1992).

P. 107, ¶ 1. Smith interviews, Jan. 14, 1993; June 23, 1993. Similar feelings were expressed at a CFA meeting in 1987, in which a survivor said, "The very idea of such a building is flawed; no matter what its design or scale, it cannot reflect the enormity of the tragedy it purports to commemorate" (CFAT, June 19, 1987, p. 29).

Architectural critic Hélène Lipstadt thought that language of veneration had kept critics from asking "obvious questions" about the museum—for example, whether the "atrium, stair and space frame" owed anything to "Freed's mastery of these elements in the Javits Convention Center" in New York. See Hélène Lipstadt, "The United States Holocaust Memorial Museum and the Critics," *Casabella*, Oct. 1993, n.p.

P. 107, ¶ 2. Hilberg interview, Aug. 29, 1992.

CHAPTER THREE

P. 109, ¶ 2. PCOHT, Feb. 15, 1979, p. 10.

P. 109, ¶ 3. Ibid., p. 79. In 1994, Menachem Rosensaft replaced his mother on the council.

P. 110, ¶ 1. Dawidowicz in ibid., p. 20; Yaffa Eliach, "The President's Commission on the Holocaust: Reflections," p. 3, "Staff Summary of Com-

missioners' Views," box 15, PCOH-mf. Other suggestions for a living memorial were made on March 21, 1979, including a film-and-tape library, an
annual memorial lecture, and a chair of Holocaust studies. ("Summary of
Views received to date (3/21/79): Museums and Monuments," pp. 12–13,
box 15, PCOH-mf.

P. 110, ¶ 2. These various comments made in "Opinions Expressed by the
Commissioners," Feb. 6, 1979," p. 3, box 15, PCOH-mf.

P. 111, ¶ 1. PCOHT, Feb. 15, 1979, pp. 79–80.

P. 111, ¶ 2. Various commissioners' comments in "Update—the Work of
the Commission, May 14, 1979," p. 4; Bruno Bettelheim, "The Holocaust—
One Generation After," in Roger S. Gottlieb, ed., *Thinking the Unthinkable:
Meanings of the Holocaust* (New York: Paulist Press, 1990), p. 380; final
quote in "Summary of Views received to date (3/21/79): Museums and
Monuments," PCOH-mf.

P. 112, ¶ 1. "Summary of Views received to date (3/21/79)," p. 5, PCOHT.
The idea of a railcar would be realized in the permanent exhibition, but, as
James Young points out, this was not the first use of a boxcar in an American
Holocaust museum. In the Dallas Memorial Center for Holocaust Studies, a
Belgian railcar was shortened by a third and put at the museum's entryway.
Some survivors objected to going through it, so a secret entrance was added for
them. See James E. Young, *The Texture of Memory: Holocaust Memorials and
Meaning* (New Haven: Yale University Press, 1993), pp. 297–98. "Update—
The Work of the Commission, May 14, 1979," p. 2, box 15, PCOH-mf.

P. 112, ¶ 2. "Update—The Work of the Commission, May 14, 1979," p. 4,
PCOH-mf.

P. 112, ¶ 3. PCOHT, Feb. 15, 1979, p. 20.

P. 113, ¶ 1. PCOHT, April 24, 1979, p. 126.

P. 113, ¶ 2. *Report to the President,* pp. 10–11.

P. 114, ¶ 1. Berenbaum to Wiesel, Oct. 11, 1979, Berenbaum files.

P. 114, ¶ 2. In these formative years, Beth Hatefutsoth (the "Museum of
the Jewish Diaspora," in Tel Aviv) and Yad Vashem were often viewed as
models for the museum in Washington. Quoted material from "Annex
Three," HMMF.

P. 115, ¶ 1. Wiesel interview, March 15, 1993.

P. 115, ¶ 2. All quoted material from Freedman memo to council members, special advisers, second generation, "Agenda for Council Meeting, Thurs-
day, April 30, 1981," HMMF.

P. 115, ¶ 3. Hilberg's self-characterization as a "footnote writer" in HMCT,
Dec. 12, 1980, p. 62. All other quoted material from his letter to Raskas,
Feb. 20, 1981, HMMF.

P. 116, ¶ 1. Robert McAfee Brown, *Elie Wiesel: Messenger to All Humanity*, rev. ed. (Notre Dame, Ind.: University of Notre Dame Press, 1989).
Quoted material in HMCT, Dec. 12, 1980, pp. 44, 51, 68. The issue of just

how "horrible" the museum should be, and how the story could best be presented to children, was considered throughout the years of planning for the exhibition. In 1982, Hillel Levine, then deputy director of the council, thought it one of his responsibilities to link the council with other federal agencies that could be helpful, to make, in his words, "the work of the council part of Washington business." To that end, in Sept. 1982 he organized, with the support of the National Endowment of the Arts, a conference convened by the National Institute of Mental Health called "Remembering and Memorializing the Holocaust: Psychological and Educational Dimensions." Thirty participants, distinguished psychologists, teachers, even Fred Rogers of *Mr. Rogers* fame, offered five recommendations: the museum should be designed primarily for adults; no children below ninth grade should visit without an adult; children should have a separate entrance, limited program, and special orientation, and there should be special "tracks" within the permanent exhibition for them. (Transcript of conference, HMMF.) The museum does include a special exhibition for children, "Daniel's Story." See "Holocaust Museum Helps Children Think the Unthinkable," *New York Times*, June 3, 1993, pp. B1, B4.

P. 117, ¶ 1. Quoted material in previous two paragraphs from Mazewski to Raskas, Feb. 24, 1981; Raskas to Mazewski, March 6, 1981; Mazewski to Raskas, March 20, 1981. I am indebted to Father John Pawlikowski for sharing this correspondence with me.

P. 117, ¶ 2. The proceedings of the conference may be found in Brewster Chamberlin and Marcia Feldman, eds., *The Liberation of the Nazi Concentration Camps: Eyewitness Accounts of the Liberators*, intro. Robert H. Abzug (Washington, D.C.: United States Holocaust Memorial Council, 1987). Remarks by Lerman and Wiesel on pp. 12, 15.

P. 118, ¶ 1. "Naftalin and Siegel's remarks in Comprehensive Staff Planning Document: 11–23–82," p. 2, HMMF; see also "Process—11–22–82," HMMF. Talisman's remarks in HMCT, Dec. 2, 1982, pp. 43–44.

P. 118, ¶ 2. HMCT, Dec. 2, 1982, pp. 2–3, 11–12.

P. 119, ¶ 1. HMCT, Aug. 4, 1983, pp. 59–61.

P. 119, ¶ 2. Drabek's comments in ibid., pp. 70–71; and letter to Council, May 8, 1983, HMMF. Drabek continued the argument into 1985. In a prepared statement for a council meeting, he wrote that, whereas in Auschwitz visitors do not learn about the Jewish victims, in the United States "people are mostly persuaded that anybody who was in Auschwitz was Jewish. It is our duty to tell the whole story." At the same time, Drabek objected to extending the boundaries to include the Armenians as Nazi victims, for, he said, "if we try to cover other genocides, we run the risk of entangling ourselves in endless political complications." (Typed corrections of Drabek statement found accompanying letter from Marian Craig, Secretary to the Council, to Drabek, Aug. 28, 1985, HMMF.)

P. 120, ¶ 1. Hilberg to Wiesel, July 28, 1983, HMMF.

P. 120, ¶ 2. HMCT, Aug. 4, 1983, pp. 75, 118.

P. 120, ¶ 3. HMCT, Aug. 4, 1983, p. 109.

P. 121, ¶ 1. Ibid.; Hilberg's comments on p. 128, Davis's on p. 80.

P. 122, ¶ 1. Ibid., pp. 149–50. Interestingly, in his comments on the Auschwitz convent controversy, Albert Friedlander, rabbi of Westminister Synagogue in London, England, expressed a similar view of the sobering function of Auschwitz. It was, he said, not a place where "prayers remove darkness. It is the place where one can remember the evil and walk away maimed." (Albert H. Friedlander, "Jewish and Christian Suffering in the Post-Auschwitz Period," in Carol Rittner and John K. Roth, eds., *Memory Offended: The Auschwitz Convent Controversy* [New York: Praeger, 1991], p. 178.)

P. 122, ¶ 2. For general background on Pfefferkorn, see "Survivor and Scholar," *Washington Jewish Week*, Jan. 21, 1982. Quoted material from memo to Micah Naftalin, Nov. 11, 1982, "Personal—Pfefferkorn," HMMF.

P. 124, ¶ 2. Pfefferkorn's approach described in memo from Cohn and Altshuler to Wiesel, Sept. 26, 1983, HMMF. All other quoted material on this plan in preceding paragraphs taken from "To Bear Witness, to Remember, and to Learn: A Confidential Report on Museum Planning Prepared for the United States Holocaust Memorial Council, February 28, 1984," HMMF.

P. 125, ¶ 1. Hilberg quoted in HMCT, March 14, 1984, p. 64; Talisman and Rosensaft in HMCT, Feb. 28, 1984, p. 74; Franklin Littell, HMCT, March 14, 1984, p. 84; Pawlikowski, HMCT, Feb. 28, 1984, p. 61; Wiesel, HMCT, March 14, 1984, p. 56.

P. 126, ¶ 1. Final quote from HMCT, Jan. 30, 1985, p. 2. All other quoted material in this and preceding paragraph from Wiesel memo to Anna Cohn, Nov. 23, 1984, HMMF.

P. 127, ¶ 1. Quoted material in this and preceding paragraph from Cohn interview, July 22, 1992.

P. 128, ¶ 1. Shaike Weinberg, "Concept Outline," May 1985, p. 6, HMMF.

P. 128, ¶ 2. Ibid., p. 8.

P. 128, ¶ 3. Naftalin to Wiesel, May 30, 1985, HMMF. Abramson quote in "Transcript of Museum Planning Meeting—7–12–85," "Museum Concept Materials (various) fy 1985" box, pp. 2, passim, 60, HMMF.

P. 129, ¶ 2. "Chairman's Guidelines for the Content Committee, assisted by Eli Pfefferkorn, August 12, 1985," pp. 4, 23; "Second Installment: Museum Concept by Elie Wiesel, August 1985"; both in Wiesel files.

P. 129, ¶ 3. Wiesel, Rosensaft, and Reagan quoted in Ilya Levkov, ed., *Bitburg and Beyond: Encounters in American, German and Jewish History* (New York: Shapolsky Publishers, 1987), pp. 44, 138, 39. After Reagan left office, council member and Holocaust survivor Kalman Sultanik, vice-president of the World Jewish Congress, kept up a correspondence with the president about his decision. In a letter to Sultanik on May 22, 1989, Reagan stated, "I did some research on my own and learned that, yes, there were some S.S.

troops buried there, but a number of them were buried in prisoner uniforms. They had been executed for trying to shield inmates from torture and the ovens." In his letter of June 13, 1989, Sultanik asked for the sources of the president's information, and Reagan responded on June 29, 1989, "I'm sorry there is no documented evidence. . . . German officials having to do with my visit were the source." Sultanik responded on Aug. 21, 1989, noting that he had checked with historians and other survivors, a "painstaking inquiry" had been done at Yad Vashem, and "no such instance has ever arisen to their knowledge." In a handwritten response on Aug. 31, the president said that he had received letters from prisoners in the death camps who were "befriended by an S.S. guard," and he was "convinced that the accounts are true." Sultanik wrote Raul Hilberg about all of this, and he responded on Sept. 12, 1989, "It is extremely unlikely . . . that several SS men would have been sentenced for having helped prisoners, then to have been executed, and their bodies to have been removed in prisoner garb to be buried in—of all places—a cemetery reserved for men who died in their military or SS uniforms." I thank Kalman Sultanik for providing me with copies of this correspondence during our interview on March 18, 1993.

P. 130, ¶ 1. Wiesel in HMCT, April 15, 1985, p. 48; Brown in HMCT, May 13, 1985.

P. 131, ¶ 1. Bookbinder in HMCT, May 13, 1985, p. 20; Hilberg in HMCT, May 13, 1985, p. 51; Wiesel in HMCT, Dec. 4, 1986, p. 93; Hilberg interview, Aug. 29, 30, 1992. Hilberg also said that the council should have told the president not to go to Bitburg, "not just because of the graves of the SS, but because of the complicity of the German Army in mass murder"; Hilberg interview, Aug. 30, 1992.

P. 132, ¶ 1. Quoted material in this and the preceding paragraph taken from "The United States Holocaust Memorial Museum: Design Concept Proposal, January 31, 1986," pp. 6, 16, 36–37, 46, 49–50, HMMF.

P. 133, ¶ 1 and 2. Quoted material in preceding two paragraphs from HMCT, Dec. 4, 1986, p. 94; Meyerhoff interview, June 22, 1993; Berenbaum interview, April 22, 1993.

P. 134, ¶ 2. HMCT, Dec. 4, 1986, pp. 157–58. My brief characterization of these discussions is based largely on the point of view expressed by the council's executive director, Richard Krieger, in memoranda to Wiesel, May 19, 1986; May 20, 1986; June 13, 1986; minutes of the museum-development-committee meeting, June 24, 1986; "Resolution of the United States Holocaust Memorial Council Museum Development Committee Terms of Reference," all in HMMF.

P. 135, ¶ 1. See, for example, Judith Miller's presentation of the museum in *One, by One, by One: Facing the Holocaust* (New York: Simon and Schuster, 1990); Robert S. Greenberger, "Power: Painful Witness," *Regardie's*, vol. 9, no. 3 (Nov. 1988), p. 61; and "Washington Holocaust Museum Completed,"

Jewish Herald, May 5, 1989; Larry Cohler, in *Washington Jewish Week*, Dec. 25, 1986, p. 8. Strochlitz comment, in minutes of the museum-development committee meeting, Jan. 7, 1987; see also Feb. 4, 1987; both in HMMF.

P. 136, ¶ 1. Carla Hall, "Arthur Rosenblatt and the Holocaust Museum," *Washington Post*, April 29, 1987.

P. 136, ¶ 2. A number of the conference papers were published in Michael Berenbaum, ed., *A Mosaic of Victims: Non-Jews Persecuted and Murdered by the Nazis* (New York: New York University Press, 1990); the quotation occurs on p. 2.

P. 137, ¶ 1. All quoted material is from "The United States Holocaust Memorial Museum: Concept Program," April 1987, pp. 1–2, 6, HMMF. The vote on Rosenthal mentioned in Abramson to Krieger, Jan. 7, 1987, HMMF.

P. 137, ¶ 2. Lerman interview, Aug. 8, 1993; Berenbaum interview, July 27, 1993.

P. 138, ¶ 1. Minutes of museum-development committee meeting, Jan. 20, 1988, p. 3, HMMF.

P. 139, ¶ 3. All quoted material in this and preceding two paragraphs taken from "Exhibition Story Outline Presented to the Content Committee, the United States Holocaust Memorial Museum, May 11, 1988," HMMF.

P. 140, ¶ 1. Minutes of museum-development committee meeting, July 27, 1988, p. 2, HMMF.

P. 140, ¶ 2. Smith telephone interview, Jan. 1, 1994.

P. 141, ¶ 1. Unless otherwise noted, Shaike Weinberg's story and all quotations by him are from Weinberg interviews, June 11, 1991; June 6, 1992; July 25, 1992. There is a concise introduction to Weinberg's view of the museum in John Strand's "The Storyteller," *Museum News*, vol. 72, no. 2 (March–April 1993, pp. 40–43, 51.

P. 142, ¶ 1. Ben Lynfield, "Birth of a Museum," *Jerusalem Post International Edition*, June 1989, n.p. Kenneth Hudson considers Beth Hatefutsoth one of the "most important museums of the twentieth century," and pointed out that Weinberg had "turned his back on the two sacred duties of acquisition and conservation. Men have been asked to resign from their clubs for far lesser misdemeanours." (Kenneth Hudson, *Museums of Influence* [Cambridge: Cambridge University Press, 1987], pp. 140, 143.)

P. 142, ¶ 2. Weinberg interview, July 25, 1992; "The USHMM—A Conceptual Museum," remarks prepared for Frankfurt Holocaust Museum Hearings, Oct. 23–25, 1991, p. 5, HMMF.

P. 142, ¶ 3. Minutes of museum-content committee meeting, June 28, 1988, p. 12, HMMF.

P. 143, ¶ 1. Martin Smith, "What a Museum Visitor Should Think About and Remember," unpublished manuscript. I thank Martin Smith for sending me a copy of his comments. Farr talks about her experiences as a film researcher in Alan Rosenthal, *The Documentary Conscience: A Casebook in Film Making* (Berkeley: University of California Press, 1980).

P. 144, ¶ 1. Smith, "What a Museum Visitor Should Think About." Appelbaum interviews, Aug. 7, 1991; Jan. 16, 1993; Aug. 9, 1993. *For the Living*, roll 85, tape 6, p. 48. See also "New Approach to Museum-Show Design," *New York Times*, Jan. 11, 1994, p. C15.

P. 145, ¶ 1. Miller interview, April 26, 1994.

P. 145, ¶ 2, and p. 146, ¶ 1. First three quotes from Smith interviews, Jan. 16, 1992, and March 17, 1993; next two from "A Call for Artifacts," HMMF; Appelbaum interview, Aug. 9, 1993; Smith memo to Berenbaum, March 13, 1989, Smith files. Discussion with Edward Dziadosz recalled in Berenbaum interview, Nov. 21, 1993; Smith and Appelbaum interviews, Jan. 16, 1993. See "A Call for Artifacts," HMMF; *For the Living*, roll 86, tape 7, p. 57; Appelbaum interview, Jan. 16, 1993; Smith memo to Michael Berenbaum, March 13, 1989. I thank Martin Smith for sending me a copy of the latter. A 1985 report to the museum on artifacts in European sites defined artifacts as "documents used in everyday life. . . . Objects and documents from . . . ghettoes . . . objects brought into concentration camps by Jewish inmates." The "extant materials" of the camps were to be represented in the museum only by photographs. Artifacts, the report said, were important in order to suggest "the individual, intimate nature of struggles to retain self-esteem under Nazi bondage, and its social overtones of solidarity." (Aline Isdebsky-Pritchard, "Report on Original Artifact Resources from the Holocaust Era in Selected European Memorial Institutions," Feb. 1985, HMMF.)

P. 147, ¶ 1. Weinberg interviews, June 11, 1991; July 25, 1992.

P. 147, ¶ 2. Berenbaum interview, Nov. 21, 1993. Lerman signed agreements regarding archival materials with the Main Commission for the Investigation of Nazi War Crimes in Poland in Aug. 1987; with the Council of Ministers, Glavarchiv, U.S.S.R., July 1988; and with the GDR (East German) Center for Archival Information in Aug. 1989. I am grateful to Miles Lerman for providing these dates.

P. 148, ¶ 1. Miles and Chris Lerman interview, Aug. 8, 1993; Smith, *For the Living*, roll 127, tape 26, p. 5.

P. 149, ¶ 2. All quoted material in the preceding three paragraphs from Hebebrand interview, July 26, 1991; correspondence with author, April 27, 1994; *For the Living*, tapes 18–19, p. 41.

P. 151, ¶ 2. Nowakowski interview, July 22, 1992. Unless otherwise noted, all quotations by Nowakowski are from my notes during our trip to Poland in Jan. 1993.

P. 152, ¶ 1. Nowakowski interview, July 28, 1993.

P. 154, ¶ 1. Balawajder and Oleksy interviews, Jan. 16, 19, 1993. The phrase "shiver of contact" used by David Lowenthal, *The Past Is a Foreign Country* (Cambridge: Cambridge University Press, 1985), p. 246.

P. 156, ¶ 3. "USHMM Communications Planning Timeline, August 1992," HMMF.

P. 156, ¶ 4. Dyer interviews, June 25, 1993; July 29, 1993.

P. 157, ¶ 1. Berenbaum interview, Nov. 21, 1993.

P. 158, ¶ 2. Quoted material in preceding two paragraphs from Dyer interview, June 25, 1993; *For the Living*, roll 61, tape 2, p. 7.

P. 159, ¶ 1. Quotes in preceding three paragraphs from Dyer interviews, June 25, 1993; July 29, 1993. Nowakowski interview, Feb. 9, 1994.

P. 163, ¶ 2. Quoted material in previous two paragraphs from author's notes, Auschwitz-Birkenau, Jan. 18, 1993; *For the Living*, roll 123, tape 22, p. 7; roll 126, tape 25, p. 2. There had been occasional rumblings of discontent when the museum removed a barracks from Birkenau. James E. Young, a member of a group serving as an unofficial advisory board to the International Auschwitz Council, noted that the museum's "foraging for artifacts" struck an "especially raw nerve among the group," which recommended that the entire Auschwitz Council approve any removal of material. Michael Berenbaum responded that the barracks taken by the museum was "to be torn down because it could not be preserved." See James E. Young, "The Future of Auschwitz," *Tikkun*, vol. 7, no. 6 (Nov.–Dec. 1992), p. 33; Michael Berenbaum's letter to the editor and Young's reply in *Tikkun*, vol. 8, no. 2 (March–April 1993), pp. 5–6.

P. 164, ¶ 1. The Mauthausen stone was donated by the Austrian government.

P. 164, ¶ 2. "Freight Car Used During the Holocaust Donated to the United States Holocaust Memorial Museum by Poland; Arrives in Baltimore," U.S. Holocaust Memorial Council news release, n.d., p. 3.

P. 165, ¶ 1. "East Germany Presents Holocaust Artifacts to the United States Holocaust Memorial Museum," U.S. Holocaust Memorial Council news release, n.d., p. 5; "East German Prime Minister de Maiziere Presents Berlin Synagogue Keystone to U.S. Holocaust Museum; Council Leaders Urge German Memorial," U.S. Holocaust Memorial Council news release, June 12, 1990.

There were strong disagreements over whether the ruins of the V-2 rocket should be used. Shaike Weinberg was opposed; both Martin Smith and later Raye Farr thought it important to include, despite its deteriorated condition. In a memo to Farr, Smith expressed his "strongest dismay that this . . . is on the 'let's drop' list. It was made by slave labor at a camp liberated by Americans. . . . It links the Holocaust with the space age and the USA. . . . It is in marked contrast to the V2 rocket at the Air and Space Museum and makes plain the different agenda our museum has when compared to other institutions." (Smith, memo to Farr, n.d., Smith files.)

CHAPTER FOUR

P. 167, ¶ 2. Miller interview, April 26, 1994.

P. 168, ¶ 1. Faith Ruffin, "The Exhibition as Form: An Elegant Metaphor," *Museum News*, Oct. 1985, p. 59.

P. 168, ¶ 3. Appelbaum quotes in previous paragraph from Appelbaum interview, Aug. 9, 1993. Adrian Dannatt, "Bearing Witness," *Building Design*, July 2, 1993, pp. 10–11.

P. 169, ¶ 1. Appelbaum interview, Aug. 9, 1993. During a design meeting on June 20, 1991, for example, Appelbaum strongly objected to a suggestion that a railing on the third floor be enlarged so that people could sit down. This, he said, would change the nature of the exhibit, even were the seating area made purposefully uncomfortable. Another suggestion, that some sort of cushioning be provided on this railing, met with strenuous objections from most of those present. (Author's meeting notes.)

P. 169, ¶ 2. In addition to Ralph Appelbaum, I thank Ann Farrington, coordinator of the permanent exhibition, for discussing the planning of the exhibition space.

P. 170, ¶ 1. *For the Living*, roll 128, tape 27, pp. 3–4.

P. 171, ¶ 3. Kramer interview, April 21, 1993. Ioanid offered an example of the way in which the museum restored the accurate history of a photograph. Ralph Appelbaum wanted to use a photograph of Buchenwald inmates waving flags while greeting liberators in a second-floor exhibit. Ioanid was uncomfortable with this, for the women were too well fed, and their hair was too neat. He fought against the use of the photograph, and eventually a researcher in his department discovered that the photo had been taken on the one-year anniversary of liberation. A photograph of a tank coming through the gates of Mauthausen was used instead (Ioanid interview, April 14, 1994).

P. 174, ¶ 2. Susan Sontag, *On Photography* (New York: Farrar, Straus and Giroux, 1977), p. 20.

P. 176, ¶ 2. Eliach interview, March 17, 1993; Quoted material from *For the Living*, roll 91, tape 4, pp. 35–36.

P. 178, ¶ 1. Quoted material in the preceding two paragraphs from ibid., p. 38; Eliach interview, March 17, 1993.

P. 178, ¶ 3. Material in the two preceding paragraphs from Yaffa Eliach, "The Ejszyszki Tower: The Tower of Faces," *Jewish Studies Network*, vol. 5, no. 1 (Spring 1991), pp. 1–2. Eliach would eventually spend more than $600,000 on the project. She is still collecting photographs and writing a history of the shtetl. "I have become intimately involved in the lives of some of these people. They call me when their roofs leak, when they need hot water in their homes. I went to Israel to be with someone who was sick and needed me." Eliach telephone interview, April 21, 1994.

Eliach estimated that, at the time the tower project was under way, she had photographs of approximately 92 percent of the townspeople; by the spring of 1994, 96 percent.

P. 179, ¶ 2. Quoted material in previous two paragraphs from Eliach interview, March 17, 1993, and Eliach telephone interview, April 21, 1994.

P. 180, ¶ 1. Eliach, "Ejszyszki Tower," pp. 3–4. Whereas many observers have called the exhibit of photographs the "tower of faces," Eliach prefers the name "tower of life."

P. 180, ¶ 2. *For the Living*, roll 83, tape 5, pp. 34, 42–43.

P. 181, ¶ 1. Miller memo, March 1, 1989 (I thank Cindy L. Miller for providing me with copies of various documents); Eliach telephone interview, April 21, 1994.

P. 181, ¶ 2. *For the Living*, roll 130, tape 29, p. 1. In the fall of 1990, the museum was still looking for artifacts to dramatize the story of the mobile killing squads. Smith wrote, "Zero artifacts thus far. Are we going to refer to the Einsatzgruppen in 'Terror in Poland'? What about the absence of gas van stuff anywhere?" (Smith to Weinberg, Berenbaum, Farr, Sept. 5, 1990, Smith files.)

P. 181, ¶ 4. *For the Living*, roll 130, tape 29, p. 1.

P. 182, ¶ 1. Eliach interviews. Miller wrote Eliach to assure her that no alteration of the photographs would take place. "We have re-figured the tile sizes to be proportional to what we calculate to be the typical dimensions of the photographs, making cropping unnecessary. This will maintain the balance between background/environment and the human subjects that you so articulately advocate." (Miller to Eliach, July 3, 1990, Miller files.)

P. 184, ¶ 2. Material in preceding three paragraphs from Eliach interviews; Berenbaum interview, July 27, 1993.

P. 184, ¶ 3. Eliach interview, March 17, 1993

P. 185, ¶ 1. Kramer interview, April 21, 1993; *For the Living*, roll 130, tape 9, p. 3. A survey done in the fall of 1993 by Peter D. Hart Research Associates, Inc., found that visitors were most moved by exhibits that were "personal." Mentioned most often were the display of victims' shoes, survivor accounts, and the tower. ("Key Findings and Recommendations from a Survey of Visitors to the United States Holocaust Memorial Museum," 1993. I thank Debbie Klingender for sending me this report.)

P. 185, ¶ 2. Miller interview, April 26, 1994.

P. 187, ¶ 1. Debbie Klingender interview, July 25, 1992; Peter D. Hart Research Associates, Inc., "Materials from Focus Groups Conducted for the U.S. Holocaust Memorial Museum." I thank Debbie Klingender and Naomi Paiss, director of communications at the council, for their willingness to share relevant materials with me.

There are 558 cards, 260 representing people who were murdered, 298 those who survived. There are cards representing euthanasia victims (2); Gypsies (3); gay and lesbian people (9); Jehovah's Witnesses (20); Eastern European Jews (364); Western European Jews (115); and Polish prisoners (47).

P. 187, ¶ 2. Müller interview, April 23, 1993. On Müller's work for the museum, see Sara Hart, "A Dark Past Brought to Light," *10 Percent*, vol. 1 (Winter 1993), pp. 36–39, 74.

P. 187, ¶ 3. Müller quoted in Ara vaan Hertum, "The Forgotten Victims," *Washington Blade*, vol. 24, no. 18 (April 23, 1993), p. 71; Gay and Lesbian Alliance to President Carter, Jan. 31, 1980. The alliance asked that the museum include "appropriate exhibits relating to the Nazi campaign against homosexuals," that there be an educational focus on "anti-gay genocide," that "openly gay [men] and lesbians be appointed to the Citizens Committee on Conscience," that there be specific remembrance of gays in Days of Remembrance proclamations, and that fund-raising "include an outreach to gay men and lesbians" (appendix to HMCT, May 28, 1980, HMMF).

P. 188, ¶ 1. Klaus Müller, "The Holocaust ≠ AIDS," *Advocate*, May 4, 1993, p. 5.

P. 188, ¶ 2. Gay victims are represented throughout the exhibition. In a display on book-burning, the text reads that among books burned were "Magnus Hirschfeld's writings on homosexuality." In the exhibit "Enemies of the State," the text notes that homosexuals were persecuted because of their "sexual orientation," and on the third floor the text of the exhibit "Who Shall Live and Who Shall Die" reads, "About 10,000 homosexuals, most of them German and Austrian, were imprisoned in the camps. They often received the hardest work assignments, as a result of which more than half did not survive. Many homosexuals were also sentenced and interned under other categories." There are also mug shots of gay victims on the third floor. In the second-floor exhibit, "Return to Life," the text reads, "Under the Allied military government, some homosexuals in Germany were forced to serve out their terms of imprisonment, regardless of the time they had spent in concentration camps. The law used by the Nazis to imprison homosexuals remained in effect until 1969." Former museum historian David Luebke had suggested in a design meeting in 1992 that this last exhibit could deal with other survivors beyond Jews. Shaike Weinberg responded that there were no artifacts to build a story around, but agreed with Luebke to put something in the text. (Design-meeting notes, March 9, 1992, HMMF.)

P. 190, ¶ 1. Quoted material in preceding two paragraphs from Farrington interview, July 28, 1993; Hebebrand interview, July 26, 1991; author's notes at design meeting, June 20, 1991; Farr interview, Feb. 8, 1994.

P. 191, ¶ 1. Miller interview, April 26, 1994; telephone interview, May 5, 1994; letter to author, May 9, 1994. In a memo to Appelbaum on Oct. 26, 1990, Miller suggested exhibits on Jewish culture before and after the Holocaust, "thereby mediating the victimization by placing it within a much broader historical context" (Miller files).

P. 191, ¶ 2. *For the Living*, roll 128, tape 27, p. 10; Smith interview, March 17, 1993.

P. 192, ¶ 1. The Warsaw Ghetto uprising does occupy a prominent place on the third floor, and on the second floor there are a number of exhibits describing armed resistance and political resistance. The very adequacy of the term "resistance" for any act other than the use of physical force is called into question by Lawrence Langer, who argued that "cultural" cries of protest against war—art and theater, for example—are ineffective against the forces of genocide. "We look at sketches of starving Jews," he wrote, "or crowds awaiting deportation to the deathcamps, of desolate children, of executions, and suddenly 'resistance' sounds irrelevant and 'culture' itself a term from an antiquated vocabulary, implying harmony, order, disciplined thought, beauty and form, thumbed from a thesaurus that never heard of the world of Theresienstadt or the events that transpired there." Artwork of the camps, which might register as acts of "spiritual resistance" for some, Langer understands "not [as] defiance but [as] a basic human need to interpret the meaning of one's own experience, or to pierce the obscurities that shroud it in apparent meaninglessness." (Lawrence L. Langer, "Cultural Resistance to Genocide," *Witness*, vol. 1, no. 1 [Spring 1987], pp. 87, 89. See also his chapter "Language as Refuge," in *Versions of Survival: The Holocaust and the Human Spirit* [Albany: State University Press of New York, 1982], pp. 1–65.)

P. 192, ¶ 2. Klingender interview, July 25, 1992.

P. 194, ¶ 1. Quote in previous paragraph from Kramer interview, April 21, 1993. Appelbaum to Farr, June 25, 1992, Miller files (memo also contains Miller's critique).

P. 194, ¶ 2. Kramer and Farr interview, June 25, 1993.

P. 196, ¶ 1. Weinberg interview, June 11, 1991.

P. 196, ¶ 2. Farr interview, April 21, 1993. The "philosophical statement" was presented to the content committee on Jan. 20, 1988, and the discussion continued on Feb. 29, 1988.

P. 196, ¶ 3. Smith telephone interview, Jan. 1, 1994; Kramer interviews, April 21, 1993; June 25, 1993.

P. 198, ¶ 1. Smith to Farr, n.d., Smith files. As it turns out, there are always people crowded up against the privacy walls, watching the changing monitor photographs intently. Museum staff reacted in various ways when I asked if they were worried that these exhibits increased the danger of voyeurism. As noted, Raye Farr said this was the only way the material could have been included in the exhibition, and she believed that it was an important part of the exhibition, a place where visitors "rapidly absorbed anguish." On the other hand, Ann Farrington said the constant crowds reminded her of "people stopped at a traffic accident" (Farrington interviews, June 23 and 25, 1993).

P. 199, ¶ 1. Sybil Milton, *In Fitting Memory: The Art and Politics of Holocaust Memorials* (Detroit: Wayne State University Press, 1991), p. 16; *For the Living*, roll 86, tape 7, pp. 69–70. There is, however, a significant amount of material on the fourth floor that offers visitors a taste of the allure of Nazi ritual. Indeed, there is a powerful interplay in exhibit segments on the rise of National Socialism between text, monitors, artifacts, and song and speech. Crowds singing martial music, and Hitler's voice lend depth to this important part of the exhibition.

P. 199, ¶ 2. Rosenfeld to Smith and Appelbaum, Feb. 16, 1989; Smith's response to Dec. 6, 1989, memo to staff on changes in exhibition nomenclature, Dec. 7, 1989; both in HMMF. The third-floor exhibition space is called "Final Solution—1940–1945."

P. 200, ¶ 1. Miller interview, April 26, 1994.

P. 200, ¶ 2. Farr interview, June 19, 1991. Berenbaum and Mais invited me to join them on their walk through the permanent exhibition, Aug. 6, 1991.

P. 201, ¶ 1. Ringelheim memo to Smith and Appelbaum, July 17, 1990; minutes of design-committee meeting, Feb. 5, 1991, HMMF.

P. 203, ¶ 1. Luebke staff memo, Nov. 6, 1991, HMMF. Another member of the museum's staff, Severin Hochberg, suggested adding generals, to show the "profound implication of the German Army in the killings," as well as "deportation bureaucrats and experts, local Fascist leaders," and "German and local churchmen who gave their blessing" (Hochberg staff memo, n.d., HMMF).

P. 203, ¶ 2. Ringelheim staff memo, Nov. 12, 1991, HMMF.

P. 204, ¶ 1. Farr interview, Jan. 28, 1992. These important segments were divided after discussion about having all of this material in one segment, "The Nazi Police State," a suggested alternative to "Totalitarianism." Some members of the design team thought the former too limiting, missing the power of totalitarianism's effect on the whole of society. At a design meeting on Aug. 2, 1991, Weinberg argued, however, that "control of minds is difficult to do visually." At a meeting on Jan. 17, 1992, splitting the exhibit was discussed; Weinberg argued that it was necessary to show not only terror but the "structure, control and regimentation of an individual's life," minutes of design meeting, HMMF. The basic design was chosen in a design meeting, Jan. 29, 1992.

P. 204, ¶ 2. For example, David Luebke's text panel, written in consultation with Raul Hilberg in the "Killers" section, reads, "They included the high-ranking bureaucrats who helped formulate and implement the 'Final Solution,' and those who identified and located the victims. Lawyers who handled the 'Aryanization' of property owned by Jews, industrialists who profited from the slave labor of concentration camp inmates, and contractors who built the gas chambers and supplied the Zyklon B—all contributed to the genocide." In a subsequent text panel, "The Guilt of Bystanders," visitors are informed that "some bystanders sought to exploit the situation of the Jews for personal gain, but most merely stood by, neither collaborating nor coming to the aid of the victims. This passivity amounted to acquiescence, and the planners and executors of the 'Final Solution' counted on bystanders' not intervening in the process of genocide."

P. 205, ¶ 1. Author's notes, Jan. 20, 1993. Ann Farrington characterizes the model as "diagrammatic and passionate, a good teaching tool." Interestingly, its size and white color make her uncomfortable. "Its scale and color," she said, "make it look like something charming, like a doll's house." (Farrington interview, July 28, 1993.)

P. 211, ¶ 1. Information in this paragraph from Linda Hunt, "Human Hair Research Brief," March 9, 1990, HMMF. The massive display of human hair, which takes up a whole wall on the second floor of one of the brick barracks in the Auschwitz Museum, is most powerful.

P. 211, ¶ 2. *For the Living*, roll 129, tape 8, pp. 4–5.

P. 212, ¶ 2. Quoted material in preceding two paragraphs from Greenwald and Morgenstein memo, Feb. 23, 1989, HMMF.

P. 213, ¶ 1. Sybil Milton, "Recommendations for Archival Accessions and Collection Development of a Holocaust Museum," 1986, pp. 9–10, HMMF. Eliach interview, March 17, 1993. Dr. Hadassah Rosensaft, a member of the council and the content committee, and survivor of Birkenau and Bergen-Belsen, whose husband, young son, parents, and only sister were murdered in the gas chambers, also extended her objections beyond hair. During a content-committee meeting on May 2, 1989, she objected to using a casting of the Mauthausen dissection table, or any part of a crematorium, even the doors. "The tools of death," she said, "should remain in the place of the crime, not [be] enshrined in our museum." Minutes of content-committee meeting, HMMF.

P. 213, ¶ 2. Rosenfeld to Smith and Appelbaum, Feb. 16, 1990, HMMF.

P. 213, ¶ 3. Rosenfeld memo, Feb. 16, 1989, HMMF. Martin Smith was less concerned about the "good manners" of the museum; in an updated memo in response to Rosenfeld, he said, "I would rather be condemned by the media than pretty up the event" (Smith files).

P. 214, ¶ 1. Minutes of content-committee meeting, Feb. 13, 1990, HMMF.

P. 214, ¶ 2. Minutes of content-committee meeting, Oct. 10, 1991, HMMF.

P. 215, ¶ 1. Design-meeting notes, Dec. 9, 1991; Jan. 8, 1992; both in HMMF.

P. 215, ¶ 2. *For the Living*, roll 129, tape 8, pp. 4–5. Likewise, Appelbaum believed that the hair was so "visceral" that "people who are compelled to tell the truth in this museum, couldn't make that final last step" (*For the Living*, roll 129, tape 8, p. 5).

P. 216, ¶ 2. Smith memo to Farr, n.d., Smith files.

P. 217, ¶ 1. Berenbaum interview, April 14, 1994. For a detailed study of United States governmental involvement with ex-Nazi organizations and individuals, and its impact on American society, see Christopher Simpson, *Blowback: America's Recruitment of Nazis and Its Effects on the Cold War* (New York: Collier Books, 1988).

P. 219, ¶ 2. David S. Wyman, *The Abandonment of the Jews: America and the Holocaust, 1941–1945* (New York: Pantheon Books, 1984), pp. 307, 334. See *Days of Remembrance: A Department of Defense Guide for Annual Commemorative Observances*, 2nd ed. (Washington, D.C.: Office of the Secretary of Defense, n.d.), pp. 86–87. In the first DOR ceremony, Wiesel said, "Not one bomb was dropped on the railway tracks to the death factories" (Days of Remembrance [DOR] brochure, April 24, 1979, p. 16). In 1981, he said, "Why weren't the railways to Birkenau bombed by either the Allies or the Russians?" (DOR brochure, April 26–May 3, 1981), p. 12). And in 1985, Senator Claiborne Pell, whose father, Herbert Pell, was the American representative to the United Nations War Crimes Commission, said, in reciting a litany of examples of American indifference, "We even refused to bomb the rail line that carried the Nazi victims to Auschwitz. We did all too little 40 years ago; what can we do now?" Wiesel, in the same ceremony, spoke of his ambivalence. "When I think of the American Army, it is always a sentiment of gratefulness, joy, that I am overcome with. But . . . somehow, the Jewish war, the Jewish agony, Jewish deaths were forgotten. . . . Our criticism of our own governments . . . is not directed only at them. . . . The Russian Army was closer to Auschwitz than the American Army. They could have sent airplanes. They could have advanced the troops. And why were they silent?" (DOR brochure, April 18, 1985, pp. 13, 24.)

P. 220, ¶ 1. Michael Marrus, "Bystanders to the Holocaust," in Ezra Mendelsohn, ed., *Studies in Contemporary Judaism*, vol. III (Oxford: Oxford University Press, 1987), pp. 217, 219; John Morton Blum, *V Was for Victory: Politics and American Culture During World War II* (New York: Harcourt Brace Jovanovich, 1976), p. 177.

P. 220, ¶ 3. Paul Fussell, *Wartime: Understanding and Behavior in the Second World War* (Oxford: Oxford University Press, 1989), p. 138. On the mechanisms of dehumanization practiced by Americans and Japanese during the war, see John W. Dower, *War Without Mercy: Race and Power in the Pacific War* (New York: Pantheon Books, 1986). H. Bruce Franklin discusses imaginative war literature in *War Stars: The Superweapon and the American Imagination* (New York: Oxford University Press, 1988), pp. 19–53. On what Americans knew about the Holocaust and when they knew it, see Deborah E. Lipstadt, *Beyond Belief: The American Press and the Coming of the Holocaust, 1933–1945* (New York: The Free Press, 1986).

P. 221, ¶ 1. James H. Kitchens III, "The Bombing of Auschwitz Reexamined," *Journal of Military History*, vol. 58 (April 1994), pp. 244–45. The conference was cosponsored by the Holocaust museum, as part of their attempt to shape a working relationship with various Smithsonian museums.

P. 221, ¶ 2. Ibid., p. 246. I thank Dr. Kitchens for a careful response to a question about the work of the people who read these photographs in a telephone interview, Oct. 27, 1993.

P. 222, ¶ 1. Ibid., p. 266. Also taking issue with Wyman was Richard Foregger, whose article "David Wyman and the Historiography of America's Response to the Holocaust: Counter-Considerations," *Holocaust and Genocide Studies*, vol. 5, no. 4 (1990), pp. 403–21, doubted that either the crematorium or the rail lines could have been destroyed, given the accuracy of weaponry. To emphasize his point, he noted that, in the attack by F-111 bombers on Muammar Qaddafi's Libyan headquarters on April 14, 1986, even with the use of the best navigational equipment and lasers to guide the bombs, "of the nine planes targeted against the . . . headquarters only two dropped their bombs; neither scored a direct hit. Bombs were dropped on the wrong targets; some landed in residential areas with the loss of 37 civilians killed and 93 wounded. . . . Reconnaissance showed very little damage to the target" (p. 415).

The British military discussions are covered in Bernard Wasserstein, *Britain and the Jews of Europe, 1939–1945* (Oxford: Clarendon Press, 1979), pp. 307–320.

P. 222, ¶ 2. Hershel Shanks, "Bombing Analysis Not 'News,' " and Kai Bird, "Bombing Auschwitz Was Feasible," *Washington Jewish Week*, June 10, 1993, n.p. I thank Dr. Michael J. Neufeld, curator in the department of aeronautics at the National Air and Space Museum, for providing me with copies of these articles, talking with me about this issue, and introducing me to James Kitchens.

P. 222, ¶ 3. Powell quote in Kitchens, "Bombing of Auschwitz Re-examined," p. 264. Browning telephone interview, Oct. 20, 1993.

P. 223, ¶ 1. Browning telephone interview, Oct. 20, 1993.

P. 223, ¶ 2. Luebke telephone interview, Jan. 8, 1994.

P. 223, ¶ 3. Wiesel's remarks found in "Part II, Presentation of the Key to the United States Holocaust Memorial Museum and Educational Center," DOR booklet, April 11–13, 1983, p. 34; Hyman Bookbinder, *Off the Wall: Memoirs of a Public Affairs Junkie* (Washington, D.C.: Seven Locks Press, 1991), p. 136.

P. 225, ¶ 1. Littell interview, April 19, 1993; HMCT, May 13, 1985, p. 63.

P. 225, ¶ 2. HMCT, April 30, 1981, p. 21; June 9, 1986, p. 95.

P. 226, ¶ 4. Smith interview, April 21, 1993. Smith wanted the exhibition to go beyond description of religious sanction or resistance to the Holocaust. He wanted it to introduce—beyond the *Testimony* film—the theological dilemma raised by the Holocaust. He noted that his article "What a Museum Visitor Should Think About and Remember," excerpted in the museum's *Newsletter*, Nov.–Dec. 1990, left out what he considered a crucial section that represented thoughts "highly personal and strongly felt." The Holocaust, wrote Smith, "took place and no revisionist nonsense will ever shake that conviction; it was one of the darkest and most evil events yet perpetrated by humankind; the scale of barbarity and suffering was huge beyond measure;

most nations and the vast majority of people didn't give a damn; most victims did very little to stop it from happening either; the people who did the killing were not very different from the rest of us; humanity—you and I—will probably do the same again unless we organize the world and our lives to prevent it; God did not prevent the Holocaust; do not trust anyone, including yourself; love your neighbor." I thank Martin Smith for providing me with an original draft of his article.

P. 227, ¶ 1. See, for example, David Chidester, *Shots in the Streets: Violence and Religion in South Africa* (Boston: Beacon Press, 1991).

P. 228, ¶ 2. Quoted material in the preceding two paragraphs from Michael Berenbaum, *After Tragedy and Triumph: Modern Jewish Thought and the American Experience* (Cambridge: Cambridge University Press, 1990), pp. 29–30. Berenbaum's chapter "The Uniqueness and Universality of the Holocaust" was also reprinted in Michael Berenbaum, ed., *A Mosaic of Victims: Non-Jews Persecuted and Murdered by the Nazis* (New York: New York University Press, 1990), pp. 20–36.

P. 229, ¶ 2. PCOHT, Feb. 15, 1979, p. 29; April 24, 1979, pp. 32, 106.

P. 229, ¶ 3. PCOHT, April 24, 1979, p. 108. In the commission's *Report to the President*, the Armenian genocide is mentioned as an example of what happens when such events do not become part of memory: "The failure to remember the past makes repetition more likely. Nothing more clearly illustrates this claim than Hitler's alleged response to those in his government who feared international opposition to genocide. 'Who remembers the Armenians?,' he asked" (p. 5).

P. 229, ¶ 4. Berenbaum, *After Tragedy and Triumph*, p. 37.

P. 230, ¶ 1. Armenian Assembly of America files (hereafter AAF); *Report to the President*, p. 26.

P. 230, ¶ 2. Greenberg interview, Aug. 8, 1991; Rabbi Irving Greenberg, *The Jewish Way: Living the Holidays* (New York: Summit Books, 1988), p. 343. Greenberg supported the inclusion of representation of the Armenian genocide in the museum. On March 8, 1979, he wrote Dr. Dicran Berberian, the executive director of the Armenian Assembly, "I know that Jews and Armenians unfortunately share in common the experience of being the victims of genocide."

P. 230, ¶ 3. HMCT, May 28, 1980, p. 51. During the 1980s, the Armenian-American community had to respond to various crises in Armenia, particularly the devastating earthquake in 1988. As a result, only part of this pledge was fulfilled. Momjian offered a payment of $100,000 on Sept. 24, 1981. The failure to fulfill the pledge was a source of some tension between the council leadership and Momjian.

P. 231, ¶ 1. HMCT, Aug. 4, 1983, p. 55. Interestingly, several of Wiesel's letters to Hilberg show that he was not yet satisfied about his own understanding of the relationship between different groups of Holocaust victims.

Responding to Wiesel, Hilberg wrote, "The killing of Armenians *was* . . . a precursor of the much greater destruction of the Jews, and I do think we are entitled to recognize this fact" (Hilberg to Wiesel, July 28, 1983, HMMF).

There was also still bitterness because, as a result of Turkish and Israeli pressure, Elie Wiesel had resigned as chairperson of an international conference on "The Holocaust and Genocide," to be held in June 1982 in Tel Aviv. (Several sessions were to deal with the Armenian genocide.) Additionally, the council retracted a financial pledge of $10,000 for the conference. See Israel W. Charny, "The Turks, Armenians, and Jews," in Israel W. Charny and Shamai Davidson, eds., *The Book of the International Conference on the Holocaust and Genocide*, bk. one, *The Conference Program and Crisis* (Tel Aviv: Institute of the International Conference on the Holocaust and Genocide, 1983), pp. 269–315.

P. 231, ¶ 2. Chambers to Bookbinder, June 6, 1983; Bookbinder to Chambers, July 7, 1983; both in HMMF. Bookbinder also corresponded with Justin McCarthy, professor of history at the University of Louisville, who had written that "the Armenian situation has no place alongside the Holocaust," and that the whole period was one of "forced migrations of Muslims and Armenians." Bookbinder responded, "Your comments reflect an obvious desire to be honest to your convictions but also to find some middle ground that would be fair all around." (McCarthy to Bookbinder, July 28, 1983; Bookbinder to McCarthy, Aug. 2, 1983; both in HMMF.) The Armenian Assembly of America included McCarthy in a list of sixty-nine American scholars who became, the assembly claimed, "part of a lobbying effort organized by the Assembly of Turkish American Associations to defeat congressional approval of a resolution to commemorate the Armenian Genocide," and listed various grants received by these scholars from the American Research Institute in Turkey and the Institute of Turkish Studies. *Journal* [of Armenian Assembly of America], vol. 14, no. 1 (Spring 1987), pp. 1, 7–9. These scholars lent their names to a 1985 advertisement, "Attention Members of the U.S. House of Representatives," that appeared in *The New York Times*, the *Washington Post*, and the *Washington Times*. The ad, buttressed by these signatories, argued that it was premature to convict the Turks of genocide, and that the role of the United States should be to press for open access to Turkish historical archives. Lerman's comments in HMCT, Aug. 4, 1983.

P. 232, ¶ 1. Freedman interview, Aug. 10, 1993; Bookbinder interview, July 29, 1991; HMCT, Aug. 4, 1983, p. 161. In a letter to Wiesel, who did not attend the Aug. 1983 council meeting, Bookbinder noted that "the Armenian tragedy was the principal episode discussed. In light of major efforts outside the Council to close the door to any kind of reference to the Armenian events," the council "reaffirmed its earlier decisions for an appropriate inclusion of this historic event," the nature of which had not yet been determined (Bookbinder to Wiesel, Aug. 9, 1983, HMMF). There was also sporadic pressure directed toward selected council members and lay leaders of the museum from Israeli officials who were concerned about their relationship with Turkey (Deukmejian and Momjian to Wiesel, April 28, 1986, HMMF).

P. 233, ¶ 1. Bardakjian to Altshuler, Aug. 24, 1984, HMMF.

P. 233, ¶ 2. Berenbaum's presentation is summarized in Deukmejian and Momjian to Harvey Meyerhoff, Dec. 23, 1991, complaining that the council was backing out of their commitment. Berenbaum also cites these "analogies" between the Armenian genocide and the Holocaust in *After Tragedy and Triumph*, p. 32.

P. 233, ¶ 3. Minutes of executive-committee meeting, Aug. 15, 1990, HMMF.

P. 234, ¶ 2. Bauer to Meed, March 17, 1991; Meed to Bauer, March 29, 1991; both in Meed files.

P. 235, ¶ 1. Minutes of museum/memorial-committee meeting April 7, 1981; Berenbaum to Elaine Heumann Gurian, Jan. 3, 1992; both in HMMF. Gurian joined the museum staff in September 1991. She had formerly been deputy assistant secretary for museums at the Smithsonian Institution, deputy director of the Boston Children's Museum, and deputy director for public-program planning at the National Museum of the American Indian.

P. 235, ¶ 2. Momjian telephone interview, Dec. 6, 1993; Adalian interview, Aug. 4, 1993. There is one other reference to Armenians, in the "To Safety" exhibit, which informs visitors that "Franz Werfel, the author of a novel about the Armenian genocide, *The Forty Days of Musa Dagh*, also emigrated to the United States."

P. 236, ¶ 3. Gregory F. Goekjian, "Genocide and Historical Desire," *Semiotica*, vol. 83 nos. 3/4 (1991), p. 219; Michael Berenbaum, "The Uniqueness of the Holocaust and Genocidal Precedents," Berenbaum files. The issue of the uniqueness of the Holocaust in relation to the Armenian genocide is the subject of Pierre Papazian's "A Unique Uniqueness?," and responses to him, in *Midstream*, vol. 30, no. 4 (April 1984), pp. 14–25.

P. 237, ¶ 1. "Armenian Terrorism: A Profile," *Department of State Bulletin*, vol. 82, no. 2065 (Aug. 1982), p. 35.

P. 237, ¶ 2. "Days of Remembrance of Victims of the Holocaust," April 22, 1981, HMMF. Reagan quoted in *Armenian Observer*, Nov. 2, 1983.

P. 238, ¶ 2. Reagan quoted in White House press release, April 1, 1985, AAF. Dickinson and Solarz quoted in Vigen Guroian, "Post-Holocaust Political Morality: The Litmus of Bitburg and the Armenian Genocide Resolution," *Holocaust and Genocide Studies*, vol. 3, no. 3 (1988), pp. 314, 319.

P. 238, ¶ 4. According to the Israeli newspaper *Ha'aretz*, Oct. 17, 1989, Jacque Kamhi, the head of the Jewish community in Turkey, hired a prominent Jewish-American attorney, Paul Berger, to lobby against the resolution. Joining in the lobbying effort were Mori Amitay, the former executive director of the American Israel Public Affairs Committee, former Assistant

Secretary of Defense Richard Perle, Washington lawyer Douglas Feith, and Mark Epstein, former Washington director of the Union of Councils for Soviet Jews. See also "Armenian Bill Draws Jewish Fire," *Washington Times*, Oct. 23, 1989; "Embassy Went Too Far in Armenian Affair" and "Turkey Seeks Help of Israel and U.S. Jews to Fight U.S. Senate Resolution Marking Armenian Genocide," *Jerusalem Post*, Oct. 24, 1989; "Between Ankara and Jerusalem," *Jerusalem Post*, Oct. 25, 1989; "The Tragedies of Other People," *Jerusalem Post*, Oct. 26, 1989; "Armenian Genocide Bill Creates Conflict for Jews," *Washington Jewish Week*, Oct. 26, 1989; all in AAF.

P. 239, ¶ 1. *Washington Jewish Week*, Nov. 2, 1989.

P. 239, ¶ 2. Daryal Batibay, "Turkey Was Not Guilty of Genocide," *Washington Jewish Week*, June 26, 1989.

P. 240, ¶ 2. I am indebted, for the use of appropriate language to talk about so-called Gypsies and their term for the Holocaust, to Dr. Ian Hancock, who notes, "*Rom* is an all-encompassing label, and there are many divisions within it." Rom and Sinti were the main tribes targeted by the Nazis, and, at the risk of oversimplification, I adopt Hancock's use of "Rom." (Letter to author, Oct. 15, 1993.)

Quotation from *Los Angeles Times*, June 26, 1984. Insofar as I can discover, there was no *intentional* exclusion of Rom from the commission or council. As several people told me, "We just didn't think about it," partly because the limits of Romani oral tradition, and the lack of a well-organized political community motivated to establish their experience as a public memory, had kept the Romani experience in the Holocaust from attracting a great deal of attention.

Simon Wiesenthal himself has long championed the equal treatment in Holocaust memory of Romani victims: "In their misfortune gypsies were on virtually the same footing as Jews" (Simon Wiesenthal, *Justice Not Vengeance* [New York: Grove Weidenfeld, 1989], p. 219).

P. 241, ¶ 1. Quoted material in preceding two paragraphs from Puxon to Wiesel, June 4, 1984; Marks to Wiesel, June 5, 1984; Kaldi to Wiesel, June 13, 1984; Wiesel to Puxon June 13, 1984; all in HMMF. Technically, of course, Wiesel was correct—appointments came from the White House—but, as we have seen, Wiesel played some role in the selection of members of both commission and council.

P. 241, ¶ 2. HMCT, July 20, 1984, pp. 10–11 and passim.

P. 242, ¶ 1. Ibid., pp. 52–53 and passim; Fisher to Reagan, July 12, 1984; Fisher and Kramer to Naftalin, Jan. 30, 1985. Fisher's letter to Reagan was referred to Jonathan Bush, general counsel for the council, who assured the White House that the council was "sensitive to this important constituency group and eager to continue to reach out and cooperate with the Gypsy community." On Aug. 23, 1984, Naftalin also wrote Fisher, offering his hopes that the July 20 meeting had established the "basis of communication and cooperation from which to proceed. . . . The story to be told must and will include the Gypsy people." (All materials from HMMF.)

P. 242, ¶ 2. Cohn telephone interview, Dec. 9, 1993.

P. 242, ¶ 3. Lloyd Grove, "Lament of the Gypsies," *Washington Post*, July 21, 1984, p. C1. Wiesenthal asked Wiesel if one of the Jewish members would resign to be replaced by a Romani representative.

P. 243, ¶ 1. Gabrielle Tyrnauer, Ph.D., "The Fate of the Gypsies During the Holocaust," report to the United States Holocaust Memorial Council, Feb. 1985, pp. 56, 57, HMMF.

P. 243, ¶ 2. Naftalin quoted in Charles Hirshberg, "Gypsies Lobby for Representation on Holocaust Memorial Council," *Washington Post*, March 9, 1986, p. A16. For Hancock's views, see, for example, Ian F. Hancock, *The Pariah Syndrome: An Account of Gypsy Slavery and Persecution* (Ann Arbor: Karoma, 1986); "Gypsies, Jews, and the Holocaust," *Shmate: A Journal of Progressive Jewish Thought*, vol. 17 (Winter 1987), pp. 8–15; "Gypsy/Roma Followup," *Shmate*, vol. 18 (Summer 1987), pp. 14–17; " 'Uniqueness' of the Victims: Gypsies, Jews and the Holocaust," *Without Prejudice: The EAFORD International Review of Racial Discrimination*, vol. 1, no. 2 (1988), pp. 45–67; "Anti-Gypsism in the New Europe," *Roma*, vols. 38/39 (1993), pp. 5–29; "The Roots of Inequity: Romani Cultural Rights in their Historical and Social Context," *Immigrants and Minorities*, vol. 11, no. 1 (March 1992), pp. 3–15; Hancock's introduction to David Crowe and John Kolsti, eds., *The Gypsies of Eastern Europe* (Armonk, N.Y.: M. E. Sharpe, 1991), pp. 3–9. See also Toby Sonneman, "Gypsies in Eastern Europe: Why We Should Care," *Humanistic Judaism*, 1991, pp. 47–49. Besides the copies of some of these articles I found in the museum's files, I wish to thank Professor Hancock for sending me both written materials and copies of some of his voluminous correspondence with council members and staff.

P. 244, ¶ 1. Marks to Wiesel, Aug. 21, 1985, HMMF.

P. 244, ¶ 2. Hancock and Megel to Holocaust Memorial Council, June 20, 1986, HMMF.

P. 244, ¶ 3. "Days of Remembrance in Memory of the Gypsy Victims of Nazi Genocide," Sept. 16, 1986, p. 4; Hancock to Wiesel, Nov. 25, 1986, published in *Shmate*, vol. 18 (Summer 1987), with Wiesel's brief reply. HMMF. In a letter to Marian Craig, director of the Days of Remembrance program, Hancock continued his criticism of this event: "At our single ceremony in September, 1986, one of your staff members was overheard telling another that the soil we had brought from Birkenau and which was used in our memorial of tears, should be 'flushed down the toilet.' We learned from a Council member who was there that Richard Krieger [the council's executive director at the time] was heard, later, to say 'this is the last time we do this for these people.' " Hancock to Craig, Nov. 19, 1990, HMMF. (Council member Harry Cargas confirmed hearing this comment in interview, Dec. 8, 1993.)

P. 245, ¶ 2. Material in the precending two paragraphs from Bob Lundegaard, "Gypsies Say Their Holocaust Story Remains Untold," *Minneapolis Star and Tribune*, July 7, 1987; Cohn interview, Dec. 10, 1993. The council published a brochure, *The Story of Karl Stojka: A Childhood in Birkenau*, to accompany the exhibition. Duna complained that the exhibition catalogue was not for sale in the museum's bookstore, not realizing that it could not be sold there, since it had been funded with federal money. None of the Days of Remembrance booklets are for sale in the bookstore, in fact.

Hancock was critical of the 1991 ceremony. In a letter to the council's executive director, Sara Bloomfield, he declared, "To arrange to have Roma light one of the six candles commemorating the six million Jews who perished, but not to have candles lit in the memory of our own dead, is reprehensible and manipulative. It gives every indication that the Roma are being used to demonstrate to the nation that they accept that their own tragedy was subordinate to the Jewish tragedy. Will a Jewish survivor light a candle for our people? Will a *Rom* even light a candle for our people? You are *still* managing Romani affairs without consulting us" (Hancock to Bloomfield, March 26, 1991, HMMF).

P. 246, ¶ 1. Hancock, " 'Uniqueness' of the Victims," p. 48.

P. 246, ¶ 2. In 1989, for example, the *Days of Remembrance Program Planning Guide, 1939–1989: 50 Years after the Eve of Destruction*, included a whole chapter on the Romani Holocaust, and Sybil Milton translated documents on the Romani experience for the Department of Defense's Days of Remembrance book. The council sponsored the showing of a film, *The Lie: Restitution to Sinti and Romani Gypsies*, in a Georgetown theater, and Duna, Milton, and several second-generation Romani spokespersons participated in a panel discussion about the film.

Quotations from Bloomfield to Duna, Oct. 4, 1990, HMMF. Bloomfield also wrote to Hancock, noting that, in response to his "variety of allegations and accusations," the council had detailed the "scope and nature" of their work in "documenting and teaching the fate of the Roma and Sinti people during the Holocaust." She concluded by stating, "The United States Holocaust Memorial Museum will do more than any single institution to help educate the American people about the tragic experience of the Romani and Sinti people during the Third Reich" (Bloomfield to Hancock, April 3, 1991, HMMF).

P. 247, ¶ 3. Milton interview, Oct. 15, 1993. See Sybil Milton, "The Context of the Holocaust," *German Studies Review*, vol. XIII, no. 2 (May 1990), pp. 269–83; "Gypsies and the Holocaust," *History Teacher*, vol. 24, no. 4 (Aug. 1991), pp. 375–87; "Nazi Policies Toward Roma and Sinti, 1933–1945," *Journal of the Gypsy Lore Society 5*, vol. 2, no. 1 (1992), pp. 1–18; and her exchange with Yehuda Bauer, "Correspondence: 'Gypsies and the Holocaust,' " *History Teacher*, vol. 25, no. 4 (Aug. 1992), pp. 511–21. Museum historian David Luebke, who wrote the text for the permanent exhibition, also argued that there was little if any difference between Jewish and Romani experience. In a memo to Marian Craig, Luebke stated, "To be sure, the 'Jewish Question' and its 'Final Solution' loomed larger in Nazi minds than did the 'Gypsy Plague.' All the same, Sinti were persecuted and ultimately exterminated on explicitly racial grounds; in this respect, similarities with the Jewish experience far outweigh differences of detail. In any case, the Nazis ceased to draw any practical, racial distinctions between Jews and Sinti from 1942 on, when most of the exterminations occurred" (Luebke to Craig, April 18, 1990, HMMF).

P. 248, ¶ 1. Ian Hancock, "Jewish Responses to the Porrajmos (The Romani Holocaust)," paper presented at Remembering for the Future International Conference on the Holocaust, Berlin, Germany, March 13–17, 1994, p. 14. I am grateful to Professor Hancock for sending me a copy of his paper.

P. 248, ¶ 2. Browning telephone interview, Oct. 20, 1993.

P. 249, ¶ 1. Henry Jenkins and Mary Fuller, "Nintendo and New World Traveling," *Civitas: Cultural Studies at MIT*, vol. 3, no. 1 (Fall 1993), p. 4.

P. 249, ¶ 3. Pawlikowski makes these arguments often in his comments at council meetings, and in correspondence with Wiesel and Berenbaum. Here I have used his letter to Wiesel, July 19, 1983, and his letter to Berenbaum, Feb. 14, 1992, in which he states, "Some of the old clichés . . . can no longer stand. This includes the statement that Jews were killed because they were Jews and the others were killed as 'outsiders.' . . . All the victims died together because they were classified as subhuman, not simply because they were outsiders" (HMMF).

P. 250, ¶ 2. Terrence Des Pres, "The Dreaming Back," *Centerpoint*, vol. 4, no. 1 (Fall 1980), p. 14.

P. 250, ¶ 3. Hayden White, "The Value of Narrativity in the Representation of Reality," in W. T. Mitchell, ed., *On Narrative* (Chicago: University of Chicago Press, 1980), p. 20. See also Hayden White, *The Content of the Form: Narrative Discourse and Historical Representation* (Baltimore: Johns Hopkins University Press, 1987), and "Historical Emplotment and the Problem of Truth," in Saul Friedlander, ed., *Probing the Limits of Representation: Nazism and the 'Final Solution'* (Cambridge, Mass.: Harvard University Press, 1992), pp. 37–53. James E. Young, *Writing and Rewriting the Holocaust: Narrative and the Consequences of Interpretation* (Bloomington: Indiana University Press, 1988), p. 15.

P. 251, ¶ 2. Minutes of content-committee meeting, May 24, 1989; Lerman memo, Feb. 8, 1988; Petersen to Lerman, June 6, 1988; all in HMMF.

P. 252, ¶ 1. Berenbaum interview, April 14, 1994.

P. 252, ¶ 2. Smith interview, Jan. 16, 1993; *For the Living*, roll 129, tape 28, p. 2.

P. 254, ¶ 1. Quoted material in the preceding five paragraphs from Bradley telephone interview, April 19, 1994.

CONCLUSION

P. 255, ¶ 1. Shlomo Katz, "An Open Letter to James Baldwin," *Midstream*, vol. 12, no. 4 (1971), p. 5.

P. 256, ¶ 2. Muhammad quoted in "Holocaust Suffering Disparaged," *USA Today*, April 19, 1994, p. 3A. See also "Comparing the Suffering of Millions," *Washington Post*, April 19, 1994; and "Muhammad Museum Visit a 'Travesty,' " *Washington Times*, April 19, 1994. While in Washington, D.C., Muhammad delivered a frightening speech at Howard University characterizing Colin Ferguson, who earlier in the year killed six people on a New York commuter train, as a "modern day Nat Turner," and declaring, "I love Colin Ferguson" ("Anti-Semitism Spewed at Howard," *Washington Jewish Week*, April 28, 1994, p. 6). In more responsible terms, American historians have recently challenged the accepted boundaries of Holocaust memory. Yale historian Jon Butler titled a chapter in *Awash in a Sea of Faith* "Slavery and the African Spiritual Holocaust." He drew distinctions between it and its twentieth-century namesake, but argued that the destruction of African religious systems in the New World "stemmed from violence and repression as well as from an open contempt for different religious beliefs, and it resulted in a cultural destructiveness of extraordinary breadth" (Jon Butler, *Awash in a Sea of Faith: Christianizing the American People* [Cambridge, Mass.: Harvard University Press, 1990], p. 157).

University of Hawaii historian David Stannard thought "Holocaust" an appropriate term to characterize the destruction of native Americans, and he criticized the traditional "Eurocentric bias that lumps undifferentiated masses of 'Africans' into one single category and undifferentiated masses of 'Indians' into another, while making fine distinctions among the different populations of Europe." Such bias, wrote Stannard, ignored the effect of genocide: "total extermination—purposefully carried out—of entire cultural, social, religious, and ethnic groups" (David E. Stannard, *American Holocaust: The Conquest of the New World* [New York: Oxford University Press, 1992], p. 151).

P. 256, ¶ 3. Dale Crowley, Jr., to United States Holocaust Memorial Council members, July 23, 1993, HMMF. A carelessly researched and inflammatory article about this issue, "Christians Offended by Film on Holocaust," appeared in the *Washington Times*, Aug. 20, 1993. Academic advisers to the museum agreed that, if anything, the museum downplayed the Christian roots of anti-Semitism.

P. 256, ¶ 4. Luebke and Ioanid to Weinberg, May 21, 1993, HMMF; Ioanid interview, April 14, 1994. The museum was heavily attacked in the nationalistic Romanian press after the opening.

P. 257, ¶ 1. Eventually, the decision was made to close on Yom Kippur. The decision, however, was not a foregone conclusion. See, for example, "Holocaust Museum to Be Open High Holy Days," *Washington Jewish*

Week, May 13, 1993, p. 8; "Holocaust Museum to Close on Christmas and Yom Kippur," *Jewish Advocate*, July 9–15, 1993, p. 6.

P. 257, ¶ 2. Interview, June 5, 1992. The question of the "Americanness" and "Jewishness" of the museum arose as well in the issue of whether the museum's cafeteria, located in the annex building, should be kosher. The decision was made to make it vegetarian. See "Holocaust Museum to Be Open High Holy Days."

P. 258, ¶ 1. Another controversy at the opening involved the invitation extended to Croatian President Franjo Tudjman, who had characterized Israelis as "Judeo-Nazis," and whose writings claimed that fewer than a million died. Both Wiesel and Simon Wiesenthal angrily denounced the invitation, and the museum responded that the State Department had directed that any head of a democratically elected government was eligible to attend. Wiesel, not satisfied, said, "His presence in the midst of survivors is a disgrace," and declared that he would not shake his hand ("Anger Greets Croatian's Invitation to Holocaust Museum Dedication," *New York Times*, April 22, 1993). On the controversy regarding Herzog, see Judith Weinraub, "Israeli Leader to Speak at Dedication," *Washington Post*, April 10, 1993. See also "Clinton Appoints Holocaust Museum Leadership," *Jewish Advocate*, June 4–10, 1993.

P. 258, ¶ 2. The resignations were not to take effect until after the opening. Reaction to Clinton's announcement found in "Holocaust Council Chief Given Notice," *Washington Post*, April 5, 1993; "Meyerhoff Is Forced Out at Holocaust Museum," *Baltimore Sun*, April 6, 1993 (in a later editorial, the *Sun* characterized the action as a "churlish sacking").

P. 260, ¶ 1. Polling data found in Peter D. Hart Research Associates, Inc., "Key Findings and Recommendations from a Survey of Visitors to the United States Holocaust Memorial Museum," 1993.

P. 260, ¶ 2. HMCT, Dec. 12, 1980, p. 109.

P. 262, ¶ 1. Grunewald telephone interview, April 19, 1994. I thank Ralph Grunewald for providing me with a twenty-page list of dignitaries who have visited the museum through April 15, 1994.

P. 262, ¶ 2. Zimmerman telephone interview, May 2, 1994.

P. 262, ¶ 4. Columnist Charles Krauthammer criticized Wiesel's move, arguing that he was calling for military action that would inexorably lead to Americans' being immersed in a ground war in the Balkans. He said as well that comparing atrocities in the Balkans to the Holocaust was an "offense against history" ("Krauthammer Swings at Wiesel," *Washington Jewish Week*, June 3, 1993, p. 6).

P. 263, ¶ 1. *Report to the President*, p. 13; HMCT, Dec. 10, 1980, p. 43; HMCT, Feb. 28, 1984, p. 62.

P. 263, ¶ 3. *World News Tonight with Peter Jennings*, ABC News transcript 3079, p. 5.

P. 264, ¶ 1. Thomas Oliphant, "Clinton's Bosnia Challenge," *Boston Sunday Globe*, April 25, 1993. The editorial war over appropriate analogies is clear from two side-by-side columns in *The New York Times*, April 25, 1994, p. A11. Ronald Steel, professor of international relations at the University of Southern California, argued in "Beware the Superpower Syndrome" that thinking about Bosnia with reference to the Holocaust, or Munich, or the domino theory is flawed. Columnist Anthony Lewis argued in "Crimes of War" that, though the scale of Serbian war crimes is different from those of Nazi Germany, comparison of Serbian and Nazi leaders "is apt."

P. 264, ¶ 2. Zbigniew Brzezinski, " 'Never Again'—Except for Bosnia," *New York Times*, April 22, 1993. The Munich analogy was expressed explicitly by Anthony Lewis's column "Peace at Any Price," *New York Times*, April 18, 1994. This "American Munich," Lewis said, "can only have the same result that it did when Neville Chamberlain and others gave Hitler part of Czechoslovakia at Munich in 1938 in return for his promise to be good henceforth: to encourage further aggression."

P. 266, ¶ 1. See, for example, John Darnton, "Does the World Still Recognize a Holocaust?," *New York Times*, April 25, 1993; Mortimer B. Zuckerman, "The Tough Options in Bosnia," *U.S. News and World Report*, May 3, 1993; Hobart Rowen, "Germany, Bosnia and Bigotry's Economic Toll," *Washington Post*, Aug. 1, 1993; and the stinging critique by Patrick Glynn, "See No Evil," *New Republic*, Oct. 25, 1993, who wrote, "At a time when a museum to Holocaust victims was opening in Washington to great fanfare, history will record that two administrations refrained, in the face of overwhelming evidence, from countering a blatant program of genocide in Bosnia whose scope and nature they fully understood." The museum's public programs also sought to mobilize Holocaust memory on this issue with a three-part series in March 1994, "Bosnia in the Light of the Holocaust."

P. 266, ¶ 2. Remarks by the president in reception to mark the dedication of the United States Holocaust Memorial Museum, April 21, 1993, HMMF. Glynn reports the blocking of the 1992 charge of genocide in "See No Evil," p. 26.

P. 268, ¶ 1. For a careful and impassioned debunking of the myth of the POWs, see H. Bruce Franklin, *M.I.A. or Mythmaking in America* (New Brunswick, N.J.: Rutgers University Press, 1993); in his *Year 501: The Conquest Continues* (Boston: South End Press, 1993), Noam Chomsky, one of the most incisive and enduring critics of the American war in Vietnam and postwar evasions, angrily writes, "Our suffering at the hands of these barbarians is the sole moral issue that remains after a quarter-century of violence."

P. 269, ¶ 1. Goffman quoted in Donald Horne, *The Great Museum: The Representation of History* (London: Pluto Press, 1984), p. 11. Tom L. Freudenheim, Adas Israel Sermon, "Ekev," Aug. 22, 1992. I am indebted to Tom Freudenheim for giving me a copy of his sermon. Similar concerns are raised by Gerald George in *Visiting History: Arguments over Museums and Historic Sites* (Washington, D.C.: American Association of Museums, 1990), when he asks, "Are museums our trophy rooms, where we show off what we have captured (art), conquered (anthropology), overcome (nature), and outgrown (history)?" (p. 24); and James E. Young in *The Texture of Memory: Holocaust Memorials and Meaning* (New Haven: Yale University Press, 1993), when he writes, "In this age of mass memory production and consumption . . . there seems to be an inverse proportion between the memorialization of the past and its contemplation and study. For once we assign monumental form to memory, we have to some degree divested ourselves of the obligation to remember. In shouldering the memory-work, monuments may relieve viewers of their memory burden" (p. 5).

P. 270, ¶ 1. Quoted material in the preceding two paragraphs from CBS News, *Sunday Morning*, March 13, 1981, transcript 781, pp. 5–7.

P. 271, ¶ 1. Quoted material in preceding four paragraphs from telephone interviews April 5, 1994; correspondence from MacDonald, April 25, 1994; and Torney's sermon "Preparing in Peace." I thank Keith Torney for a copy of his sermon. Like Brian Schnitzer, MacDonald appreciated what it was like to live through the Christmas and Hanukkah season with a menorah in the window wondering when a rock might come. "And that absolutely transforms your understanding of what it is to be a target or a minority person"(*Sunday Morning*, p. 6).

P. 271, ¶ 2. Chief of Police Wyman quoted in "Billings, Montana: A Case Study in Community Response to Hate," *1993 Audit of Anti-Semitic Incidents* (New York: Anti-Defamation League, 1994), p. 19. I wish to thank Alan Schwartz of the Anti-Defamation League for providing me with a copy of this information. See also "Montana Outrage Stalls Skinheads," *New York Times*, Feb. 20, 1994.

INDEX